INDIANS IN BRITAIN

CASS SERIES: THE COLONIAL LEGACY IN BRITAIN
Series Editor: Peter Catterall
Institute of Contemporary British History, London
ISSN: 1467-0518

The British Empire was a significant historical phenomenon which had a major effect on both the territories it colonised and the colonisers themselves. What, however, of the experience of the imperial subjects who came to the metropole? How did this shape perceptions of empire and of Britain? And what impact did they have upon Britain, both during the heyday of empire and in its aftermath? In seeking to explore these questions, this series will contribute to an understanding both of empire and of the impact and legacy of race relations in Britain.

1. Shompa Lahiri, *Indians in Britain: Anglo-Indian Encounters, Race and Identity, 1880–1930.*

Institute of Contemporary British History

ICBH

The Institute of Contemporary British History was founded in September 1986 to stimulate research into and analysis of recent history, through conferences, publications, and archives and other research tools, which will be of value to decision-makers, students and the wider public. It aims to be both a centre of excellence for research into recent British history and a source for advice and information for researchers and those with a general interest in the field.

INDIANS IN BRITAIN

Anglo-Indian Encounters, Race and Identity
1880–1930

Shompa Lahiri

Queen Mary and Westfield College, London

FRANK CASS
LONDON • PORTLAND, OR

First published in 2000 in Great Britain by
FRANK CASS PUBLISHERS
Newbury House, 900 Eastern Avenue
London, IG2 7HH

and in the United States of America by
FRANK CASS PUBLISHERS
c/o ISBS, 5804 N.E. Hassalo Street
Portland, Oregon, 97213-3644

Website: www.frankcass.com

Copyright © 2000 S. Lahiri

British Library Cataloguing in Publication Data

Lahiri, Shompa
  Indians in Britain: Anglo-Indian encounters, race and
  identity, 1880–1930
  1. East Indians – Great Britain – History – 19th century
  2. East Indians – Great Britain – History – 20th century
  3. East Indians – Great Britain – Social conditions
  I. Title
  305.8'91411'041

ISBN 0-7146-4986-4 (cloth)
ISBN 0-7146-8049-4 (paper)
ISSN 1467-0518

Library of Congress Cataloging-in-Publication Data

Lahiri, Shompa, 1969–
  Indians in Britain: Anglo-Indian encounters, race and identity.
  1880–1930 / Shompa Lahiri.
      p.   cm.
  Includes bibliographical references (p.   ) and index.
  ISBN 0-7146-4986-4 (cloth). – ISBN 0-7146-8049-4 (paper)
    1. East Indians – Great Britain – History – 20th century.   2. East
  Indians – Great Britain – History – 19th century.   3. East Indians –
  Great Britain – Ethnic identity.   4. Great Britain – Ethnic
  relations.   I. Title.
  DA125.S57L34   1999
  305.891'411041'09034–dc21   99-24206
                                                               CIP

Typeset by Vitaset, Paddock Wood, Kent
Printed by
Creative Print and Design (Wales), Ebbw Vale

Contents

Foreword

'OVERSEAS students' place themselves at the intersection of two cultures, in a highly unequal encounter. Individual students are walking representatives of their own nation and cultural identity, but they are immersed in an all-embracing host environment. The reaction is inevitably a highly ambivalent one, in which elements of attraction and antipathy, or at the very least doubt, war with each other. Some are seduced into wholehearted admiration; others repelled into forms of social or religious, political or intellectual aversion. If they are able to band together into groups, then they often find it possible to learn more about their own cultures and identities than would have been possible at home. They are either communally attracted to some aspect of the host culture, such as radical politics, or commit themselves to forming a carapace of cultural identity, which enables them to ward off the dangers of absorption. But in the process they adopt complex multiple identities, partly conditioned by mimicry, partly by heightened aware-ness of the 'traditions' of home which might otherwise have been par-tially obscured to them.

Shompa Lahiri's book is an invaluable examination of the variety of ways in which Indian students reacted to Britain and the British to them. For such Indians, the processes were complicated by the fact of British rule in India as well as by the social, religious and intellectual ferment which was taking place within the sub-continent itself. From 1843, when the first Indian student arrived in Britain, to the inter-war years of the twentieth century, when the numbers had reached the scale of a small flood, Indians were subjected to various forms of cultural arrogance, racial discrimination and social disdain. They were inevitably trans-formed in the process and there can be little doubt that nationalist politics were strongly influenced as a result. Apart from the celebrated examples of M. K. Gandhi and Jawaharlal Nehru, many other figures who were to be significant in Indian politics, administration, education and law passed through the same crucible.

Another major group who experienced these cultural cross-currents was the soldiery. David Omissi's excellent book *Indian Voices of the Great*

War has recently allowed them to be heard. Shompa Lahiri's *Indians in Britain* examines a more influential group over a longer period. Her work is marked by a striking sensitivity and understanding of the plight of individuals, of their excitements and fears, aspirations and disappointments. As well as analysing the condition of the male majority, she also fascinatingly explores the often different experiences of women students. While acknowledging the value of much recent work in post-colonial studies, she recognises a plurality of voices and a striking diversity of reactions. Another of Shompa Lahiri's major insights lies in the extent to which British culture has been significantly modified in the process. The British are still grappling with their post-colonial legacy, not least with the possibilities, prejudices and violence of a multi-cultural society not yet wholly at ease with itself. This illuminating book will contribute greatly to the understanding of the history of Indo-British contacts and to much else besides.

Professor John M. MacKenzie
March 1999

Series Editor's Preface

THIS is the first book to appear in a new series, *The Colonial Legacy in Britain*. This object of this series is to explore what happened when the empire, in the form of some of its subjects, came to Britain. What was the nature of the encounter between colonial subjects who came to Britain and their hosts, both in the heyday of empire and in its aftermath? What were the characteristics that shaped this encounter; was it determined primarily by categories of race or by such matters as class, education or status? How far did the experience of Britain affect, disrupt or reaffirm mythic images, both of the mother country of the empire and of the territories from which colonial subjects journeyed to the heart of empire? How did the British, in the form of both officialdom and the population as a whole, react to their arrival? What impact did such encounters, not at the imperial periphery but at the heart of empire, have upon the images of empire carried by their British hosts? And what was the legacy, both if and when the colonial subjects returned to their homelands and for the British? The series thus certainly aims to provide a species of imperial history. But it is primarily concerned with exploring empire and the experience of empire through the social and cultural encounters between colonisers and colonised which took place in Britain as a by-product of that empire. The thrust, then, is as much upon diasporic studies and the history of identity.

The present work makes an important contribution to the exploration of many of the themes with which this series is concerned. It could be read simply as an important pioneering piece of empirical work on the aspirations of the Indian students who came to Britain in the nineteenth and early twentieth centuries, and of the opportunities India afforded them when they completed their studies. As such, it casts light, for instance, on the rather uneven process of Indianising the Indian Civil Service under the Raj. But, above all, it is an assessment of the nature of the encounter of these Indian students with British society. This is carefully contextualised, demonstrating, for instance, how much events in India impinged upon the nature of this encounter. Indeed, this distant but uniquely significant context almost emerges as the key variable in the encounter, hardening British reactions to the students as the situation for the British in India seemed to be deteriorating from the late nineteenth century and in the process helping to produce the more politicised student returnees detected in this account. But this is not the only variable instanced and explored here.

One of the strengths of this book is that it considers the nature of the encounter from both sides. The result is an account which does not reduce its character to a series of simple and simplistic equations. The encounter was broadly unequal, but it also varied in nature across time and in different settings, all of which are carefully examined here. And there are also facets which affect both sides of the encounter. For instance, while the British could certainly indulge in Orientalist assumptions about the essential characteristics of the Indians, similar assumptions could also be entertained by the student visitors. The exaggerated expectations of England held by some students could thus also be seen as a species of essentialism, albeit one encouraged by imperial propaganda. For both sides the disabusal of this essentialism could prove a deeply disillusioning experience, with consequences for the hardening of political attitudes detected in this work. Not that the nature of the encounter was as negative as this might imply, as this subtle and well-researched analysis makes clear. It produced a range of reactions on both sides, shaped by the political context, expectations and the immediate environment. In examining these, drawing on new and detailed empirical study, Shompa Lahiri's work makes an important contribution towards developing a more sophisticated understanding of the nature of the colonial encounter.

Peter Catterall
Series Editor
June 1999

Preface: Identity and Colonial Encounter

THIS book discusses the grappling of two cultures and the discourses through which they constructed each other. By focusing on one particular episode in the long history of colonial encounter – the Indian student presence in Britain – it is possible to see how the concepts of race, identity, politics and empire were historically constructed. The study will also examine the relationship between the expectations of encounter and its outcomes. While the bulk of the book analyses motivations, perceptions, attitudes and reactions, the conclusion seeks to demonstrate how colonial encounter in imperial Britain impacted on Indians and British.

This study has a much wider significance than simply an account of student experiences. Indians educated in Britain, although small in number, had a disproportionately large influence on the course of British imperial and South Asian history. In the context of South Asian history, Indians trained in England played a crucial role in the development of modern India. They (including women) took up employment in key positions within the administration of British India; they acted as a bridge between the British and the Indian masses; they were instrumental in the nationalist movement and they were disseminators of western thought and custom in India. Indians parallel other groups of African and Asian nationalists who, as students, underwent crucial formative experiences in Britain and other parts of Europe. An understanding of the early Indian presence in Britain sheds light on issues surrounding more recent attitudes and the treatment of the British South Asian population and, by extension, other black diaspora groups. The study also provides useful tools for an historical investigation of the development of 'Englishness' and race relations in Britain, as well as overlapping with work on the representation of non-Europeans in British popular culture and the importance of race and class within imperial and nationalist politics.

Although there is little scholarship on the history of Indians in Britain,[1] literature on Indian nationalism, including the work of Anil Seal, S. R. Mehrotra and J. R. McLane, has made references to the way the first generation of Congress activists focused their attention on London through the work of the British Committee and the plethora of short-lived societies which preceded it, such as the Free India Society, the London Indian Society and the British India Society. The founding members of the Indian National Congress – W. C. Bonnerjee, Pherozeshah Mehta, Badruddin Tyabji, Manmohan and Lalmohan Ghose, Surendranath Banerjea and Anandamohan Bose – all met in England, while studying for either the Bar or Indian Civil Service, where they came under the influence of Dadabhai Naoroji, 'businessman-cum-publicist'. Harish P. Kaushik has highlighted this chapter in the Indian National Congress's development.[2] Tapan Raychaudhuri's arguments about the Bengali intelligentsia's ambivalence towards the West provide a useful background for an examination of Indian students in Britain.[3] But, apart from J. D. Hunt's *Gandhi in London* and a few articles by Stephen Hay,[4] scant attention has been given to the specific educational experience of Indians in Britain and the formative nature of their residence.

The lack of research on the Asian diaspora in Britain, within both British social and imperial history, has been attributed to the difficulty of locating primary source material. My own experience, however, shows that, while relevant material may lie hidden in government records, newspapers, periodicals, diaries, travelogues, autobiographies and novels, retrieval is not an impossible task. The under-representation of South (and South East) Asians within the small but growing field of 'black' British history has fed the myth that the Asian presence in Britain and Europe is a post-war phenomenon. This book seeks to restore South Asians (the largest ethnic minority in Britain) to the British historical landscape.

Another aim of this study is to challenge traditional frames of reference by re-examining the relationship between metropole and periphery, in this case Britain and India.[5] Firstly, in opposition to the vast majority of studies which privilege metropolitan influence on the colony, this study reverses the traditional direction of influence and focuses on a centripetal analysis, radiating from the colony.[6] The colonial subject – Indian students and sojourners – moved from the periphery to the heart of empire, transgressing the spatial, cultural and political binary divisions of nation and empire. This temporary migration from East to West enabled the periphery physically to enter the centre via the bodies of travelling colonial subjects. Imperial/colonial relations are no longer located exclusively in the context of a colonial backdrop; Britain also serves as a 'space of colonial encounters'.[7] Louise Pratt limits her concept of 'contact zones' to the colonies, but for the purposes of this study the concept has been extended to incorporate the imperial metropole.

Secondly, by removing the artificial binary divisions that have polarised studies of centre and periphery, the study is able to explore the interactive nature of imperial/colonial relations. Events and attitudes in Britain and India ricocheted off each other producing a circle of events encompassing both colonial and metropolitan societies. An integrated approach, which considers both sides of the encounter, avoids the trap of producing a one-sided analysis, focusing on either an exclusively British or Indian perspective. The histories of India and Britain are, in Edward Said's words, 'intertwined and overlapping'.[8]

Anglo-Indian metropolitan encounters provide an opportunity to test theories of identity and related concepts. This study questions the use of psychological theories of identity as tools for the historical analysis of self-formation. Kopf's deployment of Eric Erikson's psychological concept of 'identity crisis' to study the development of the Brahmo Samaj in nineteenth-century Bengal[9] and Ashis Nandy's psychological biographical approach, using the notion of the 'divided self' and 'schism',[10] imply that an identity is in crisis if an individual exhibits or expresses indeterminacy. On the contrary, identity evolves through contradiction and ambivalence. As Stuart Hall has persuasively argued,

> all of us are composed of multiple social identities, not of one ... we are all complexly constructed through different categories, of different antagonisms, and these may have the effect of locating us socially in multiple positions of marginality and subordination, but which do not yet operate on us in exactly the same way.[11]

However, Hall fails to appreciate the historical provenance of this flexible model of identity, by claiming that the fracturing of identity is unique to the modern age. This study counters this view by demonstrating how a permeable concept of identity may be applied to the past. Specifically it explains how Indian students in Britain were able, in most cases, to accommodate their eastern and western selves in a constructive and continuous process, compared with the British, who suffered from greater divisions, alternating from inclusive and exclusive conceptions of Englishness.

But this reconfiguration of identity was rarely smooth for Indians. While England formed an important vector in the development of a national Indian identity, through English education and acculturation, negative reactions to residence in England also contributed to the growth of politicisation and national consciousness. Sudipta Kaviraj's comments about the development of Indian nationalism in the late nineteenth century relate to Indian students in Britain: 'From being a negative reaction to colonial power, it turns positively into a consciousness of a new identity.'[12] Indian students in Britain were faced with three possible options. The first was total identification with British life and values. At the other extreme was total rejection of the West and the elevation of the Indian self to gain a sense of parity and value. The last option was a synthesis of Indian and British cultures, attempting to incorporate the best of both traditions. In this study I shall show that, while in the long-term most students identified with the last option, nevertheless the divisions between the three approaches are not clear. Students incorporated all three stances at various stages, and the position of each stance relative to the others, was dependent on environmental and internal considerations.

Biological and cultural hybridity are prominent themes in this study. Contemporary debates about the subject focus on the work of Robert Young.[13] He argues that inner dissonance in nineteenth-century constructions of Englishness is reflected in the obsession with hybridity, explicitly in the issue of sexual union between black and white, particularly in the writings of the nineteenth-century racial theorists Gobineau and Matthew Arnold.

There are parallels with British official discourse on Indian students. As I shall show, fear about sexual union of the races – miscegenation – did overshadow official attitudes towards Indian princes and students. The way to avoid sexual contact was through social distance,[14] but a black presence, in the form of a growing Indian student population, compromised this ideal. Firstly, it inverted the common formulation of miscegenation, which usually involved white men and Indian women, complicating rigid sexual, racial and class hierarchies. If, as Young has argued, theories of race and miscegenation were also covert forms of colonial desire for the 'other', British fear about the predatory nature of the Indian student is an example of how this desire was projected on to the Indian male. But British concern about female sexuality, from which Indians had to be protected in England, also acted as a complicating factor. Secondly, there was the question of access. In India the British remained largely segregated from the Indian masses, a key means of preventing miscegenation, but in London students were exposed to greater opportunities, particularly within the lodging-house environment.

Just as biological hybridity refers to the union of two races, cultural hybridity refers to the union of two cultures. This study will focus on how the perception of cultural hybridity was constructed in official and popular discourse. As Young's work does not engage with this theme directly, it has only partial relevance to this study. Indians who studied in England were, as a result of their western training, a product of cultural fusion between India and Britain. Their bilingualism was yet another visible symbol of hybridity. This process has been described variously as 'westernisation', 'anglicisation', 'mental miscegenation'[15] and 'denationalisation'. Kenneth Jones has utilised the concept of acculturation to signify men who were 'influenced by the specific culture of England'.[16] Although this concept is useful to the study of Indians in Britain, it is important not to underestimate the resilience and the strength of Indian cultural traditions. Attraction to the West, an important facet of the English-educated student's psyche, created ambiguity, producing more difficulties for some than others.

Notions of cultural hybridity engage with Homi Bhabha's theory of mimicry. Bhabha uses an English-educated Indian, employed by the British in the Indian Civil Service (Babu) as an example of what he terms a 'mimic man': 'He is the effect of colonial mimesis in which to be anglicised is emphatically not to be English.'[17] He is also the bearer of hybridity. Many of the Indians who entered the colonial bureaucracy in India were educated in Britain, which overlaps with the subject group of this study. Bhabha's analysis of the ambivalence present in the coloniser's attitudes to the colonised – 'resemblance and menace'[18] – captures some of the dissonance present in British dealings with Indians in Britain. However, he tends to universalise and concentrate on psycho-analysis, at the expense of adequately explaining the historical processes which constituted a British-educated Indian.

Although this study is informed by theory, as I shall show, its findings do not entirely support theoretical constructions. For example, Ronald Inden's model of 'essentialism',[19] which argues that the British perception of a static India determined by caste denies Indians human agency, is useful as it shows why the British viewed factors which attempted to subvert inherent predetermined essences, in this case residence in England, as harmful to the 'Indian mind' and consequently detrimental to students. However, Inden's model is too rigid and simple to take into account the contradictory elements of British attitudes to Indian students. While British views about Indians were influenced by essentialism, especially in Anglo-Indian fiction, where the only 'true' Indian was the one who adhered scrupulously to Indian tradition, Indian students were still expected to exercise some agency by modifying their behaviour to assimilate into collegiate life in Britain and actively imbibe the values of the English education system. Thus the legacy of Macaulay's education policy,[20] with its seeming advocacy of hybridity, jostled uncomfortably with deep-seated essentialism and resulted in ambivalence in British attitudes towards Indian students.

A key aim of this book is to show how a study of Indians in late nineteenth- and early twentieth-century Britain can place contemporary discussions of race and identity within an historical framework of analysis. Even before large-scale migration took place after the Second World War, Europe, and specifically Britain, accommodated small, but visible, black colonial populations. Exploration of Anglo-Indian relations in Britain shows how race and class intersected, producing confusions of category, inverting hierarchies, as well as reinforcing the existing axis of domination and subordination.

The study is divided thematically and chronologically, reflecting the whole travel process, by starting in India and moving to Britain. The first chapter discusses Indian motivation for travelling to Britain by charting the development of a travel culture in India and the way in which pragmatism combined with the less substantial search for 'authentic' metropolitan British society produced high expectations. Chapter 2 investigates how the shifting cleavages of race and class, as experienced by students, played off each other to simultaneously compound and confuse power structures within a metropolitan setting. The third chapter explores the context of British attitudes towards Indians in Britain, examining the representations of Indians in the various media of British popular culture, including the press, the theatre and above all novels. Chapter 4 analyses the reciprocal nature of British policy towards Indians in India and Britain, marked by inconsistency and ambivalence. Students were viewed as posing a sexual and political threat to metropolitan British society and British hegemony in India, as well as being victims of potentially damaging forces in British society. Thus students became the targets of control and protection. Chapter 5 assesses Indian reactions, both positive and negative, to first-hand contact with Britain, characterised by identification and resistance. The chapter also focuses on politicisation and the development of national consciousness among Indians in Britain. Finally, the conclusion evaluates the impact of colonial encounter in Britain, on both the British and the Indians. Brief biographical information on selected students is also provided.

Driven by the need to historicise adequately,[21] the Introduction will concentrate on the historical context of the South Asian presence in Britain, providing a framework, wherein the development of British policy and student responses may be contextualised.

NOTES

1 Books on the subject include R. Visram, *Ayahs, Lascars and Princes: The Story of Indians in Britain 1700–1947* (London: Pluto Press, 1986). This was intended as an introduction to the subject. B. Maan, *The New Scots: The Story of Asians in Scotland* (Edinburgh: Donald, 1992). The following articles have appeared: M. Sherwood, 'Race, Nationality and Employment among Lascar Seamen 1660 to 1945', *New Community*, 2, 17 (1991),

pp. 229–44; A. Dunlop and R. Miles, 'Rediscovering the History of Asian Migration to Scotland', *Immigrants and Minorities*, 9, 2 (1990), pp. 145–67.

2 H. P. Kaushik, *Indian National Congress in England* (New Delhi: Friends Publication, 1991). A similar book covering the 1930s and 1940s is K. C. Aurora, *Indian Nationalist Movement in Britain 1930–1949* (Delhi: Inter-India Publications, 1991).

3 T. Raychaudhuri, *Europe Reconsidered: Perceptions of the West in Nineteenth Century Bengal* (New Delhi: Oxford University Press, 1988). Other studies of this kind include I. Abu-Lughod, *Arab Rediscovery of Europe: A Study in Cultural Encounter* (Princeton, NJ: Princeton University Press, 1963). It has been pointed out to me that much of the material in this book relates to Bengalis. Although this was not intentional – reflecting as it does the sources available – neither is it surprising, given the regional breakdown of the student population (see Table 2) and, perhaps more importantly, the fact that 'the Bengali intelligentsia was the first Asian social group of any size whose mental world was transformed through its interactions with the West', Raychaudhuri, *Europe Reconsidered*, p. ix.

4 J. D. Hunt, *Gandhi in London* (New Delhi: Promilla, 1993); S. Hay, 'Between Two Worlds: Gandhi's First Impression of British Culture', *Modern Asian Studies*, 3, 4 (1969), pp. 305–19 and 'The Making of a Late Victorian Hindu: M. K. Gandhi in London (1888–1891)', *Victorian Studies*, 33 (1989), pp. 76–98.

5 M. Sinha, *Colonial Masculinity: The 'Manly Englishman' and the 'Effeminate Bengali' in the Late Nineteenth Century* (Manchester: Manchester University Press, 1995), p. 9.

6 J. M. MacKenzie, *Propaganda and Empire: The Manipulation of British Public Opinion 1880–1960* (Manchester: Manchester University Press, 1984), p. 2.

7 M. L. Pratt, *Imperial Eyes: Travel Writing and Transculturation* (London: Routledge, 1992), p. 6. 'Contact zones' are 'the space in which peoples geographically and historically separated come into contract with each other and establish on-going relations.'

8 E. W. Said, *Culture and Imperialism* (London: Vintage, 1994).

9 D. Kopf, *The Brahmo Samaj and the Making of the Modern Indian Mind* (Princeton, NJ: Princeton University Press, 1970).

10 A. Nandy, *The Intimate Enemy: Loss and Recovery of Self under Colonialism* (New Delhi: Oxford University Press, 1983).

11 S. Hall, 'Old and New Identities, Old and New Ethnicities', in A. D. King (ed.), *Culture, Globalisation and World-System* (Basingstoke: Macmillan, 1991), p. 57. Hall's concept of identity is based on the Gramscian notion of the war of position.

12 S. Kaviraj, 'The Imaginary Institution of India', in P. Chatterjee and G. Pandey (eds), *Subaltern Studies: Writings on South Asian History and Society*, Vol. 7 (New Delhi: Oxford University Press, 1992), p. 12.

13 I am using this word at the risk of 'reutilising the exact vocabulary of Victorian racialism'. R. J. C. Young, *Colonial Desire: Hybridity in Theory, Culture and Race* (London: Routledge, 1995).

14 K. Ballhatchet, *Race, Sex and Class Under the Raj: Imperial Attitudes and Policies and their Critics, 1793–1905* (London: Weidenfeld & Nicholson, 1980).

15 B. Anderson, *Imagined Communities: Reflections on the Origins and Spread of Nationalism* (London: Verso, 1983), p. 91.

16 K. W. Jones, *The New Cambridge History of India: Socio-Religious Reform Movements in British India* (Cambridge: Cambridge University Press, 1989), p. 3.

17 H. Bhabha, 'Of Mimicry and Man – The Ambivalence of Colonial Discourse', in F. Cooper and A. L. Stoler (eds), *Tensions of Empire: Colonial Cultures in a Bourgeois World*

(London: University of California Press, 1997), p. 154
18 Ibid.
19 R. Inden, *Imagining India* (Oxford: Blackwell, 1990).
20 Macaulay's 'Minute on Education' stated the intention of creating a class of Indians who were Indian in appearance, but English in mentality. See Anderson, *Imagined Communities*, p. 91.
21 Sinha, *Colonial Masculinity*, p. 11.

Acknowledgements

THIS book is a revised version of my doctoral dissertation, undertaken in the History Department of the School of Oriental and African Studies, University of London. I would like to thank the staff of the India Office Library, the British Library: Bloomsbury and Colindale, the British Communist Party Archives, Cambridge University Library, Edinburgh University Library, Fawcett Library, Society of Friends, London, University College, Library, Victoria League, the Wellcome Institute and also Professor Richard Sorabji.

I am grateful to my research supervisor, Professor Peter Robb. for his guidance. Professor Tapan Raychaudhuri, Dr Peter Catterall and Professor James Manor have also provided useful comments and suggestions, which I have incorporated. Professor John MacKenzie deserves a special acknowledgement for contributing a foreword. He also dispensed invaluable advice and criticism on earlier drafts of this book. I would like to take this opportunity to thank Frank Cass for having the courage and vision to publish this book. Lastly, I am indebted to my family, especially my sister, for providing encouragement and support; without her this book would not have been possible.

Glossary

Acomment is necessary about the spelling of Indian names. It is common to have many different spellings for the same surname. To avoid confusion I have, in most cases, retained the original spelling used at the time in both the endnotes and the main text.

Bilat Pherat   a person who has returned from England, known as 'England-returned'
Brahmo Samaj   nineteenth-century religious reform movement in West Bengal
Duga Puja   main religious festival of West Bengal held in October or November
Majlis   Indian student society at the Universities of Oxford and Cambridge (word derived from Persian word for Parliament)
Parsi   follower of the Zoroastrian religion, chiefly from western India
Prayasitta   purification ceremony performed by Hindus returning from England to regain caste
Shastra   Hindu scriptures codifying all branches of knowledge
Vakil   Indian-trained advocate of law
Zenana   women's quarters within a house or palace closed to strangers; this practice was common in both nineteenth-century Muslim and Hindu households in India

Introduction

THE Indian presence in Britain preceded the arrival of immigrants in the period after the Second World War. From the middle of the nineteenth century the Indian population consisted of roughly five main, transient groups: students, princes, soldiers, ayahs and lascars.[1] The mid-nineteenth-century Indian community also comprised a number of litigants seeking justice in British courts, as well as economic migrants (although as British subjects they were not technically migrants), who had come to make their fortune in London by whatever means they had at their disposal. This usually involved petty trade, frequently resulting in destitution. Indians who had lost civil suits in India believed that only in the heart of the empire, London, would they be able to obtain some kind of redress. Many litigants were Privy Council appellants; consequently, it was their final appeal. Others 'appealed' to the Crown, Parliament and British public opinion. Oomar Khan is a typical example of blind faith in British justice. He had come to England in 1891 to appeal against a legal decision concerning a land suit but was advised to return to India as it was impossible for any authority to intervene on his behalf. Khan refused and was put into custody when he attempted to see the Queen at Balmoral. He deceived doctors by feigning sickness and when a second passage home was arranged for him, he still refused to go. The British authorities were powerless to deport such men, whose presence one official described as 'dangerous'.[2]

Ayahs and lascars came to Britain for employment. The word 'ayah' originated from the Portuguese word for tutor *aio*. These women acted as nurses and attendants to English families on the long voyages to and from India, but were often abandoned in England. An institution known as the 'Ayahs' Home' was established in Aldgate during the late nineteenth century. When its owners, Mr and Mrs Rogers, could no longer afford to maintain the building it fell under the auspices of the

London City Mission in 1900 and relocated to Hackney. The institution was described as a 'Home of Nations'.[3] Nannies from all parts of Asia resided within its walls. According to one source, 80 or more guests visited the home in 1926. The Mission took advantage of this opportunity to preach to a captive audience and some conversions took place. Life in the Home was described as 'sedate': the residents would visit the parks in London in groups of two or three, and indoors they would look at newspapers or play a native game *pachis* – similar to ludo.[4] Most ayahs stayed for an average of six to eight weeks, while they awaited a passage back to India. They did not necessarily travel back to India with the same family that had initially engaged them; new employers would approach the Ayahs' Home looking for the services of an ayah. Some women visited England numerous times during the course of their working lives.

The London City Mission also took an interest in the spiritual welfare of lascars (sailors). The Mission appointed Joseph Salter to preach the gospel to them and he wrote two books about his work in the 'oriental quarters' (the East End and Shadwell) and the docks of London.[5] Abraham Challis replaced Joseph Salter. St Luke's Mission in the Victoria Docks put the Reverend E. B. Bhose in charge of lascars in the 1880s. He visited them daily on board ship and in hospital and also established a Sunday school. Bhose died in 1905, after 20 years' work with lascars. In 1897 Aziz Ahmed, an Indian Christian, founded an independent mission in Glasgow from funds he had raised. But Ahmed's object was not primarily to convert non-Christians. He wrote: 'Our work aims at making lascars better men. We do not interfere with Islam or Roman Catholicism. As a layman I try to give the best advice to Indian seafaring men, for the good of their souls, minds and bodies.'[6] Another Indian Christian was so impressed by this ethos that he established a mission in Birkenhead.

The success of evangelical work among the mainly Muslim lascars was limited. Although approximately 20,000 lascars visited Britain in 1912 alone,[7] their stay in Britain was not often long, unless they deserted and settled in Britain, which a significant number did. Most clung tenaciously to their religion, Islam. In 1908 the Indian Seamen's Institute, also known as the Lascars' Institute, was established as a non-residential club to supplement the work of the Asiatic Home for Strangers. K. Chowdhury, a meteorologist at Manchester University, headed it. In the six months ending June 1910, 4,180 seamen visited the club.[8] It was used principally as a social institution and information centre, where the men could obtain news about their districts from newspapers and new arrivals.

EARLY INDIAN STUDENT POPULATION

By the time the first Indian students came to Britain in the mid-nineteenth century, an itinerant Indian population of ayahs and lascars already existed. The first Indian student may have been Reverend Dhunjeebhoy Naoroji, a Parsi convert to Christianity, who arrived in 1843.[9] He was educated at the Free Church College, Edinburgh, and ordained in 1846. Shortly afterwards Wazir Beg, 'the son of a Mohammedan Messman' from Poona, followed Naoroji to theological college in Edinburgh, where he was also ordained, eventually becoming a Presbyterian minister in Australia.[10]

In 1845 four Bengali Hindus accompanied Dr Goodeve, Professor of Anatomy in Calcutta, to University College, London. The East India Company agreed to fund all their expenses. The college authorities named the four students as 'Dwarkanath Bose, Chunder Seal, Bholanath Bose and Soojee Coomar Goodeve Chuckerbutty'.[11] All obtained diplomas at the Royal College of Surgeons and two took degrees in medicine at the University of London. Chunder Seal did not proceed beyond a bachelor's degree, although he did attain a respectable position in the list of those who graduated with honours. Bholanath Bose was awarded a medical diploma with distinctions in chemistry. All four doctors were praised for pursuing their studies with 'assiduity and intelligence'[12] and acquitting themselves well during their sojourn. However, Dr Chuckerbutty, who stayed in Britain longer than the other three (returning to India in 1850), was singled out for gaining 'the esteem of all who became acquainted with him'.[13] He eventually became an assistant surgeon in the East India Company's medical service.

A decade later in 1856 Bombay sent three Parsis – Rustomjee Byramjee, Kharsedjee Rustomjee Camajee and Munchejee Hormusjee Camajee – who joined the medical faculty of University College, London.[14] This initial trickle of students was welcomed on the grounds that residence in England would provide useful experience beyond the realms of academic qualifications: 'Even in cases of failure to obtain the special object, a compensation, not unlooked for by its recipients, will be found in the knowledge, associations and experiences derived from a course of education in this college, and a few years residence in the "Metropolis of the British Empire".'[15] As I shall show, this stance contrasted sharply with later official policy.

Between 1865 and 1885 approximately 700 men from Bengal travelled to England.[16] The responses of these early pioneers varied. Manmohan Ghose, who came to Britain to study for the Indian Civil Service with Satyendranath Tagore in the early 1860s, wrote: 'We have no other

enjoyment or occupation but our studies.' He complained about the
'English diet of cold beef and ham' and craved one of Bengal's national
dishes *macher jhal* and *bhat* (fish curry and rice). The cold, damp climate
caused him to suffer ill health. These assaults on his physical and mental
well being provoked him to write:

> I shall never be happy until I return home and see you all. Several reasons
> have conspired to make me unhappy in this country. It will please God to
> take me back to my native country so I may enjoy peace of mind. The
> recollections of past days only extract tears from my eyes. I am no longer
> the same in body and mind. If the task we have willingly undertaken had
> not been imposed upon us by the interests of nation, I should not have
> thought it worthwhile to sacrifice my body and mind.[17]

By contrast, a decade later a Muslim student was greatly impressed
by what he had seen of England. Unlike Ghose, who longed to leave
Britain, Syed Mahmud, a student at Cambridge and Lincoln's Inn,
dreaded the prospect of departure from a country he had come to
admire fervently:

> It was with pain [he lamented] that I looked forward to being separated,
> perhaps for many years to come, from a society in which I had spent four
> years of the most important portion of my life with great happiness and
> advantage … It was neither the great mechanical power of England, nor
> even her wealth that produced in me feelings of the greatest admiration.
> It was the refinement of the English society and its institutions that I took
> the greatest interest in and admired most … I can not conceive a nobler
> human being than an English gentleman of good birth and good
> education.[18]

STUDENT NUMBERS AND COMPOSITION

No census was ever taken of the number of Indian students in Britain.[19]
Consequently, figures vary enormously and accurate statistics are
difficult to obtain. The figures in Table 1 give some indication. They have
been amalgamated from several sources and the intervals between years
are not consistent.

The problem of procuring exact figures is rooted in the transient
nature of the Indian student population. On average, students stayed
for about three to four years. But this does not take into account
variations in individual circumstances and the length of courses, which
could radically extend or shorten the period of residence. Edinburgh

Table 1: Students in Britain

Year	Number	Year	Number
1873	40–50	1900	336
1880	100	1907	700–80
1885	160	1913	1,700–800
1890	200	1922	1,500
1894	300–80	1927	1,800

Sources: *Journal of the National Indian Association* and Indian Student Department Reports.

University posed particular complications. There were a sizeable number of Indian medical students who were not members of the university but were studying for diplomas from the Royal College of Physicians and Surgeons in Edinburgh and Glasgow. Many of these candidates spent a brief period in Edinburgh, sometimes only a matter of weeks, to take their examinations. In addition, statistics did not always include students at private tutors (known as 'crammers'), school children or industrial trainees in factories. Also, the names of students studying at university and for the Bar could easily be counted twice. From 1903 Indians visiting England, in whatever capacity, were required to carry identity certificates which contained information about family background, pecuniary status and object of visit. The certificates were partly introduced in response to the rising number of destitute Indians in Britain and partly to provide a useful vetting device. The scheme was an abysmal failure, however, as the majority of students neglected to obtain a certificate. It was finally abandoned in 1913.[20] Records of these certificates do not therefore provide an accurate indicator of the size of the student population.

Although complete returns are not available and the figures are to some extent a matter of conjecture, nevertheless it is clear that, excluding the war years (when passages were strictly rationed by the government), the number of Indian students arriving in Britain increased annually. K. Chowdhury of the Indian Seamen's Institute estimated this influx cost £45,000 per year in fares. He noted that numbers increased especially steeply in the last six or seven months of 1909 when 85 Indians arrived in one steamer alone. He believed the total number of arrivals was 300, 'in addition to six or seven hundred already in residence in various parts of the country',[21] giving a total of approximately a thousand students in 1909, a figure compatible with Table 1. The increase may be attributed to the decision taken by the Council of Legal Education to raise the standard of admission in 1911. The expected

changes brought an unprecedented rush of Indian applicants, anxious
for enrolment before the new rules were enforced.

While the Indian student population formed a tiny section of the
British population as a whole at any one time, the statistics in Table 2
reveal the enormous interest shown by the inhabitants of all the main
Indian provinces in studying in Britain. In 1912 the Indian Student
Department received statistics from six regional advisory committees,
comparing the number of enquiries made about higher-educational
opportunities in Britain with the number of students who were
successful and actually went to Britain.[22]

Table 2: Enquiries and Successful Student Departures for Britain

	Calcutta	Dacca	Bombay	Madras	CP[1]	Punjab
Enquiries	203	200	56	368	122	59
Successful	22	5	21	37	0	2

Note: [1] CP = Central Province
Source: (IOL) Indian Student Department Report 1914, p. 969.

The National Indian Association published intermittent lists of
Indians in Britain in its *Journal* from 1885 to 1900. These lists provide an
insight into the social composition of the Indian student population of
Britain during the last quarter of the nineteenth century. Tables 3, 4 and
5 give a regional, subject and religious analysis of Indian students. In
1885, of the 160 Indians listed, 114 were students. The remainder were
either schoolboys, visitors or unknown. The typical student for this year,
and indeed throughout the period, was a Hindu law student from either
Bombay or Bengal. However, the most unexpected aspect of these tables
concerns the high number of Muslims and Parsis. Muslims constituted
approximately 25 per cent of the Indian population, but Table 5 shows
that from 1894 the proportion of Muslim Indians travelling to England
consistently exceeded 25 per cent. The steep rise in students from the
north-west of India suggests that members of the Muslim intelligentsia
in these areas were abandoning their traditional suspicion of English
education and becoming increasingly attracted to the West. The Parsis,
who formed a tiny percentage of the Indian population and were
concentrated mainly in Bombay, came to England in disproportionately
high numbers. The tables reveal that at their peak they formed over 25
per cent of Britain's Indian student population and in 1885 Parsis even
out-numbered Muslims. The enormous over-representation of this
community suggests strong links between Parsis and England.

Table 3: Regional Analysis

	1885	1887	1890	1894	1896	1900
Bengal	58	50	53	101	104	45
Bihar				43	48	
Bombay	54	49	63	98	113	83
Madras	4	3	13	15	13	20
North-West Province	19	25	20	17	24	23
Punjab	12	14	31	49	49	43
Central Provinces	0	2	5	1	3	3
Native States	9	13	18	15	15	n.k.

Table 4: Subject Analysis

	1885	1887	1890	1894	1896	1900
Law	53	74	102	50	149	150
Medicine	38	33	30	31	29	30
Science, agriculture, engineering	23	10	4	5	0	9
Indian Civil Service	0	7	12	23	21	29
School	0	0	15	0	0	12

Table 5: Religious Analysis

	1885	1887	1890	1894	1896	1900
Hindu	69	79	122	149	155	144
Muslim	31	45	52	87	81	91
Parsi	38	36	45	53	53	57
Sikh	4	1	0	0	0	0
Christian	0	0	0	17	15	24
Brahmo	0	0	0	0	0	4

Source: *Journal of the National Indian Association*, 1885–1900

STUDIES

Indians in Britain mostly studied law, medicine, for the Indian Civil Service and for industry. Manmohan Ghose was the first Indian to be called to the Bar (i.e. to be admitted as a barrister) in 1866, followed by a string of other well-known names, including Michael Madhusudan Dutta, Badruddin Tyabji and W. C. Bonnerjee. The popularity of law among Indian students was due to the privileged position English-trained barristers exercised over Indian-qualified pleaders. Bar examinations were even said to be easier than legal examinations in India.

Despite this advantage, Indian students still used the services of a coach to guarantee success. S. S. A. Cambridge, a barrister of Gray's Inn from British Guyana, tutored many Indian students.[23]

From 1877 to 1886 the number of advocates in the three presidencies rose significantly. In the Bengal High Court it increased ninefold from four to 37, including eight Muslims. The number of advocates in Bombay more than doubled from 12 to 27 and in Madras there was an equivalent increase from five to 12.[24] This general expansion is seen more clearly after 1886. From this date Indian advocates in the Allahabad High Court started to outnumber Europeans by two to one, rising to 15:1 between 1921 and 1925, when only two out of 30 barristers were Europeans. For the years 1866 to 1928 75 per cent of the barristers appointed to the Allahabad High Court were Indian. The numbers of Muslims and Hindus were roughly equal, although Muslims appeared to have dominated for much of the period, particularly between 1896 and 1905.[25]

According to one student, Indians showed a preference for the Middle Temple, which was commonly known as the 'Indian Inn'.[26] It offered more scholarships than other Inns of Court and the Middle Temple's deposit was only £50, half the amount charged by the other Inns. This lessened the burden of paying a lump sum, which included admission fees. Yet financial considerations were not the only factors which informed a student's choice of Inn; library facilities and opportunities to meet eminent lawyers were also important.

The foreign element, classified as either Irish or Indian, grew substantially during the first decade of the twentieth century. By 1913 half the barristers called to Gray's Inn were from overseas. Overall they increased from 39 per cent of admissions in 1900 to 64 per cent in 1910.[27] This is reflected in Edward Dicey's observations in 1909, when he was a resident bencher and dined in the Inns of Court: 'The change from the days when I was myself a student, which struck me the most in the aspects of the Hall, was the fact that the native students, instead of being in a minority, as in former years, had become an enormous majority.' Dicey described how of the 17 students called to the Bar from Gray's Inn 'fifteen were Indians or Oriental and only two were white'.[28] After the First World War the lifting of travel restrictions caused an influx of students from India. J. A. Shearwood complimented Indian students on their general success at examinations: 'comparatively few failures are recorded, which is the more remarkable when it is remembered the examinations are held in a language which is not their mother tongue, and few of them have had the advantages of our public school training'.[29]

Three of the students who completed their medical education at University College, London, in the 1840s described earlier, joined the Uncovenanted Medical Service on their return to India. The Indian

Medical Service was not thrown open to competition until 1853. By 1860 only two Indians had been successful, subsequently the numbers passing the entrance examination increased. Most Indians studying medicine attended Edinburgh University. Several reasons contributed towards its popularity. Firstly, it was comparatively inexpensive compared with London. Secondly, it was better known to Indians than other medical schools. Many former students had become missionaries and doctors in India. Thirdly, it was possible for Indian students to do one part of their examination, modern languages, in their own vernacular. According to one Indian doctor, Indian medical colleges had higher admission standards,[30] a parallel with the situation in law. Although the number of Indian medical students was also high; many came, as we have noted, for only a few weeks or months, to sit examinations or attend classes. According to Sir T. R. Fraser, Professor of Clinical Medicine at Edinburgh, only a small minority remained there for more than a year.[31] The statistics available for 1902 to 1906 reveal that the number of medical students fluctuated between 70 and 82.[32]

Some of the Indian doctors who qualified in England obtained fellowships at the London medical colleges. Dr Hormusji Manekji Masin was the first student from Bombay to obtain a fellowship from the Royal College of Surgeons in England. Dr Mangaldas Mehta became a Fellow of the Royal College of Obstetricians and Gynaecologists and was knighted in 1936 for his services to medicine. He had worked in hospitals in London and Dublin since arriving in 1905. Gandhi's physician, Dr Jivaraj Mehta, studied in England for seven years, helping to establish the London Indian Association, a welfare centre for Indians in London.

Satyendranath Tagore was the first Indian to pass the Indian Civil Service examination in 1863 at University College, London. After his success was announced Cama and Company sent a donation of £3,000 to the college. Before 1922 ICS examinations took place exclusively in London.[33] Indian candidates had to spend between one to two years on probation at university in London, Oxford or Cambridge. Compulsory residence in a British university was introduced in 1876, when Lord Salisbury reduced the maximum age for ICS candidates from 21 to 19. The papers of the Viceroy of India, Lord Ripon, show that officials were concerned to secure suitable English candidates. An Oxbridge education was believed to provide unique moral and educational benefits. But Indian nationalists pointed to Lord Lytton's dispatch in 1878, which stated that 'the recent reduction of the age for competitive examination will practically render competition of natives educated in their own country a matter of exceptional difficulty'.[34] Whether the intention was to exclude Indian candidates or not, the effect was disastrous. Only one Indian succeeded out of ten hopeful candidates between 1876 and 1883.

Indians were handicapped in many ways. They were obliged to compete – in the English language against Englishmen – barely a year after matriculation, as well as to harness financial resources and to muster the courage to travel abroad at a young age. Numbers started growing after the age limit was raised again.

The idea of sending Indian students to Britain for technical instruction was first mooted at the Simla conference presided over by the Viceroy of India, Lord Curzon.[35] From 1904 the Indian government awarded ten scholarships for a duration of two years, every year. By 1912 222 students had been granted scholarships. This increase was reflected in the number of Indian students attending centres of technical education in Britain. Glasgow University had no technical students before 1905, but by 1913 60 were registered. Over the same period the size of the Indian student population of the Manchester School of Technology multiplied roughly fourfold. Birmingham University had only 23 Indians attending in the equivalent period.[36]

WOMEN STUDENTS

The vast majority of Indian students in Britain during the late nineteenth and the early twentieth century were male. However, as the twentieth century progressed, the number of Indian women students began to grow slowly.[37] The first Indian women came to Britain in the nineteenth century. According to National Indian Association figures, there were ten Indian women in Britain in 1887.[38] Most had accompanied their husbands, but four girls were attending school. Two years later, while the number of females remained stagnant, three were engaged in higher studies. By 1896 the number of women in England had trebled. Although only three were identified as medical students, a regional breakdown was provided: the majority came from Bengal (14) and Bombay (14) with two individuals from Punjab and the North-Western Province.[39] At the turn of the century 25 Indian women resided in Britain, 24 from Bombay and one from Calcutta. Thirteen were schoolgirls, nine were medical students and three had come for teacher training.[40]

Toru Dutt, the poetess, and her sister Aru were the first Bengali Christian women to travel to Britain with their parents in 1870. They may have been the first Indian women students in England. The sisters attended higher lectures for women at Cambridge University; as females they were prohibited from enrolling at the time. The lectures were supplemented by private tuition.[41] In 1879 another Indian Christian,[42] Susan Rajahgopal, Senior Assistant Mistress to the Government Female Normal School, Madras, was enabled by Miss Carpenter's Fund for

Indian Female Education to spend a year in England in order to study pedagogy.[43] The Government of Madras approved the scheme and agreed to finance the sea voyage and two-thirds of her pay during her stay. She received the remainder on her return.[44] The success of the scheme led the Madras government to send two more teachers, Anne Shunmugum and Henrietta Bernard, from the same school, in 1881. Other Indian women corresponded with the National Indian Association, in the 1870s, about studying in Britain. Anandamohan Bose requested a scholarship on behalf of a Bengali Hindu widow from Calcutta who wanted to become a teacher. She was granted £10, half the amount given to Susan Rajahgopal. When the daughter of Durga Mohan Das wished to study at Girton College, Cambridge, the Association asked Girton whether she could be exempted from summer examinations.[45]

By 1906 Bengal had fallen behind both Madras and Bombay in the field of female education and teacher training. To redress this imbalance the Government of Bengal decided to send two Indian women to be trained in England in order for them to return to India and teach in a training college for women teachers, to be established in Calcutta in connection with Bethune College. The Director of Public Instruction in Bengal, A. Earle, argued that even if the college were not built these women would be 'invaluable for employment as Assistant Inspectors of girls schools'.[46] They were given an allowance of £150 per annum for their two-year course and passages to and from India.

One of the students was Mrs Sarala Bala Mitter, a Hindu widow, graduate of Calcutta University and teacher at Bethune College. She attended Maria Grey Training College in England. According to Sarala's end-of-term assessment she had little difficulty fitting into the college or halls of residence and was very popular with her fellow students. She failed her practical teaching course, but improvement was predicted.[47] Earle believed that it was important to send a Muslim candidate as well. Miss Atia Fyzee (a relative of Badruddin Tyabji) won the scholarship. But, despite possessing 'plenty of mental powers and ability',[48] she was plagued by ill health in England. Consequently, her college attendance suffered and her results were poor. A year later Sarojini Das was able to secure a government scholarship, following intervention by her father. At 27, Sarojini had numerous qualifications as well as experience of teaching in Calcutta. She also suffered from ill health. Nevertheless she successfully took the Cambridge Teachers' Examination in December 1908 and studied kindergarten methods at the Froebel Institute.[49]

Despite the Government of Bengal's initiative, 'the crying need'[50] for suitably trained women teachers remained a stumbling block in the education of girls in the province. In 1909 a ladies committee in Calcutta, called the 'Mahila Samiti', established a scheme to raise sufficient money for training teachers in England. It was hoped that Indian women would introduce improved methods of teaching organisation in Indian schools, on their return.[51] Sympathisers of the scheme in London formed the Indian Women's Education Association. Lady Muir Mackenzie was elected president. Initially the body was exclusively female in composition and its president felt that this feature contributed to its success: 'What is so particularly interesting about the Indian Women's Education Association is that it is Indian women themselves who carry on the work.'[52] *The Times* reported that its ultimate objective was to establish a college in Calcutta.

The first scholar of the Association was Mrs Rajkumari Das. She spent a year (1917–18) at the London Day Training College, where her progress was praised, especially in view of the language difficulties she faced.[53] By 1931 the Association had provided 13 scholarships, one per annum. Candidates for scholarships were judged on both family background and academic qualifications. The poor quality of teachers in India was blamed on their low caste origins. The Indian Women's Education Association sought to raise the whole status of the teaching profession by offering Indian women of the 'cultured classes',[54] who were graduates of an Indian university, scholarships to enable them to train in England. The Association's membership was aware that as a small organisation its influence was limited. In fact, it was the only unofficial body funding teacher training for Indian women in England. One member, Mrs Sen, described its work as 'a mere drop in the ocean'.[55] Nevertheless, she believed that the impact of such training was immeasurable, not only on teachers in India but in terms of 'the value of contact, by travel and observation with ideas and methods ... differing from those prevailing in India'.[56] The flourishing careers of many of its scholars were regarded as proof of the Association's considerable success.

The National Indian Association's statistics show that several Indian women came to Britain to study medicine. In 1894 the Dufferin Fund provided scholarships for six to obtain experience in English hospitals for a period of two years. Two of these women were Indian, Miss Govindu Rajulu and Miss Miriam Singh; both came from Madras and qualified in Edinburgh. Other women who qualified in Britain included Annie Jagannadhan, who went to Edinburgh's School of Medicine for Women in 1888 and returned to India with a triple qualification in 1892 to take up the post of house surgeon at Cama Hospital in Bombay. Two years later she died of tuberculosis. Motibai Kapadia also studied in

Britain; on her return she was put in charge of the Victoria Hospital in Ahmedabad, remaining in the post for 36 years. Dr D. J. R. Dadabhoy was the first Indian woman to obtain a diploma in tropical medicine from the University of London. Dr Jensha Jhirad won the Tata Scholarship, when it was extended to women. After qualifying at the London School of Medicine for Women in 1916, she took up several posts in hospitals around the country. In 1919 she returned to India with an MD in obstetrics and gynaecology from the University of London, the first Indian woman to take examinations in this subject.[57]

Dr Rukhmabai also trained at the London School of Medicine for Women, qualifying in 1894. Before coming to Britain she had been involved in a celebrated court case, involving the restitution of conjugal rights. Rukhmabai had married her husband, Dadaji Bhibaji, when she was 11 and he was 19, but she continued to live with her family. Finally after 12 years had passed, Dadaji demanded that she live with him. Rukhmabai refused on the grounds that she had had no say in the marriage and found him personally repugnant.[58] Her husband brought a case against her and the court found in his favour, ordering Rukhmabai to live with her husband. It is unclear what followed, but Rukhmabai finally came to England through the exertions of an English woman doctor, Dr Pechey Phipson, who was attached to a women's hospital in Bombay. In England Rukhmabai lived with the Liberal MP W. S. B. Mclaren and his wife, who undertook to raise funds for her medical studies.

By 1920, as a result of the growing numbers of Indian women students in Britain, the London School of Medicine for Women, in co-operation with the India Office, opened a hostel for Indian women medical students. Miss L. M. Brooks was the warden. The shortage of rental accommodation after the First World War meant that 'In some cases they had to wander from place to place seeking admission and even when this had been gained it has been for a few weeks only.'[59] The Secretary of State for India provided the hostel with an interest-free loan of £1,000.

While most Indian women came to study either medicine or teaching, some came to study in a private capacity. For example, Renuka Ray enrolled at the London School of Economics in the 1920s. Cornelia Sorabji[60] was the first woman of any nationality to study law at a British university (Oxford). Indian women were not eligible for government scholarships when she applied in 1889,[61] therefore a private fund was set up for her in England. Another Indian, from the Tata family, who was called to the Bar in 1923, when it was opened to women, followed Cornelia Sorabji.

BRITISH INITIATIVES

Any discussion of the background of Indian students in Britain between 1880 and 1930 is incomplete without reference to key committees and government bodies set up to deal with this group. As will become clear, the students were frequently regarded as a 'problem' in official circles by the early twentieth century, if not before. The official spotlight was first placed on Indian students in 1907, when the Lee Warner Committee was established to investigate the whole issue of the position of Indian students in Britain. Although students had provoked attention before then, this was the first time the issue was deemed serious enough to warrant a governmental inquiry. The general feeling was that Indian students had failed to make the most of their residence in England. Oral and written testimony was taken from 65 Europeans and 35 Indians in London, Cambridge, Oxford and Edinburgh.[62]

Some students felt that there was no justification for the inquiry; others viewed the Committee as a cover for spying.[63] When the Lee Warner Committee finally completed its report, all sides agreed that the nature of its findings warranted its suppression. On 4 March 1908 Lord Minto, Viceroy of India, wrote to Lord Morley, Secretary of State for India: 'the [Indian] Home Department were a good deal taken aback at certain statements in it, the publication of which they declare would without doubt put the fat into the fire again'.[64] There was consensus that passages in the report could be open to misrepresentation and might offend Indians. Fifteen years later the Lee Warner Report was published as an appendix to the 1922 Lytton Report, which had re-examined the position of Indian students in Britain. Even after such a long time the Government of India had been extremely reluctant for such a frank and controversial report to be published. Finally, the Secretary of State for India, Lord Peel, overrode any opposition to publication. In a letter to Peel, Lord Lytton, the Parliamentary Under Secretary to the India Office, advocated a more open and less secretive approach. He could not comprehend the Government of India's 'nervousness' on the subject and regarded their sensitivity to Indian opinion as excessive.[65]

Before 1909 there was no official organisation to oversee Indian students in Britain, only voluntary associations existed. The National Indian Association in Aid of Social Progress and Female Education in India, referred to earlier, was founded in 1871. The objects of the Association were stated on the front page of its journal: 'To extend a knowledge of India in England and an interest in the people of that country. To co-operate with all efforts made for advancing education and social reform. To promote friendly intercourse between English people and the people of India.'[66] The Northbrook Society, established in the 1880s, was also interested in Indian visitors to Britain. Other societies were established by Indian students themselves, including the London Indian Society and the Indian Society. In 1909, implementing the Lee Warner Committee's recommendations, an Advisory Committee and Bureau of Information were established in London under the chairmanship of Lord Ampthill and the executive control of T. W. Arnold. The Bureau provided information on educational matters, furnished references, provided lists of suitable lodgings and kept in touch with India. The Advisory Committee was concerned with guardianship of students, publication of handbooks and arranging receptions.

In 1912 the Indian Student Department was created at the India Office. As in the case of the other official organisations, the British authorities had had to be jolted out of their complacency, in this case by the outcry following the assassination of Sir William Curzon Wyllie, Political ADC, by an Indian student, Madan Lal Dhingra. British officials felt obliged to put Indian students under a framework of institutional control. In 1913 local advisers were appointed to Indian students at Oxford, Cambridge, Manchester, Glasgow and Edinburgh. Later, after formal representation by students against these advisers, the university authorities took over.

NOTES

1 Indians also came in the capacity of visitors and businessmen, such as K. R. Cama and Dadabhai Naoroji. Naoroji was Britain's first Indian MP (Liberal). He was also professor of Gujarati at University College, London, writer, historian, economist, founder of the London Indian Society, social reformer and keen Zoroastrian. A considerable number of Indian craftsmen attended exhibitions in Britain, see Ch. 3 for exact numbers.
2 India Office Library (IOL)L/P&J/6/296, No. 278, 1891.
3 J. Newcombe Goad, *White into Harvest* (London: Morgan & Scott, 1927), p. 97.
4 *London City Mission (LCM) Magazine*, Vol. 88 (1922), A. C. Marshall.
5 J. Salter, *The Asiatic in England: Sketches of Sixteen Years Work among Orientals* (London: Seely, Jackson & Halliday, 1873) and *The East in the West or Work among the Asiatics and Africans in London* (London: S. W. Partridge, 1896).
6 T. R. Underwood, 'Work among Lascars in London', *East and West*, 4 (1906), p. 467.
7 *LCM Magazine*, Vol. 77 (1912), p. 145. This figure included men from various parts of the Far East and Africa.
8 *Indian Magazine and Review*, No. 477 (September 1910), p. 248.
9 Ardashir Wadia came to Britain in 1840 to study marine engineering and a year later his two cousins Jehangir Naoroji and Hirjeebhoy Merwanji Wadia followed him to learn about shipbuilding. Their experiences are recounted in *Journal of a Residence of Two Years and a Half in Great Britain* (London: William H. Allen, 1841). But none of

these men attended university or any other institutes of education; they merely observed the operation and methods employed by British industry.

10 *Edinburgh Review*, Vol. 217, No. 443 (January 1913), F. H. Brown.

11 Chakrabarty took the name of his mentor Dr Goodeve.

12 University College, London (UCL), Annual Report 1846.

13 Proceedings of UCL Annual General Meeting, 28 February 1855.

14 Rustomjee Wadia later joined them.

15 UCL, Proceedings of AGM, 25 February 1857.

16 Kopf, *Brahmo*, p. 195.

17 Ibid., p. 97.

18 *Indian Magazine*, No. 26 (February 1873), p. 271.

19 (IOL) V/24/832, Indian Student Department Report, 1928, p. 28. D. C. B. Drake, the *Indian Mirror*, 9 December 1885, speculated that 1.5 to 2 per cent of the whole educated class had at one time been to England.

20 (IOL)L/P&J/6/1275, No. 3864, 1913.

21 K. Chowdhury, 'The Indian Student in England', *Student Movement*, 12 (1910), pp. 86–8.

22 (IOL) Indian Student Department Report, 1914, p. 969.

23 *West Africa*, 24 June 1922, p. 660.

24 A. Seal, *The Emergence of Indian Nationalism: Competition and Collaboration in the Later Nineteenth Century* (Cambridge: Cambridge University Press, 1968), p. 126. Again, the evidence suggests that the majority of Muslims in Britain came from the north-west of India.

25 G. F. M. Buckee, 'An Examination of the Development and Structure of the Legal Profession in Allahabad, 1866–1935' (PhD, University of London, 1972), p. 160.

26 S. Satthiandhan, *Four Years in an English University* (Madras: Varadachari, 1893), p. 161. Observation made by C. Krishnan.

27 R. L. Abel, *The Legal Profession in England and Wales* (Oxford: Blackwell, 1988), p. 69.

28 E. Dicey, 'Hindu Students in England', *Nineteenth Century and After*, 66 (August 1909), p. 353. Dicey (1832–1911) was a respected and influential journalist. He had edited the *Observer* newspaper and was a regular contributor to *Nineteenth Century and After*, specialising in the politics of eastern Europe. Although he was called to the Bar in his youth, he did not practise. But he did take up residence in chambers at the turn of the century, which forms the basis of the article. See L. A. Gordon, *Brothers against the Raj – A Biography of Sarat and Subhas Chandra Bose* (New Delhi: Penguin, 1990), p. 23 for an analysis of the number of Indian students at the three Inns of Court between 1909 and 1915. According to these figures, Lincoln's Inn was the most popular with 374 (total number attending over the six-year period), followed by the Middle Temple with 267, and finally Gray's Inn had 152 Indians. Although the figures do not support Satthiandhan's remarks for the nineteenth century, Dicey's number of 15 for the number of Indians at Gray's Inn in 1909 is similar to Gordon's figure of 19. Gordon's book also contains a reference to the number of Bengalis at the Middle Temple, p. 624.

29 *Indian Magazine*, No. 585 (April 1918), p. 61. I have been unable to find out more about J. A. Shearwood.

30 (IOL) Report of Indian Students Committee [Lytton Report], Part 1 (London, 1922). Hereafter known as W1757. Appendix 4 (see note 34). Report contains 1907 Lee Warner Report. Hereafter known as Appendix 4.

31 (IOL) L/P&J/6/845, 1908 (unpublished evidence volume of Lee Warner Report), p. 261.

32 Ibid., p. 271. Appendix to Dr Fraser's statement.

33 In 1922 it became possible to sit ICS examinations in Allahabad, followed by Delhi six years later.

34 British Library (BL), Ripon Papers, Add. Mss. 43,580, Lord Lytton (Viceroy of India, not to be confused with his son, mentioned above, who chaired the 1922 committee into Indian students), 2 May 1878, p. 263.

35 Numerous Parsis came to observe the workings of British industry, including, shipbuilding, textile, engineering, steel and soap manufacture in the mid-nineteenth century. See note 9.

36 (IOL) V/26/865, Indian Technical Student Committee Report, 1912 (London, 1913), p. 10.

37 Indian universities accepted women students before British universities. The University of Madras admitted women in 1876 and the University of Calcutta removed restrictions in 1878; London was a year behind in 1879.

38 *Indian Magazine*, No. 169 (January 1887).

39 Ibid., No. 306 (June 1896), p. 313.

40 Ibid., No. 349 (January 1900), p. 71.

41 H. Das, *Life and Letters of Toru Dutt* (London: Oxford University Press, 1920).

42 Many of the first generation of Indian women students were Christian, including Cornelia Sorabji, Mary Bhore and Pandita Ramabai. (The last converted to Christianity while a student and teacher at the Cheltenham Ladies College.) But these ladies were not as devout as Manorama Bose, who came to England in 1882 to pursue a teacher-training course. Entries in her diary show that she maintained a rigorously Christian lifestyle, attending church and bible classes to the exclusion of everything else. (IOL) MSS. Eur. F. 178/69.

43 *Journal of the National Indian Association* reported the arrival of two sisters in 1877 to study pedagogy.

44 (IOL) MSS. Eur. F. 147/3, Committee Meeting of NIA, 26 November 1879.

45 Ibid., Committee Meeting, 8 January 1878.

46 (IOL) L/P&J/6/772, No. 2394, 1906.

47 Ibid., Principal of Maria Grey College, Miss Alice Wood, 25 March 1907.

48 Ibid., Certificate for end of autumn term, 19 December 1907.

49 (IOL) L/P&J/6/823, No. 2722, 1907.

50 W. Wedderburn and K. G. Gupta, *Female Education in India*, 10 February 1916.

51 Ibid.

52 *Indian Magazine*, No. 511 (July 1913), Annual Meeting of NIA, 1913, p. 185. I have not been able to find out more about Lady Muir Mackenzie.

53 Ibid., No. 566, February 1918.

54 Fawcett Library Papers (FL) Indian Women's Education Association, *General Meeting and Report for Two Years ending October 20, 1932*, pp. 7–8.

55 *Times Educational Supplement*, 22 July 1920, p. 403.

56 (FL) Indian Women's Education Association, 1932.

57 Wellcome Institute: Medical Women's Federation Papers, SA/MWF, Box 16.

58 In fact, the court case shows Rukhmabai's motivation was much more complex. See *Advocate of India*, 14 April 1887 and *Bombay Gazette*, 29 June 1887.

59 *Times Educational Supplement*, 22 July 1920, p. 403.

60 Her sister Alice studied medicine at Great Ormond Street Hospital, London, and became a medical missionary in India.

61 (IOL) L/P&J/6/260, No. 1430, 1889.

62 (IOL) L/P&J/6/845, p. 4.
63 Ibid., Satya. V. Muckerjea and M. N. Chak, p. 254.
64 (IOL) MSS. Eur. D. 573/4, 43-1908.
65 (IOL)MSS. Eur. F. 160/10, 3 August 1922. Lord Victor Alexander George Bulwer-Lytton (1876–1947) became Governor of Bengal in 1922 after chairing the Committee.
66 (IOL) MSS. Eur. F. 147/4.

— 1 —

Indian Purposes: Travelling Subjects

TWO apparently contradictory processes were taking place in the late nineteenth and the early twentieth century. In Britain there was a steady increase in the number of Indian students, while in India the perception of western superiority was undergoing erosion. Evidence for a rejection of the West can be seen in all spheres of life: socially there was increased racial animosity; politically, there was an assertion of indigenous Hindu identity and the rise of nationalism; lastly, there was a keener sense of economic exploitation. Before leaving India many students were exposed to all three.

REJECTION OF THE WEST

According to the established view, one aspect of Indian life few Indians managed to escape, regardless of status, caste or wealth, was racial discrimination. Senior British officials were not blind to the indignities suffered by Indians; Sir Henry Cotton mentioned the abuses and assaults inflicted on the local population by the British community and noted that the more educated the Indian, the more he was disliked by Englishmen, because he wanted to be treated as an equal.[1] Ill-treatment of Indians, such as ejection from first-class train compartments and common assault, were regular occurrences. Another aspect of the problem was racial exclusion. Indians were debarred from advancement within government service, even though they had suitable quali- fications. Pherozeshah Mehta, Brojendra De, W. C. Bonnerjee and Surendranath Banerjea were all passed over for promotion. Matters came to a head during the Ilbert Bill controversy, the legislation intended to give Indian judges and magistrates criminal jurisdiction over resident Europeans. Racism provoked a dual response: not only did it imbue Indians with a strong sense of colour and nationality, it also offered an area of emotional identification between different classes of Indian, which united them and to a certain degree overrode sectional interests.

Despite racism, alliances between English officials and well-placed

Indians were fostered in the form of patron/client relations.[2] These
relationships were used to facilitate travel to and education in Britain,
particularly for students arriving in the nineteenth century. W. C.
Bonnerjee was assisted by an English lawyer, Cockerel Smith. Aurobindo
and Manmohan Ghose lived with an English friend of their father (K.
D. Ghose), who acted as their guardian. Pandita Ramabai was encouraged and supported during her residence in England by the Sisters of
Wantage Mission. However, Gandhi does not fit this model: he had no
contact with the British before making his decision to go and study in
England. 'For the first time in my life', he wrote, 'I had an interview with
an English gentleman [Mr Lely]. Formerly I never dared to front them.
But thoughts of London made me bold.'[3] Gandhi was unable to secure
any financial support for his venture from Lely, a British official.

The fundamental contradiction between British and Indian interests
was most apparent in the economic context, promoted in the 'drain of
wealth' theory. Dadabhai Naoroji first propounded the theory in 1867.
He argued that nearly a quarter of India's revenues were expropriated
by Britain; as a result, India was 'being continually bled'.[4] The drain
argument was a tangible symbol of British exploitation and its simple
adversarial message had widespread appeal. The impression grew that,
while Indians were faced with increased hardships from famines and
an additional taxation burden, they were still obliged to pay for British
home charges and contribute to the artificial export surplus. Naoroji
and his associates argued that only self-rule would arrest the drain and
allow the growth of native industries and traditional handicrafts, thereby removing any hindrance to Indian economic development. These
theories were put into practice when British goods were boycotted in
Bengal during the Swadeshi era (1905–08). By burning British imports,
Bengalis were able to show their physical rejection of the West and their
commitment to Swaraj.

The negative factors of racism and economic exploitation were not
enough to stimulate the creation of national consciousness in India.
Cultural nationalists looked for more positive ways in which the East
could assert its superiority over the West. The glorification of ancient
India was given intellectual credibility by the work of scholars such as
Max Müller. The theosophical movement of Olcott, Blavatsky and
Besant all praised eastern spirituality over western materialism. All over
India it was possible to see the assertion of a specifically Hindu identity.
In western India, Balgangadhar Tilak spearheaded opposition to the
Age of Consent Bill, complaining about British interference in Indian
cultural practices. In northern India, the religious reform movement
Arya Samaj argued the superiority of Hinduism based on Vedic infal-
libility, and in southern India Annie Besant influenced the English-

educated. The development of overtly patriotic literature in the nine-
teenth century, particularly in the historic novels of Bankim Chandra
Chatterjee, did much to instil pride in Bengalis and popularise the
Bhagavad Gita. Another Bengali, Swami Vivekananda, reinterpreted the
Vedanta. He rejected all western models as alien to the Indian situation,
advocating instead renunciation (*sanyasa*) and social service. The cult of
Sakti, associated with the goddess Kali, was also unique to Bengal. This
Hindu religious revival alienated Muslims, but even within Islam Sufi
eclecticism was suffering a decline in popularity, leading to a return to
fundamentals.

While 'new Hinduism' provided a religious stimulus, Japan's victory
over Russia in 1904 demonstrated eastern military might. A contemporary Indian underground revolutionary pamphlet read: 'Indians,
look the fire is burning in Japan and Russia has retreated before its
blazing heat.'[5] Inspired by the Japanese victory, Sarala Devi Ghoshal
opened a fencing academy in Calcutta. She had already opened a school
for physical education two years earlier to infuse her fellow countrymen
with a sense of patriotism.[6] Other events in the world were also noted
in India, such as the development of anti-colonial movements in Turkey,
Egypt and Ireland, the Russian Revolution, the Chinese Boxer rising
and the introduction of representative institutions in colonies such as
Barbados, the Philippines and New Zealand.

Why was it that Indians chose to travel to Britain during a period
when the West was losing its attraction? I shall answer this question by
examining student motivation for studying in Britain. This chapter will
illustrate how functional motives for travel to Britain were accompanied
by the quest for 'authentic' imperial culture. But first it is necessary to
look at the background to this development. Travel is crucial to theories
of colonial encounter mentioned earlier. By investigating why people
travel, what they see, changing perceptions of themselves and others
towards them, it is possible to see the effects of travel on self-image and
identity.

MOVEMENT FOR FOREIGN TRAVEL IN BENGAL

The increase in the number of Indians travelling to Europe by the early
twentieth century may be attributed, in part, to the gradual lifting
of the Hindu taboo on sea voyages. In 1894 a group of self-appointed
Bengalis formed a standing committee to investigate the thorny topic
of sea travel. The committee consisted of three judges and two doctors.
The credentials of the committee secretary Maharaj Kumar Benoy
Krishna were impeccable. He represented one 'of the most respectable

orthodox Hindu families of Calcutta',[7] which no doubt added substance to the committee's hopes of being taken seriously by religious fundamentalists. The Indian press reported the growth of meetings in support of sea voyages. Five well-attended and enthusiastic meetings were reported in Calcutta. The movement was also able to elicit the support of high-ranking British officials such as Sir Alexander Miller, the legal member of the viceregal council.

> I am sure [he wrote to Maharaj Bahadur] it would be very useful to English public opinion if they saw more of Hindoo gentlemen. The English idea of a Hindoo is too frequently taken from some Bearer or Ayah, who has accompanied his or her employer to England, and even the young men who come over to read for the Bar, or at Universities, do not mix enough with English gentlemen to affect the feeling of society there. This is partly from their being so few in number, and partly also, no doubt, from difficulties of language, which induce them to stick a good deal together.[8]

The Hindu sea-voyage movement in Bengal launched a two-pronged attack on its opponents. In a pamphlet it sought to show, firstly, the advantages of foreign travel, while countering religious objections, and, secondly, it accused its orthodox critics of inconsistency in regard to their treatment of returnees.

The sea-voyage movement was able to show an historical precedent for foreign travel. Evidence from the Report of the Sixth National Social Conference in Allahabad was used. One delegate claimed that:

> Under the Peshwa's rule, two Brahmin agents ... had gone to England 110 years ago and on their return they had been taken back into orthodox society. Fifty years ago an agent of the Satara Rajah's, who had gone to England, had been similarly received back into society. Since then there had been a regular series of accumulated precedents, in which the head of Acharayahs of different sects had made the same pronouncements time after time after most serious deliberations.[9]

Sea voyages were, as the *Indian Mirror* pointed out on 20 August 1892, common in ancient India. The committee's aim was to proceed in its own words 'on the very safe lines of recommending a voyage by sea when it is performed under Hindu conditions of life'.[10] Consequently a crucial plank of the movement's argument was that it was practicable to live in Hindu fashion on board ship or in a foreign country. For this purpose several Anglo-Indian officials and the Indian press were cited to show that vegetarianism could be maintained in England without inconvenience.[11] For example, Hindu traders who travelled as far afield as New York and Hong Kong had not been outcast, because they travelled with a quantity of dried food and drank purified water.[12]

The movement for foreign travel was not just a turn of the century phenomenon. As early as 1871 Satyendranath Tagore on his return from Europe advocated foreign travel:

> It is only when we see a state of society completely different from our own [he argued] and far more improved and civilised, not only see it, but are influenced by it, that we begin to realise our own shortcomings by contrast. When, for instance, we see the position occupied by the fair sex in European society, we feel how degraded is the condition of our own ladies. As more of our people are attracted to Europe, they will naturally imbibe liberal and enlightened ideas, and come back as missionaries of western knowledge and civilisation.

He looked forward to the time 'when "Westward ho!" will be the general cry of our people, when parents will not consider the education of their sons as finished before they have passed through a course in one of the English universities'.[13]

The standing committee also argued that residence in the West was essential in order to internalise fully the ideas propounded by English education: 'English education and the new environment brought forth by modern civilisation have created in the minds of the people of this country new ideas, which they admire, but feel it difficult to assimilate, to make their own. Sea voyage and residence in western countries help the sojourners there to assimilate these ideas.'[14] A government official argued in a similar vein when he claimed that 'to get the best out of a distinctively English culture it is obviously essential to visit England itself'.[15] The committee concluded: 'We thus see sea voyage as a necessary supplement to the education which the people are now receiving.'[16]

Foreign travel had profound political and economic implications. The supporters of sea voyages were keen to point out that it was the England-returned who constituted the progressive elements in Indian society and 'the moving spirit of the National Congress'. Thus foreign travel was viewed as an essential component of modernity and progress. The economic aspect of the question was also stressed: 'There is a growing desire ... in some quarters to make excursions to the West for commercial purposes ... People may feel themselves driven by sheer necessity to try their fortune in remote countries ... come back home with added qualifications and augmented resources.'[17] One newspaper warned that restrictions on foreign travel had already exacted a high price: 'The immemorial prohibition of the Hindu to cross kalapani [the black waters of the sea] has sealed his doom, has effected his political extinction, and left him an intellectual roué.'[18]

The main area in which the committee needed to persuade its orthodox opponents of the validity of its cause was that of religious dogma. The committee consulted a large number of pundits; 68 signed the following statement:

> As residence in England and other foreign countries does not come within the category of heinous transgressions, involving degradation (*patita*), and heavy penances are not provided for it, and there is nothing even by parity of reasoning to consider it a heinous transgression, a person, who resides in England and other foreign countries, without committing any heinous transgressions should not be considered fallen (*patita*).[19]

A further 42 pundits signed a similar statement stating that a Hindu should not be outcast if he adhered to the *shastras* when abroad. However, pundits were divided about food consumed out of necessity. Two schools of thought existed: one view stipulated that 'the sin can be expiated, but that the person who commits the sin cannot again associate with his caste-fellows'; the other took a less inflexible stance. While it was impossible to forgive the sin, 'the performance of expiatory ceremonies would allow the offender to mix socially with his caste-fellows'.[20] A contributor to a Calcutta magazine argued that the *shastras* did not explicitly forbid sea travel: 'On the contrary God Himself is given the title of "the Steersman", "He who holds the tiller".' Furthermore, 'one of the best known tales in Bengali literature was the tale of Srimanta, the merchant', who beheld the goddess, Kamala, while sailing to Ceylon.[21] Nearly a decade before the pamphlet was published, the Principal of Lahore College, Dr Leitner, had purchased a college at Maybury, England, with a view to establishing an 'Oriental University'. The primary object of the college was to allocate suitable facilities to ensure against loss of caste.[22]

At grassroots level it was difficult to find much coherent or systematic opposition to foreign travel. Bankim Chandra Chatterjee, an author and leading member of Bengali Hindu society, consulted by the committee wrote: 'I have not come across a single instance in which the journey to Europe was abandoned out of respect to the authority of the *shastras*.'[23] If this is to be believed, critics of foreign travel were not as powerful as supposed, and supporters of sea voyages had already partially won the argument. Chatterjee, however, admitted that most of those who had returned from Europe 'remained outside the pale of Hindu society'. Bankim had little sympathy for such individuals, arguing that their ostracism was self-imposed. 'On their return to this country', he claimed, 'they voluntarily keep away from Bengali society by adopting European habits and customs ... Those who on their return from Europe did not adopt this course have in many instances been re-admitted into Hindu society.'[24] Bankim's criticism of the England-returned was part of a wider backlash which was taking place in late nineteenth-century Bengal. Tapan Raychaudhuri has shown in his book *Europe Reconsidered* that perceptions of England and of the West in general admitted both criticism and, in the cases of Bhudev Mukhopadhyay and Bankim Chandra Chatterjee, rejection of some western values in favour of Indian ones.[25]

The standing committee was able to record in some detail the glaring contradictions and anomalies which existed in regard to the whole question of outcasting and adherence to Hindu orthodoxy. The consumption of food forbidden by Hindu scriptures had, according to the committee, 'been pretty common in Hindoo society' for some time, without such men being outcast. The practice had been growing in Bengal, not just among students and schoolboys but even among leading members of the community. It was reported that, 'In their own private residences or those of their friends, European or Native, in garden houses, in hotels kept by European or Mohammedans, on steamers, in railway refreshment rooms, numbers of Hindoo gentlemen dine in the European style, and the orthodox members of society find it convenient to connive at these practices.'[26] Restaurants that served European dishes were said to be increasing near offices and theatres. Similarly pipe-water, which had been frowned upon, was regularly consumed 'by Hindus of unquestioned orthodoxy', along with in some cases wines, spirits, medicines as well as European and Muslim confectioneries.

It was not just in private life that some groups of Hindus adopted new western habits; public life too was not immune from encroachment. Some dedicated Anglophile nationalist leaders, many of whom had studied in Britain, caused difficulties for the organisers of the annual meeting of the Indian National Congress by obliging them to make special arrangements for delegates who lived in 'European Style'. The committee concluded:

> Hindoo society has exhibited nothing like consistency, observed no definite principle, in dealing with those of its members who have made voyages to Europe. The same men that recognise them on one occasion do not recognise them on another. They dine with them today and decline to dine with them tomorrow ... [T]he utmost that the ultra-orthodox members of the community seek to do is to omit to recognise only the travelled men, while they permit themselves to mix freely with men who have been tainted by association with the chief offenders.[27]

At a fundamental level the sea-voyage controversy focused attention on whether it was practicable or desirable to maintain an orthodox Hindu lifestyle, at the cost of individual freedom of movement. The importance of the issue is made clear by the following statement:

> It cannot be a matter of indifference to the Hindoo community if the gentlemen who come back from Europe ... are to be received back into society or excluded from it ... no subject can be of greater national importance than the discussion of the limits which custom may have prescribed to the liberty of movement of the men who compose the nation.[28]

Although the standing committee attacked religious zealots for the hypocrisy and inconsistency of their stance on the issue, nevertheless it was concerned to avoid alienating such an influential group. As a result, it argued that it was possible to reap the benefits of foreign travel without the wholesale adoption of western habits.

THE QUESTION OF SEA VOYAGES OUTSIDE BENGAL

Lucy Carroll's article on the sea-voyage controversy in early twentieth-century northern India suggests that it was not so much the localised nature of opposition which flared up in the cases of two returnees, Ganesh Prasad and Parmeshwar Lal, which demands attention, but rather the tremendous breadth of support for foreign travel among north Indians. Groups usually classified as 'traditionalist', in terms of the social reform debate in India, voiced their support for sea travel and certain philanthropic kayastha taluqdars paid for students to study in Britain.[29]

In areas outside Bengal, particularly the north-west of India, a much more relaxed, *laissez-faire* approach to foreign travel appears to have been the norm. According to the newspaper *Kayastha Samachar* there was little opposition to Indians returning from Europe at the turn of the century: 'The majority of those who have come back from Europe have refused to perform any expiatory rites, and although certain individuals have kept themselves aloof from them for a time, the bulk of the community have never raised any difficulties and matters in the course of a few years have smoothly settled down.'[30] However, one group that did express their resentment and jealousy was the Indian-trained *vakils*. Not only did British-trained barristers block their promotional path, but they also enjoyed many privileges over *vakils*, pushing them into second place.[31]

When the Bengal sea-voyage movement requested the opinion of the Indian Union of Allahabad, the Bengalis were accused of hypocrisy on the issue. It was, they felt, inappropriate for Bengalis, not known for their rigid adherence to religious doctrine, to attempt to take the moral high ground on this question. The issue of foreign travel excited little attention in Allahabad, which prompted one of its residents to write:

> In these provinces the question is not of so much importance. The kayasthas, various classes of Brahmans and other caste-men have taken 'England-returned' barristers, merchants and other persons without much fuss about it. If the highest caste Brahmin goes to England and *lives carefully in orthodox Hindoo style*, ready to listen to the dictates of the orthodox Hindoo community – no one will have the slightest objection in taking him back ... [S]o we have not much anxiety for our men here, who may go to England for the country's cause.[32]

It is here that the Union of Allahabad's irritation spilt over:

> But the orthodoxy of Bengal, it seems, is differently constituted. Some of these have raised a hue and cry ... over this question, which would not raise them much in the estimation of their sensible fellow-countrymen both in and out of Bengal. There are Hindus ... who are better Hindus than modern Bengalees, generally speaking, can ever claim to be. They observe the rigid discipline of caste ... observing Hindu rites as strictly as they can be observed. What is the average Bengal Hindu of today, to these truly orthodox scions of the Aryan race?[33]

Striking comparisons were made between what was perceived as the rather meagre endeavours of Indians crossing the Pacific, English boys cycling around the world and Japanese students filling up European universities. It was argued that restrictions on travel were 'unnatural' in an age when voyaging was universal; instead they had become an unbearable burden to many. The Union concluded: 'Native youth must travel or see themselves distanced by the youth of far less civilised people than the bengalee.'[34] Paradoxically, the north Indian newspaper *Bharat Bandhu* had, in 1881, before the sea-voyage movement had been launched in Bengal, actually viewed Bengalis as more advanced on this issue. It had called on north Indians to send their sons abroad for fear of Bengali and Muslim competition.[35]

Bombay's liberal attitude to foreign travel was remarked upon by a south Indian Brahmin as early as 1884: 'In Bombay presidency going to England has become common enough, and there is no difficulty with regard to the social restoration of the traveller.'[36] This does not tally with

Gandhi's experience in the 1890s; although most of those travelling from
Bombay in the nineteenth century were Parsis, who entertained no
religious objections to foreign travel and to whom the observation
would appear more applicable. The south Indian Brahmin noted that
'overpowering resistance' existed in his own homeland. But here, as in
Bengal, there was inconsistency on the question of outcasting. He cited
the following anecdote to illustrate his point: 'One of the barristers now
practising at Bangalore is a Brahman, whom the Smartas have excom-
municated. But his Brahman servant, who had lived with him in
England for years, had been, after some probation and after certain
ceremonies, taken back into the bosom of his caste and family.'[37]

It is clear from the great personal cost involved that few Indians can
have taken lightly the decision to travel to Britain. Not only was there
the prospect of ostracism from the community in which the young man
(or in some cases woman) had grown up, but, in addition, excom-
munication from close family members was not uncommon. The
pioneer travellers Sasipada Banerji and his wife were both stoned and
abused when embarking on their journey. Others, such as W. C.
Bonnerjee, were forced to adopt clandestine methods in order to flee
their parental home and receive training in England. In the age of high-
speed transport it is easy to forget the long and arduous voyage which
had to be endured. No amount of preparation or imagination could
equip Indian newcomers to Britain for the change in lifestyle and
environment they would encounter.

Despite these hurdles, expectations of England and the numerous
advantages it could offer were high. R. C. Dutt and his compatriots
Surendranath Banerjea and B. L. Gupta were well aware of the risks
they were taking; Dutt summed up their thoughts while travelling on
the steamer to Britain in a letter to his brother:

> We had left our homes and our country, unknown to our friends, unknown
> to those who are nearest and dearest to us, staking our future, staking all,
> on success in an undertaking which past experience has proved to be more
> than difficult. The least hint about our plans would have effectually
> stopped our departure; our guardians would never have consented to our
> crossing the seas; our wisest friends would have considered it madness to
> venture on an impossible undertaking. Against such feelings, and against
> the voice of experience and reason, we have set out in this difficult
> undertaking – stealthily leaving our homes – recklessly staking everything
> on an almost impossible success.[38]

Nevertheless, the incentives appeared to have outweighed the obstacles,
provoking Satyendranath Tagore to write as early as 1871: 'there are

strong inducements, which impel our people to visit England ... We find that our professional advancement, even social rank and position depend on it, we are emboldened to embark on the enterprise at considerable sacrifice, even at the risk of loss of caste.'[39]

UTILITARIAN MOTIVES

The growth of an Indian student population in Britain, in the nineteenth and the twentieth century, was in many respects an inevitable accompaniment of the imperial process. India's colonial relationship with Britain led to a situation where employment in government service was dependent on qualifications, which were obtainable only in Britain. Thus most of the Indians who came to Britain did so to gain qualifications, in order to be called to the Bar or join the Indian Civil Service or the major professions. The 1858 British proclamation promised impartial admission to government posts on a non-racial basis. As discrimination debarred entry into public and private enterprises, the professions and government service began to look more attractive.

At a practical level all those wishing to enter government service were forced to sit examinations in Britain. British-qualified barristers enjoyed privileges over their Indian counterparts, the *vakils*. This distinction was most prominent in Calcutta, where advocates trained in England had substantial advantages over *vakils*: they had the right to take the leading brief and they could appear for a client without power of attorney. There was no distinction between the two in Madras, which may explain why fewer individuals went to Britain from southern India. As already noted, the evidence suggests that the Bar examinations in England were at one point easier than pleader examinations in India. Pandit Bhagwadin Dube, Reader in Law at Allahabad University, claimed that 'It is well known that Bar examinations are not as difficult as those for legal degrees in India.'[40] When Dr Katju took the High Court pleader examinations in 1906 only 15 out of several hundred passed.[41] Furthermore the British official Curzon Wyllie argued: 'the Bar examinations should be made more difficult', as Indian students who had been unable to pass the pleader's examinations had been successfully called to the Bar in England.[42] This is supported by the alleged remarks of an Indian parent: 'I am sending my son to England because he has failed thrice in his examinations here.'[43] In many cases students whose parents had intended them for other professions in the words of one student, Sheikh Abdul Kadir, 'drifted to the Bar because it was the easiest thing to do'.[44]

The poor quality of legal education in India was reflected in the actions of leading Bombay barristers. Badruddin Tyabji, K. R. Cama and

N. V. Gokhale were so alarmed at the low standards of Bombay University Law School that they attempted to establish a rival institution, which would force the university to improve its standards.[45] An Indian who had been called to the Bar, Cumruddin Latif, believed the teaching was better in England, as the principles and not just the letter of the law were taught.[46] According to one pleader, law lectures in India were devoid of any reference to legal textbooks or precedents.[47]

In addition, all foreign qualifications were believed to have greater market value, offering brighter career prospects and increased financial rewards. Mohammed Said Khan was enticed by 'good pay' and 'good living' into journeying to England, to sit for the ICS examinations.[48] C. S. Venkatachar, another ICS probationer, who came to Britain in the 1920s admitted: 'My entry into the Civil Service was mainly a means of furnishing myself with a career with handsome emoluments and a pension at the end of it.'[49] Medicine was also a lucrative profession. In the late nineteenth century many Bengali Brahmos went to Britain to study homoeopathy as well as for the Indian Medical Service. This stint abroad enabled men such as Prafulla Chandra Roy and Dwarkanath Roy to build up reputations and 'carve out small fortunes for themselves as respected physicians' in Calcutta.[50]

No profession provided greater financial incentives than the law. The growth in the volume of litigation in the nineteenth century enabled England-returned barristers to exact high fees for often lengthy court cases. At the top end of the salary range were men such as C. R. Das and Motilal Nehru, who were able to live lavishly on their incomes. Badruddin Tyabji's income rose astronomically from Rs7,170 per month in 1868 to Rs122,360 per month in 1890,[51] on par with the most senior British officials in India. The stories surrounding the extravagant lifestyles of such men probably encouraged many others to embark upon legal careers. In 1888–89, 551 out of a total of 1,956 barristers and pleaders were earning over Rs2,000 and the equivalent figure in Bombay was 129 out of 542.[52] As one observer concluded in 1916:

> In the early twentieth century it is still true that the lawyers are the spoilt children of Bengal life. They make an income entirely disproportionate to their abilities, thus an able lawyer will make five or ten times as much in a year as an equally able doctor, and even an incapable lawyer will make a better income than capable members of other professions.[53]

The presence of a few Indian High Court judges by the end of the nineteenth century demonstrated that it was possible to scale the heights of the legal profession. This was not possible in the Indian Civil Service until the twentieth century, when Indians such as Satyendranath

Prasanna Sinha, an England-returned barrister, was appointed to the legislative council and Ibrahim Ramantulla became acting Governor of Bombay presidency in the 1920s. These material and promotional prospects had encouraged a hundred Indians to study at Lincoln's Inn between 1861 and 1893, 'increasing from one a year at first, to five or six annually towards the close of this period'.[54]

Not all of those who had been called to the Bar in England received wealth and prestige immediately on their return to India. Muhammad Ali Jinnah was unable to obtain a single brief for three years after his return from England. Gandhi and C. R. Das also took a long time to establish successful practices. Indian barristers were dependent on Indian solicitors to supply them with clients. Tyabji was fortunate in this respect, as his brother was a prominent solicitor. But most Indian barristers had to contend with a widespread preference on the part of litigants and solicitors for English barristers, who, it was believed, would exert greater influence over judges. Also a British qualification was not always a guarantee of success in an increasingly overcrowded profession. In 1896 there were 121 advocates practising in the Calcutta High Court. This figure had risen to 457 by 1916. In Bombay the number had increased from 84 to 248 over the same period.[55] Those who sought qualifications from Britain hoped that they would provide them with a much needed competitive edge.

Thus while Britain offered potential economic and career benefits for Indian students, India on the other hand provided few educational incentives. The uncontrolled growth of higher education following the Hunter Commission in 1882, which advocated the increase of private colleges, had led to a fall in standards. The Sadler Commission concluded:

> It is widely believed that the standards of attainment represented by the examinations of the universities has shown a steady decline. Such assertions are difficult to test or prove, but the enormous numbers of ill-trained candidates who have been sent from the schools to the entrance examination, and from the colleges to the higher examination make this conclusion appear probable.[56]

Lecturers were underpaid and overworked with poor conditions of tenure and pay. Classes were overcrowded and students received little guidance. It was clear that Calcutta University, with a drop-out rate of 50 per cent, believed to be the highest in the world, was failing its students, half of whom were never getting 'beyond the stage of school work',[57] owing to the low standards of secondary schools. Only 36.7 per cent of Indian students matriculated in the decade 1887 to 1897. A government report on the progress of education for the post-war years claimed that the superiority of British degrees was not due to the course of study pursued in India but in the methods of study.[58] This was a reference to the most common complaint levelled at universities; namely that they emphasised examinations, cramming and the memorising of facts parrot fashion, at the expense of analysis and intellectual development. The extent to which standards had dropped on a national level may be debatable, but it was the perception of 'intellectual deadness' and the numerous defects present in the Indian higher education system which acted as stimulants for students considering studying in Britain. Many British officials believed that the only way to halt the exodus was to improve educational standards in India.

INTELLECTUAL CONSIDERATIONS

It is possible, when looking at the wider motivation behind a student's decision to study in Britain, to overemphasise the obligatory aspects of the decision. The issue is a great deal more complex. Undoubtedly, most students arriving in Britain were aware that career advancement within the British power structure was dependent on qualifications from Britain. However, intellectual considerations were in many cases equally as important, or in the case of Dr Pherozeshah Mehta more important. He told Mohandas Karamchand Gandhi: 'We came to England not so much for purposes of studies as for gaining experience of English life and customs.'[59]

When one examines the statements given by students about their reasons for going to Britain, most stress the equal weight given to material and intellectual considerations. One of the pioneer Indian students in Britain, W. C. Bonnerjee, described how a visit to England allowed him to accomplish several objectives within a single act: 'I had offered to me a glorious opportunity of at once educating myself in England, seeing the world and getting called to the English Bar.'[60] Similarly, Pandit Bhagwadin Dube, when questioned by the 1907 Lee Warner Committee on the subject, replied that he had come to England, firstly, to be called to the Bar and, secondly, to see English life.[61]

The President of the Cambridge Majlis also argued that, while the primary objective of every Indian student in Britain was 'obtaining a sound education and qualifying themselves for work in some profession on their return', equally they were 'anxious to mix freely with Englishmen and see English life, for which they had come charged with intense admiration'.[62] The spread of English education by the late nineteenth century in India had ensured that most of the young men embarking on a sojourn in England were familiar with English history and literature. As a result, in the words of the 1910 Committee on Distressed Colonial and Indian Subjects: 'Many of them have thereby imbibed a reverence for civilisation and political institutions of this country.'[63]

English literature fuelled the desire of Indians to see the fictitious England portrayed in books. For M. C. Changla one biography alone was enough. Lord Morley's book *The Life of Gladstone* was, he wrote, 'a combination of biography and history and when I read it, the ambition grew that I should go to Oxford, possibly to the college in which Gladstone studied – Christ Church – and also enter public life and participate in Parliament'.[64] The Assamese historian S. K. Bhuyan, discussing his time in London, pointed out that his wish to visit Britain had been nurtured from a very young age. When he was 8, Bhuyan's high school teacher asked the class who entertained ambitions of going to England. Both Bhuyan and his friend stood up. Bhuyan was not unique among his peer group. He wrote that, 'A visit to England formed part of the future plans of ambitious children and youth of those days; and a man returned from abroad, known generally as a "Bilat-Pherat", commanded considerable distinction in society, whatever might be his actual achievement.'[65] As the years passed, Bhuyan's thoughts focused more on England. The following lines of a poem he composed during his adolescence summarise his thoughts at the time:

> I sigh for distant Albion's shore,
> The more I sigh, my will is more.
> Whose glens are green, whose people white,
> Afar extends whose terrestrial light.
> O, how I long there once to land,
> Helpless, save in way I planned.
> Anoint these dreams of future date,
> I long to go, but there is Fate.
> Gracious God, I know not how,
> To praise Thee and to bow Thee now.
> Forgive my follies, be my guide,
> Keep me guarded by your side.
> Oft in youth and oft in age,
> Check my pride, egotism and rage.
> Thou art my Father, Thou wilt show,
> The means to get it, the way to go.
> To the distant land I sigh for now,
> With desires which I know not how.[66]

His passion for England, like Changla's, stemmed from his love of romantic English literature. He wrote: 'My acquaintance with the gems of English thought roused in me an earnest desire to see the land, where so many great poets and authors were born.' Nevertheless, Bhuyan was clearly aware of the potential employment opportunities when he explained the dual benefits of such a trip: 'Besides, the laurels gained in a British university were useful from a material point of view, as they would entitle the possessor to a superior appointment in the Indian Civil Service, educational or administrative.'[67]

K. K. Banerjee believed that he articulated the views of 'thousands of educated Indians' when he described the intense disappointment he felt at having to abandon his hopes of studying in Britain. Although his father did not actually forbid him, nevertheless the prospect of the whole family's losing caste was an effective deterrent. Banerjee's father could appreciate his son's ambition, but the price to be paid for individual self-improvement was too high and Banerjee was reluctantly forced to agree. When asked to choose between family and personal ambition he chose family: 'Naturally I had to tell him that no I would not go to England.'[68] He was so distressed that he dreamt he was appearing in an examination at Charing Cross station. Although he had never set foot in England he could conjure up visions of it before his eyes. Similarly, a law student at the Middle Temple, Ram Gopal, was able to visualise 'the glories of London in all the strange and glowing tints'. His imagination proved inadequate: 'But when I set foot for the first time in London, oh, what a different spectacle presented itself! – a spectacle that far surpassed the picturing power of imagination.'[69] The proliferation of books and pictures of England-led Indians such as Banerjee to feel that they were intimately acquainted with the country. This is testimony to the success of English education as an instrument of acculturation.

A trip to Europe for an Indian had begun to acquire the same function that the Grand Tour of Europe had once fulfilled for a European, namely a way of completing a gentleman's education. J. C. Muckerji, an Indian student, spoke of the latent belief among Indian parents 'that the only thing necessary to make a man of his young ward is to fit him out to England'.[70] For some, travel to Europe had become part of their rite of passage, with the idea that a boy who had left on the steamer would return to India a man. However, as numbers increased throughout the twentieth century, England was no longer the haunt of a privileged minority. In 1913 a British official in Lahore claimed that a phenomenon which he called 'travel fever' had taken hold of whole districts and large groups of students from one area would go abroad to study the same subject.[71]

At the core of all motivation was the attraction felt by subjects of the empire to the metropolitan centre of the British Empire, England, or

more specifically London, the largest city on earth for much of the period
in question. The metropolis acted as an irresistible magnet to those who
lived at the periphery. An Indian student articulated this view clearly
in 1920: 'As colonials living on the periphery of the empire Indians are
naturally attracted to the metropolis. The English are the ruling people
in India and naturally ambitious Indian youth want to come to the centre
of the life of these people, just as they used to go to Delhi in olden days.'[72]
Metropolitan England had symbolic value; it was the fount of all
standards, power, justice, art, taste, culture and career advancement, as
well as the seat of imperial government. Dadabhai Naoroji's speech,
entitled 'England's duties to India', listing the benefits of British rule in
1867 described in a tentative way what students expected to find in
Britain: 'law and order', 'university education', 'material progress',
'social elevation' and, above all, political freedom.[73] To early liberal
nationalists such as Naoroji and the other founding fathers of the Indian
National Congress, who had all met in England, the West and particularly Britain was India's 'significant other'. Although British rule
was often the subject of criticism, nevertheless it was Britain that
provided the yardstick by which to measure India's achievements and
aspirations.

Indian nationalist historians and writers such as John Mcguire, David
Kopf and J. H. Broomfield[74] have argued that the affinity of Indians who
went to England for English literature and culture, shown above, was
a product of the distortions of colonialism, brought about by the inter-
nalisation of ruling-class values, in order to maintain British hegemony
in India. Within this framework the desire to visit Britain may be seen
as an exaggerated case of 'the acceptance of the objectification of one's
own culture as projected by the protagonists of the dominant culture'.[75]
Whether interest in Britain among English-educated Indians was a
manifestation of a type of 'false consciousness' or not, and clearly the
rise of nationalism demonstrates that acculturation was incomplete,
nevertheless its existence is clear.[76] The attraction of England operated
on different levels: it was possible to experience England vicariously,
through the writings of Indians who had resided in Britain, and
England-returned Indians were also influential.

INDIAN WRITING ON ENGLAND

The writing of individuals who had visited England in the capacity of
visitor or student provided insight into English life. Although many
were straightforward travelogues, with a short description of the places
visited and little comment, nevertheless they performed a useful

function. R. B. Nadkarni wrote in the preface of his European journal
that the object of his book was 'to remove the bar of prejudice against
foreign travel'.[77] While this was not always explicitly stated, the main
aim of those who published their experiences of Europe was to promote
foreign travel to an educated Indian audience. Furthermore, these
earlier travellers demonstrated that it was possible to maintain caste
in England. Even before the Hindu sea-voyage movement became
properly organised by the late nineteenth century, a south Indian lady,
Pothum Janakummah Ragaviah, who visited England with her
husband, wrote in her journal: 'I can testify from my own experiences
that England is a very healthy country for Hindus.'[78] A visitor to
England, the Reverend P. M. Chowdhury was also able to adhere to a
vegan diet.[79] Diarists made comparisons between India and Britain,
praising certain aspects of British life, including the treatment of women,
the athleticism of English students, general cleanliness, London, law
and order, enterprise and industry.

Satthianadhan presented an extremely glowing picture of his four
years at Cambridge, which no doubt did much to whet the appetites of
potential Indian students. He assured students of a warm welcome and
a guarantee of friendship from Oxbridge students:

> Here no sooner does he enter his college, than he finds himself in the midst
> of a refined circle of young men, who are eager to associate with him; here
> he mingles freely with men probably far above his station in life. There are
> no invidious distinctions of rank or race, the reverence with which men
> regard wealth or station being counteracted by the admiration they
> entertained for the aristocracy of moral or intellectual excellence.[80]

Furthermore, according to Satthianadhan, an Indian's nationality
would actually assist him in making friends: 'his being a foreigner is an
additional advantage which wins their friendship more readily'.[81]
Satthianadhan testified to the genuineness of these friendships by
recounting the time that he had been visited (when unwell) by his
college friends, and how he had been invited to their homes during
vacations. Not only were Oxbridge students welcoming, but college
life itself had the added bonus of freedom and independence. Such
advantages were not, he believed, available in London or Edinburgh.
Only at Oxford or Cambridge could an Indian student fulfil the object
that had led him to travel to England: 'the desire to see the grand "old
country", to fully understand what English life is, and to form for
himself an idea of English society and manners – in other words to share
in the social life of the people'.[82]

Although it is not clear how many people studied these books and
how influential they were, those that did come across the publications

may well have been attracted by the representations of Britain and Europe. However, admiration was often offset by criticism of the English weather, food and more fundamentally a general lack of spirituality, manifesting itself in excessive concern for material acquisition. These books written in the nineteenth century had a dual purpose: not only did they provide a guide for potential Indian students, pointing out possible pitfalls, giving advice on customs and appropriate behaviour in given situations, as well as a visual picture of Britain; they also gave a first-hand account of Indian experience of British society, as well as the type of reaction this contact produced.

PRESTIGE OF THE ENGLAND-RETURNED

Although English history and culture, as revealed to Indians through literature, inspired those wishing to visit England, books alone were not enough to convert desire into action. They tantalised the Indian reader with romantic visions of a sanitised Britain, where justice and democracy could be found in the enlightenment tradition. But for many it was the example of an England-returned or some kind of family intervention that proved decisive. Some parents believed that England would provide their children with a fresh start, turning to success efforts which had met only with failure in examinations in India. Gopi Chettar Menon was one such individual. His father had been told that 'ne'er do-wells sometimes turned a new leaf in England'.[83] Similar thinking about the rejuvenating qualities of England encouraged the Government of Bengal to send Nogendranath Sengupta, a suspect in the Mussulman-para Bomb case, to be educated in Britain at government expense.[84] Prakash Tandon in his autobiography *Punjabi Century 1857–1947* referred to a Bengali student who travelled with him to England claiming to be an ex-terrorist. The student told other Indians on board – whether falsely or in earnest – that his visit to Britain had been contrived as an experiment 'by an English police officer, who had recommended him for painting murals in India House in London, in the hope that a stay in England would wean him from politics'.[85] To what extent this is true is unclear. There are parallels here with Indian princes, who were sent to Britain by the Government of India in the hope that residence in Britain would have a corrective influence.[86] Ironically, India and the colonies in general had long been seen as places where the wayward sons of English gentlemen were sent, usually following an indiscretion, in order to redeem themselves before returning to Britain.

Many of those who visited England were following in the footsteps of other family members. Once one member of the family had broken the taboo of foreign travel, he cleared the path for others to follow suit. Before settling in Britain in the late nineteenth century, the father of Rajani Palme Dutt had already established family connections with Britain. Two of his more illustrious ancestors Toru Dutt, the poet, and R. C. Dutt, president of the Indian National Congress and author, had both lived and studied in Britain. In the case of J. N. Chaudhuri, who spent his childhood in England; both his mother[87] and his father had been educated in England. When grandparents are included, the Bonnerjee family show a minimum of three generations educated in Britain from the middle of the nineteenth century up to the 1920s. B. K. Nehru, following in the footsteps of his cousin, Jawaharlal Nehru, was keen to point out that for upper-class families it was *de rigueur* to send their children to England. It was taken for granted that he would follow in the family tradition.[88]

The prestige of those who had returned to India proved extremely influential. One Indian student, Jagmanderlal Jaini, wrote of the favourable impression he had gained of two men who had returned from England. It led him to conclude: 'any intelligent Indian, preferably of a strong moral character and with a frank open receptive mind would be infinitely benefited by a residence in England'.[89] K. K. Banerjee was aware that 'India gave preference to those persons who had crossed the seas and had been educated in England or in Scotland'. He reflected: 'there is just that lurking admiration and love for those persons who had been there, probably their outlook on life had broadened and they were much wider than ourselves'.[90] Another Indian speaking of his student days in England, some 20 to 30 years after, described how his decision to study in England was activated by an England-returned:

> There was a fellow who returned from England, who was an officer in the Mardan where I was studying, and he was being treated just like a European with good pay, good living and all that, while we were sort of treated lower status ... I thought that, well, if I go to England and be like him it is a good career.[91]

As late as 1922 one Indian highlighted the importance of England to India, a country a fraction of the sub-continent's size, as a place where reputations were made and lost. J. N. C. Ganguly, a student at Birmingham University, told the Lytton Committee of a feeling prevalent in India 'that unless a man became known in England he was not worthy of consideration'. He cited the case of Rabindranath Tagore, 'whose fame in India dated from the growth of his reputation in England'.[92] The situation was no different in 1898, when R. C. Dutt was on his second trip to England. He wrote to his brother: 'It is frightfully uphill work to establish your name and get a footing in the crowded and unsympathetic world of London, especially if your speciality is Indian subjects, which tire Englishmen to death.'[93] Despite a varied and successful career in government service in India, it was to London that he went to find 'distinction and fame' in the 'fag-end' of his life. These cases show how important the example of other Indians travelling to England was in influencing family members and the community at large.

PARENTAL ASPIRATIONS

As I have shown, many Indian parents viewed Britain as a window of opportunity for their children. Obtaining qualifications in England was rarely an individual enterprise; students carried with them the hopes and expectations of their parents.[94] Motilal Nehru's letters to his son in England provide a useful insight into parental motivation. Motilal had visited England twice in 1899 and 1900, before accompanying his son in 1905. He was very impressed by what he had seen of the country. In addition, he was strongly committed to foreign travel, an issue that had split Kashmiri Brahmins into three camps. Motilal's refusal to perform the *prayaschit* or purification ceremony on his return to India led to the establishment of the most radical of the three groupings, known as Moti Sabha or Satya Sabha. The other two groups included the Dharma Sabha, composed of orthodox Brahmins, who vehemently opposed foreign travel, and, in the middle, the Bishen Sabha (named after Bishen Narayan, an England-returned barrister) whose members agreed to perform the purification ceremony.

Although Motilal had amassed a fortune as a *vakil*, his failure to gain academic distinction may have been a source of regret.[95] Perhaps he felt that his son's success in England could compensate him in some way. A letter to Jawaharlal just before Motilal returned to India, having settled his son at Harrow, shows that he had great ambitions for his only son. He expected that an English public school and Oxbridge education would provide suitable foundations for these aspirations. In buoyant mood, he bullishly exclaimed: 'I am going back to India with the firm conviction I have sown the seeds for your future greatness and I have not a shadow of a doubt that you have a great career before you.'[96] When he wrote this not a single Kashmiri had won a place in the Indian Civil Service. Motilal coveted this prize for his son,[97] but not purely for self-aggrandisement. Jawaharlal would bring glory and honour to himself, his family, his province and his nation. Thus Nehru's hopes for his son had wider ramifications, beyond the private and the personal.

Motilal felt that only a thorough immersion in British society would enable Jawaharlal to achieve the goal set for him. He encouraged his son to cultivate friendships and make contacts in England which would be useful to his future career. Motilal wanted his son to be both a social and an academic success. With the former uppermost in his mind, he wrote to Jawaharlal at Harrow: 'Make friends with your immediate neighbours in the house – occasionally entertain them on holidays and half-holidays – in a word try to be a general favourite as you are bound to be without my telling you.'[98] This advice was repeated when Jawaharlal entered Cambridge: 'Entertainment of the leading people at Cambridge now and then is a very necessary item of expenditure. I want you to be the most popular young fellow and most distinguished graduate of Cambridge.'[99]

Motilal was keen for his son to gain as much exposure to English life as possible from his residence and not confine himself exclusively to Indian society in Britain. Consequently he wrote to his brother Bansi Dar Nehru – who also had two sons, Brijlal and Shridhar, studying at Cambridge at the same time as Jawaharlal – expressing his concern that the three cousins should not live together in or out of term time: 'I do not want the boys to live together. They should of course meet occasionally and even pass a few days together off and on but if they are constantly together they might as well have remained in India.'[100] This attitude was indicative of that of many parents who instructed their sons to avoid Indian companionship in Britain and mix exclusively in English society,[101] in order to reap the full benefit of their stay. This was partially connected to parental fears about their offspring becoming entangled in 'extremist' politics. Both Motilal Nehru[102] and S. G. Velinker,[103] a prominent Bombay lawyer, wished to prevent their sons from joining the Majlis.

Motilal had great faith in the English educational system.[104] A university education, unaccompanied by public school, would have adequately provided the necessary qualifications for a place in the Indian Civil Service, a more common course of action among parents. But Motilal had high expectations. When his son complained of homesickness he attempted to console him by stating the purpose of their enforced separation: 'It's a question of making a real man of you',[105] he wrote. Motilal believed that only an English public school combined with university could transform his shy, pampered child into a Renaissance man, equipped to deal with all aspects of life. At Harrow 'fagging' was part of the ordeal intended to produce an all-rounder, able to look after himself and show deference to his elders. The irony of this school custom was apparent to Motilal when he wrote: 'I am so anxious to know what menial services are exacted at Harrow from the only and dearly loved son of a man who employs more than 50 servants in India.'[106]

Motilal subscribed to Dr Arnold's dictum that 'real men' were made through the training of both the mind and the body. As a result, he encouraged his son to take part in the sporting life of Cambridge: 'You must join the Union Society at once and also a boat club. Pass every minute of available time in the open air – either on the river or on the turf.'[107] Motilal had never studied in England, yet he had internalised British masculine and sporting values to the point that he was disappointed when his son failed to relate any fights he had been involved in at Harrow:

> I am very glad indeed to hear of your achievements at the Rifle Range and the sham fights and will be very pleased to read your account of the Field Day you were about to have when you wrote last. It is these things which go to the making of men and I am happy to find that you take a keen interest in them ... I am a little surprised at your not having yet found yourself mixed up in a 'real' fight with some boy or other ... It will by no means be discouraging to me to hear it.[108]

Motilal's emphasis on aggressive behaviour is an example of how 'colonial masculinity' was appropriated by the colonial elite.[109] Although Motilal was anxious that his son should acquire the fighting and social skills of 'real men', nevertheless he made it quite clear that he was not prepared to accept a European daughter-in-law or Eurasian grandchildren.

Motilal was acutely aware that by studying in Britain his son was taking his first step in rising within the British career structure in India. He also felt that Jawaharlal would gain invaluable experience by firsthand contact with Britain, urging him to observe and learn from his surroundings in order to glean the maximum benefit from his time in England: 'Try and keep in touch with all your surroundings, and do not let anything happen under your very nose without knowing it and receiving some impressions from and about it. Experience is nothing but the sum total of impressions received from time to time by close observation.'[110] Motilal had pinned all his hopes and dreams on what his son would become – a member of the establishment, and the type of man he would be – a prototype English gentleman. But Jawaharlal did not quite fulfil these ambitions. Firstly, he studied for the Bar instead of the Indian Civil Service[111] and, secondly, while he may have become more acculturated, his increased radicalism prevented him from becoming a 'mimic man' establishment figure.

Erosion of caste restrictions, pragmatism, parental aspirations and curiosity about the West, specifically England, all motivated Indians to study in Britain. Attachment to English literature and thought and a general attraction to western metropolitan society suggests that the increasing rejection of the West in Indian society was partial. To claim there was an unqualified rejection would be too simple and fail to grasp the ambiguities and complexities present within Indian attitudes. Rejection and admiration of the West co-existed; consequently Indian students in Britain had little difficulty in disengaging their abhorrence of British rule from their aesthetic appreciation of English culture. The West was a crucial vector within the Indian self. Even the most ardent cultural nationalists 'received ample doses of English education and protective patinas of western modernity'[112] and exhibited some interest in first-hand contact with British society, if only to justify their criticisms.[113]

It is possible to see how all these factors operated in the motivation of one man, M. K. Gandhi. Although Gandhi's situation was by no means typical, he does, nevertheless, provide a useful insight into the types of influences and pressures affecting students. British rule had made Gandhi's prospects of succeeding his father as Prime Minister of Rajkot uncertain. Hopes of job security and of restoring the family's beleaguered fortunes lay with entry into the higher imperial services, which involved residence in Britain. However, it took the intervention of a family friend, Mavji Dave, to plant the idea in Gandhi's mind and the example of Dave's England-returned son, Kevalram, who had not only saved time and money by going to England but had also gained that indefinable glamour of being an England-returned, with all the prestige and mystique it entailed.

Gandhi described his own motivation for studying in England in one word, 'ambition'; but he had already been seduced by the allure of England: 'Before the intention of coming to London for the sake of study was actually formed', he wrote in his London diary, 'I had a secret design in my mind of coming here to satisfy my curiosity of knowing what London was.'[114] The intellectual and material factors intermingled when he wrote: 'If I go to England, not only shall I become a barrister (of which I used to think a great deal) but I shall be able to see England, the land of philosophers and poets, the very centre of civilisation.'[115] The positive images of England Gandhi had gained from eight years of English education appear to have overridden the negative impressions he had of zealous missionaries, in his own words, 'pouring abuse on Hindus'.[116]

What the Gandhi case shows more than anything else is the power of human agency in defying convention and pursuing an independent course of action, although it is clear from his case that without last-minute financial intervention his trip would have been aborted. Gandhi, like many other students, encountered strong religious opposition. While in England he wrote for the Vegetarian Society's journal, listing the difficulties he had encountered before leaving India, as 'money, consent of my elders, separation from relations and caste restrictions'.[117] It is interesting that after obtaining the consent of his mother, uncle and father-in-law he experienced little opposition to his plans in Rajkot, his hometown; but in Bombay, at a caste meeting of Patels, he faced active hostility. Gandhi was convinced that malice and jealousy rather than religious scruples lay at the root of these objections.[118] Obstacles served to embolden him: 'I must write had it been some other man in the same position which I was in, I dare say he would not have been able to see England. The difficulties which I had to withstand have made England dearer to me than she had been.'[119] Finally, as Stephen Hay has noted, Gandhi's motivation went beyond self-interest. He was inspired 'by the spirit of reform', as reflected in his farewell school speech: 'I hope that some of you will follow in my footsteps and after you return from England, you will work wholeheartedly for big reforms in India.'[120]

Students' accounts of their own motivation stress the equal importance of material and intellectual factors. Indians were forced to travel to Britain in order to climb the greasy pole of ambition. In the 20 years before 1885, when the numbers of Indians going to Britain was small, 700 men went to England from Bengal alone, largely to compete for the ICS.[121] Nevertheless, even when the legal profession became over-congested in India and the 'glittering prizes' Indian students were expecting on their return to India did not materialise, the numbers travelling to Britain continued to grow (excluding the war years), despite government attempts to curb them. It was the perception that a British qualification was the ticket to success rather than the realities of the labour market in India which continued to prevail, exemplified in D. N. Bonerjee's opinion that 'the English hall-mark had advantages remedial measures could not overcome'.[122] Equally, curiosity about the West is inadequate as an explanation, especially as hostility to British rule had become more pronounced and better organised after the First World War. Only both elements together can provide a satisfactory explanation. Indians travelled, in part, to utilise the educational opportunities available to them in metropolitan Britain and thereby reconstruct Indo-British relations. Education offered on the one hand the prospect of social mobility and a broadening of mental horizons, but on the other it bound them more tightly to the colonial system of rule. They were also motivated by the desire to appropriate European culture – a kind of reverse colonialism.

NOTES

1 S. Gopal, *British Policy in India 1858–1905* (Cambridge: Cambridge University Press, 1984), p. 121. Sir Henry Cotton (1845–1915) occupied various senior posts in the Government of India before returning to Britain to become MP for Nottingham East in 1906. He served on the Lee Warner Committee.

2 C. A. Bayley, *The Local Roots of Indian Politics: Allahabad 1880–1920* (Oxford: Clarendon Press, 1975).

3 M. K. Gandhi, *The Collected Works of Mahatma Gandhi*, Vol. 1 (Delhi: Government of India, 1958), p. 7.

4 B. Prasad, *Indian Nationalism and Asia* (Delhi: B. R. Publishing, 1979), p. 4.

5 R. K. Ray, 'Moderates, Extremists, Revolutionaries in Bengal, 1900–1908', in R. Sissons and S. Wolpert (eds), *Congress and Indian Nationalism* (Berkerley: University of California Press, 1988), p. 67.

6 Ibid., p. 66.

7 The Standing Committee on the Hindu Sea-Voyage Question, *The Hindu Sea -Voyage Movement in Bengal* (Calcutta: S. N. Banerjee, 1894), p. 43.

8 Ibid., p. 20.

9 Ibid., Justice Mahadeb Gobind Ranade, p. 36.

10 Ibid., p. v.

11 Ibid., p. 48.

12 Ibid., p. 41.

13 *Journal of the National Indian Association*, No. 6 (June 1871), p. 108.

14 Ibid., p. 49.

15 Ibid., p. 20.

16 Ibid., p. 49.

17 Ibid., p. 1.

18 Ibid., p. 49.

19 The Standing Committee on the Hindu Sea-Voyage Question, *Hindu Sea-Voyage Movement*, pp. 1–2.

20 Ibid., p. 7.

21 *Indian Magazine*, No. 527 (November 1914), p. 271. Krishna Lal Mukane.

22 *The Times*, 8 April 1884.

23 The Standing Committee on the Hindu Sea-Voyage Question, *Hindu Sea-Voyage Movement*, p. 17.

24 Ibid., p. 17.

25 Raychaudhuri, *Europe Reconsidered*.

26 The Standing Committee on the Hindu Sea-Voyage Question, *Hindu Sea-Voyage Movement*, p. iv.

27 Ibid., p. v.

28 The Standing Committee on the Hindu Sea-Voyage Question, *Hindu Sea-Voyage Movement*, p. 1.

29 L. Carroll, 'The Sea Voyage Controversy and the Kayasthas of North India, 1901–1909', *Modern Asian Studies*, 13, 2 (1979), pp. 298–9.

30 Ibid., p. 268.

31 Ibid., p. 287.

32 The Standing Committee on the Hindu Sea-Voyage Question, *Hindu Sea-Voyage Movement*, p. 44.

33 Ibid., p. 44.

34 Ibid., p. 44.
35 *Bharat Bandhu*, 11 March 1881.
36 *Journal of the National Indian Association*, No. 157 (January 1884) pp. 26–7.
37 Ibid., No. 162 (June 1884), p. 279.
38 J. N. Gupta, *Life and Work of Romesh Chandra Dutt* (London: J. M. Dent, 1911), p. 18. After an outstanding career in the ICS, Dutt retired in 1847, aged 49. Two years later he became president of the Indian National Congress. He also wrote novels, books on history and economics, and lectured in Indian history at University College, London.
39 *Journal of the National Indian Association*, No. 6 (June 1871), p. 108.
40 (IOL) L/P&J/6/901, No. 3923.
41 S. Schmitthener, 'A Sketch of the Development of the Legal Profession in India', *Law and Society Review*, 3, 2 and 3 (1968–69), p. 365.
42 (IOL) L/P&J/6/901, No. 3923.
43 *The Times*, 7 March 1911.
44 (IOL) Appendix 4, p. 95.
45 Schmitthener, 'The Legal Profession in India', p. 364.
46 (IOL) Appendix 4, p. 95.
47 Schmitthener, 'The Legal Profession in India', p. 364.
48 (IOL) MSS. Eur. T. 109.
49 (IOL) MSS. Eur. T. 112.
50 Kopf, *Brahmo Samaj*, p. 112.
51 Seal, *Emergence of Indian Nationalism*, p. 128.
52 Ibid., p. 129.
53 J. C. Jack, *The Economic Life of a Bengal District: A Study* (Oxford: Clarendon Press, 1916), p. 91.
54 Schmitthener, 'The Legal Profession in India', p. 366.
55 *Thacker's Indian Directory*, 1896 and 1916.
56 Calcutta University Commission Report, 1917–19 (Calcutta, 1919), p. 64.
57 Ibid., p. 330.
58 Quinquennial Review of the Progress of Education in India, 1917–22, p. 70.
59 M. K. Gandhi, *An Autobiography* (Harmondsworth: Penguin, 1982), p. 33.
60 Manicklal Muckerjee, *W. C. Bonnerjee – Snapshots from his Life and his London Letters* (Calcutta: Deshbandhu Book Depot, 1944), p. 2.
61 (IOL) L/P&J/6/845, p. 89.
62 Ibid., p. 197.
63 Report of Committee on Distressed Colonial and Indian Subjects, Cd 5133 (London, 1910), p. 16.
64 M. C. Changla, *Roses in December* (Bombay: Bharatiya Vidya Bhavan, 1978), p. 3.
65 S. K. Bhuyan, *London Memoirs from a Historian's Haversack* (Assam: Gauhati Publication Board, 1979), p. 1. Bhuyan, son of a minor Indian official, gained a PhD from the School of Oriental and African Studies, University of London. He was also a poet and biographer.
66 Ibid., p. 2.
67 Ibid., p. 6.
68 (IOL) MSS. Eur. T. 79/2.
69 S. Hay, 'The Making of a Late Victorian Hindu: M. K. Gandhi in London 1888–91', *Victorian Studies*, 33 (1989), p. 79.
70 (IOL) L/P&J/6/845, p. 98.

71 (IOL) Indian Student Department Report 1913–1914, p. 9.

72 (IOL) L/P&J/1707, No. 6900, 20 August 1920.

73 C. L. Parekh (ed.), *Essays, Speeches and Writings of Dadabhai Naoroji* (Bombay: Caxton Printing Works, 1887), p. 27.

74 J. Mcguire, *The Making of a Colonial Mind: A Quantative Study of the Bhadralok in Calcutta 1857–1885* (Canberra: Australian National University, 1983). Kopf, *Brahmo Samaj*. J. H. Broomfield, *Elite Conflict in a Plural Society: Twentieth Century Bengal* (Berkeley: University of California Press, 1968).

75 Raychaudhuri, *Europe Reconsidered*, p. 136.

76 General curiosity about the West in Indian society is discernible from Motilal Nehru's comments on his return from Europe in 1905 after leaving his son Jawaharlal at Harrow. Motilal wrote: 'There was a regular stream of visitors with all sorts of idle questions as to what I saw in various countries of Europe I visited.' R. Kumar and D. N. Panigrahi (eds), *Selected Works of Motilal Nehru*, Vol. 1, *1899–1918* (New Delhi: Vikas, 1982), p. 85, 7 November 1905.

77 R. B. Nadkarni, *Journal of a Visit to Europe in 1896* (Bombay: D. B. Taraporevala, 1903).

78 P. J. Ragaviah, *Pictures of England* (Madras: Ganz Brothers, 1876), p. 4.

79 P. M. Chowdhury, *British Experiences* (Calcutta, 1889), p. 21.

80 Satthianadhan, *Four Years in an English University*, p. 24.

81 Ibid., p. 23.

82 Ibid., p. 22.

83 K. P. S. Menon, *Many Worlds: An Autobiography* (Delhi: Oxford University Press, 1965), p. 14.

84 (IOL) L/P&J/6/1423, No. 52, 3 March 1916. Nogendranath Sengupta hailed from an orthodox Hindu family in Noakhali. He grew up during the Swadeshi era and became involved with the revolutionary movement in Bengal. He played a key role in the Mussalmanpara bombing case. After his acquittal Sengupta was sent to England by Cornelia Sorabji for further education, where he converted to Christianity. On returning to India in 1922, he worked in government service.

85 P. Tandon, *Punjabi Century 1857–1947* (London: Chatto & Windus, 1961), p. 204.

86 See S. Lahiri, 'British Policy towards Indian Princes in Late Nineteenth and Early Twentieth-Century Britain', *Immigrants and Minorities*, 15, 3 (1996), pp. 214–32.

87 W. C. Bonnerjee's daughter, graduate of the Sorbonne and Newham College, Cambridge.

88 (IOL) MSS. Eur. T. 113.

89 J. Jaini (ed. M. Amy Thornett), *Fragments from an Indian Student's Notebook: A Study of an Indian Mind* (London: A. H. Stockwell, 1934), 4 November 1903, p. 28.

90 (IOL) MSS. Eur. T. 79/2.

91 (IOL) MSS. Eur. T. 109. The last part of this quote refers to 'widening' of mental horizons, not physical size.

92 (IOL) W1757, p. 53.

93 Gupta, *W. C. Bonnerjee*, 13 January 1898, p. 299.

94 There were exceptions: the nineteenth-century student pioneer W. C. Bonnerjee obtained no support from his father and was obliged to run away from home.

95 B. N. Pandey, *Nehru* (London: Macmillan, 1976), p. 27.

96 Kumar and Panigrahi, *Selected Works*, Vol. 1, *1899–1918*, p. 78, 16 November 1905.

97 Ibid., p. 80, 20 October 1905, 'I think I can say without vanity that I am the founder of the fortunes of the Nehru family. I look upon you, my son, as the man who will build upon the foundations I have laid. In about two years you will be in a position

to pass a few months among your old surroundings at Allahabad ... Laden with the Honours within your reach at Harrow, and budding into a vigorous manhood.'

98 Ibid., p. 76, 30 September 1905. Motilal was disappointed when he wrote: 'You do not also speak of any friendships that you formed at Harrow', p. 107, 26 March 1906.

99 Ibid., p. 132, 30 July 1907.

100 Ibid., p. 88, 12 November 1905.

101 *The Times*, Editorial, 19 November 1906, p. 5.

102 Kumar and Panigrahi, *Selected Works*, p. 129, 26 July 1907.

103 Changla, *Roses*, p. 34.

104 Jawaharlal Nehru did not share his father's enthusiasm for English education. When he heard restrictions were to be placed on the number of Indians at Cambridge, he wrote: 'I suppose all this would simply make Indian students go to continental and other countries and to my mind this will be a good thing. They will then be more fit for doing something than if they have been to Oxford or Cambridge.' S. Gopal (ed.), *Selected Works of Jawaharlal Nehru*, Vol. 1 (New Delhi: Jawaharlal Nehru Memorial Fund, 1984), p. 66, 18 March 1909.

105 Kumar and Panigrahi, *Selected Works*, 20 October 1905, p. 80.

106 Ibid., p. 79.

107 Ibid., p. 129, 26 July 1907.

108 Ibid., pp. 92–3, 23 November 1905.

109 See Sinha, *Colonial Masculinity*.

110 Ibid., p. 89, 16 November 1905.

111 It was actually Brijlal, Motilal's nephew who was the first Kashmiri to enter the ICS.

112 S. Wolpert, 'Congress in Perspective', in R. Sisson and S. Wolpert (eds), *Congress and Indian Nationalism* (Berkerley: University of California Press, 1988), p. 23.

113 Bankim Chandra Chatterjee planned to visit Europe. Raychaudhuri, *Europe Reconsidered*, p. 343.

114 M. K. Gandhi, *The Collected Works of Mahatma Gandhi*, Vol. 1 (Delhi: Government of India, 1958), 12 November 1888, p. 3.

115 Ibid., p. 54.

116 Gandhi, *Autobiography*, p. 24.

117 *Indian Magazine and Review*, No. 248 (August 1891) p. 387.

118 Ibid., p. 390.

119 Gandhi, *Collected Works*, p. 12.

120 S. Hay, 'The Making of a Late Victorian Hindu: M. K. Gandhi in London', p. 76.

121 Kopf, *Brahmo Samaj*, p. 195. Kopf noted: 'of the twelve outstanding Brahmos of the beginning of the century, five were educated in England and a further two had visited England', pp. 115–16.

122 (IOL) L/P&J/6/845, p. 25.

— 2 —

Indian Experience: Race and Class at the Heart of Empire

INDIAN students' experiences varied considerably, according to their expectations on arrival and their reception in England. The incredibly high aspirations harboured by many students have already been described. It was perhaps inevitable that the reality of life in England did not match up to student expectations. In the late nineteenth century racial discourse was grafted on to existing assumptions about the hierarchical nature of an increasingly class-conscious society. In this chapter I shall focus on how the shifting categories of race, class and poverty affected Indian experiences of Britain and impaired relations with the host community, to both subvert and accentuate existing uneven patterns of power and subordination. But first I examine the intellectual experiences of students.

In some cases lecturers did have an enormous impact on individual students. R. C. Dutt, one of the pioneering Indian students in Britain, was deeply impressed by his college professors: 'I shall never forget the kindness which we have received from them, they have been more like friends than teachers to us.'[1] Javed Majeed has shown how important John McTaggart Ellis McTaggart, who taught at Cambridge, was to the development of his pupil, the Sufi poet Muhammed Iqbal.[2] Cornelia Sorabji admired her tutor, Benjamin Jowett, Master of Balliol College, Oxford, immensely; he became her mentor during her years in England. Cornelia's relationship with Jowett was intellectually very close. The conventional teacher/pupil relationship was transcended and Jowett became almost a surrogate father, attending to her academic and spiritual needs. After Jowett's death Cornelia wrote: 'He had a way of finding out your interests and views, and making you show him your self … He touched the spring of what was best and most lasting in one, and one knew all that was expected of one was to be natural.' Cornelia considered some of Jowett's views old-fashioned. She wrote:

He revered women and did not wish them to forsake their sphere. 'There is plenty', he said, 'for them to do where God has placed them.' Although he did not think learning unsexing ... I think he fancied you might do anything as long as you were modest, earnest, religious, gentle and true.[3]

Nevertheless, many of her opinions echoed those of Jowett. Like him she did not support the suffragette movement and rebuked her rival, Rukhmabai,[4] for 'seeking notoriety and fame' and 'opposing existing laws and breaking loose from proper restraints',[5] by foisting her scheme for female education in India on a British official.

As a student at the London School of Economics (LSE) in the 1920s, Renuka Ray was deeply influenced by the anti-imperial stance taken by Dr Eileen Power, lecturer in international history. Numerous other Indians and non-Europeans at the LSE after the First World War were inspired by Professor Harold Laski, who displayed a strong interest in Indian independence. Many years later Renuka Ray wrote in her auto-biography:

> His course 'On the History of Political Ideas' was fascinating and kept us spellbound. Yet it was his seminars rather than his inspiring lecturers that were truly exciting. Even today I remember how he could draw out his students and provoke them into discussions, which were most stimulating.[6]

On the other hand, with these exceptions, there are conspicuously few references to individual lecturers in autobiographies, diaries or letters. This may be indicative of the general lack of rapport between Indian students and the English men and women they encountered, a point to be discussed in more detail later.

Much of the Indian student's time in England was devoted to following courses of study, although this was not always true for law students. Gandhi conscientiously read every textbook on his book list, but studiousness was rare and unnecessary as '[t]he curriculum of study was easy'.[7] Students had to take examinations in Roman law and common law, as well as papers on English and colonial constitutions, legal history, evidence, civil and criminal procedure and equity. Indians were permitted to study Hindu and Muslim law only after 1907. According to Gandhi, few Indian students read the textbooks prescribed, preferring instead 'to pass the Roman Law examination by scrambling through notes on Roman Law in a couple of weeks, and the Common Law examination by reading notes on the subject in two or three months'.[8] Even those who failed were given three or more chances to pass within a year. But most candidates did not fail; Gandhi calculated the pass rate in Roman law at 95 to 97 per cent, with a minimum of 75 per cent in the final examination. The only other requirement was to attend six dinners per term.

The content of the Indian Civil Service syllabus changed more drastically than the law courses from the late nineteenth to the early twentieth century. In the first part of the period greater weight was given to arts subjects: 'Almost two-thirds of the total possible marks were allocated to papers in languages, literature and history ... Natural and moral sciences were included only as supplementary subjects.'[9] However, by 1900 science had moved from the margins of the curriculum to virtually equal status with the arts. Clive Dewey has noted that universal truths were less entrenched in examination papers and there was a progressive movement towards greater debate. As a result, Indian students who sat the Indian Civil Service examination were presented with alternative propositions; they were encouraged to question, analyse, compare and contrast issues which had previously been taken for granted.

The enormous impact this process must have had on the intellectual and political development of Indians can only be surmised. Subhas Chandra Bose alluded to the importance of the books he had studied for the ICS examination when he wrote about the modern European history course, for which he was required to read original sources such as Bismarck's autobiography, Metternich's memoirs and Cavour's letters: 'These original sources, more than anything else I studied at Cambridge, helped to rouse my political sense and to foster my understanding of the inner currents of international politics.'[10] Like Nehru and many other Indian students, he saw the parallels between these nineteenth-century European nationalists and India's struggle for self-determination. It was inevitable that 'inflammatory' works which appeared on course reading lists, such as Milton's *Areopagitica*, on the freedom of the press, Mill's *On Liberty* and Burke on discontent and American taxation, would provoke young men living under colonial rule to question why these admirable principles were not applied to India.

RACIAL PREJUDICE

Indian students' experience of racial discrimination in Britain was also at odds with notions of justice, equality and civil rights imbibed from textbooks and British rhetoric. Racial theories first gained currency in Britain in the middle of the nineteenth century, when they were advanced by anthropologists and ethnologists. Craniology and comparative anatomy were intended to give academic credibility to theories of black inferiority. This biological determinism confirmed the validity of generalising about group characteristics, the desirability of racial purity, the need to control inferior elements within a race and the justice of imposing British civilisation on so-called 'backward' nations such as India. These theories served to link the two variables of class and race, by justifying class rule – the government of the rich over the poor – as a basis of domestic policy and racial superiority as a determinant of colonial policy towards non-European subject peoples. The British obsession with classification is illustrated by Sayyid Ahmed Khan, a judge and founder of Aligarh College, who was asked during a visit to the India Office in 1869 to identify himself from a meticulously constructed, anthropological survey of India.[11]

Racial prejudice, defined by Michael Banton as 'an emotional and rigidly hostile disposition towards members of a given group',[12] affected students at a personal level as well as institutionally, impinging on key aspects of their lives such as accommodation and admissions. While it may have varied in its extent – some fortunate students came through completely unscathed – its effects were nevertheless insidious. One of the earliest recorded cases was that of Upendra Krishna Dutt. Unlike the majority of Indians who came to Britain in the late nineteenth and the early twentieth century, Dutt, father of Rajani Palme Dutt, was not a transient sojourner. He had come to England in order to study and eventually settled in Cambridge to practise medicine. Consequently he was a true precursor of the Commonwealth immigrants. Although Dutt's family was not affluent, a wealthy Brahmin took an interest in him when he was a small boy. As a result, he was obliged to leave his home, where he was the eldest son, and go and live with the Brahmin. He was educated to a high standard and then returned to his paternal home. After matriculating from Calcutta University he won the Gilchrist travelling scholarship in January 1876. The enormity of this achievement can only be fully appreciated if one takes into account that only one such scholarship existed for the whole population of British India.

Dutt first encountered incivility when travelling to England on a steamer in 1876: 'Why do you call me Babu? In my country only servants call me Babu ... "What should we call you then?" "Upendra Babu" was the quiet reply.' Dutt contrasted this behaviour with that of Australians who later boarded the vessel: 'In Ceylon all were transferred to another P&O steamer coming from China; here a host of Australians came aboard and their friendly attitude, treating all fellow passengers as equals, made a marked contrast with the ill manners of the Anglo-Indians.'[13]

After eight years in Britain Dutt emerged in 1884 as a qualified doctor. His academic career was littered with prizes and firsts. He had obtained a first-class honours degree with gold medal and won a scholarship to St Mary's Hospital. However, despite his undoubted merit, he found application after application for a post or in answer to an advertisement for a doctor's assistant turned down. In the words of his son to whom he related his early experiences: 'Acceptance and selection on the basis of qualifications and testimonials turned into hasty discovery that the position was no longer available as soon as the interview took place.'[14] Dutt wrote in his memoirs of the existence of a colour bar: 'No one would have me on account of colour.'[15] The desperation felt by other non-European doctors in Britain faced with the same problem is shown in the case of an Afghan doctor. He had also qualified in England and had searched unsuccessfully for a position. Finally he resorted to suicide by shooting himself. When Dutt went in person to answer an advertisement for a doctor's assistant in a poor part of East Ham, he was told he had no chance and that he was destined to meet the same fate as the Afghan doctor. But Dutt persevered doggedly. Eventually he found a position as an assistant in Leicester. This was followed by another post working with 'a rather unscrupulous money-making doctor'. Bury Hospital employed him as a house surgeon and eventually he took up practice in a working-class area of Cambridge.

Dutt differed from most of his contemporaries in that the discrimination he faced was in finding employment, whereas the majority of the early student population returned to India shortly after completing their studies. A few of these students even believed their race was an asset rather than an impediment. For instance, in 1888 an anonymous student from Madras wrote:

> I am glad to say the welcome I received here, and the manner in which I am treated here, and the benefits I am now receiving here, remove from my mind the fear of being outcasted. I am not slighted for my colour, nation, or my caste. The more I have of difference, the more I am respected. Hence I wish my colour turned from brown to black.[16]

Kunwar Maharaj Singh, who went to Harrow with his brother in the 1890s, also claimed that his nationality was an advantage: 'not only was there not an atom of prejudice against us, but the sympathies of Masters and boys were actually in our favour, and even at Oxford, where in my time there were about a dozen Indians in all, I found no trace of antipathy'.[17]

By the twentieth century Indian students were no longer so fortunate in their reception and the warmth of the British welcome had distinctively cooled. Student testimonies from the Edwardian period reveal that the situation had worsened. Many of the Indian witnesses questioned by the Lee Warner Committee reiterated Major Hasan's view, that the biggest problem facing Indian students was 'prejudice of race and colour'.[18] N. S. Subbarao, President of the Indian Majlis, who had been living in St John's College, Cambridge for five terms gave especially illuminating evidence to the Committee. He cited numerous instances of subtler forms of racial prejudice. Although English undergraduates were friendly towards him in private, they did not want to be seen with him publicly. Sometimes the racial prejudice would betray itself unintentionally; Subbarao gave several interesting examples of this. He had been told by one of his English acquaintances that he was 'an exceptional sort of nigger'.[19] Subbarao described this statement as an attempt by the man to 'justify himself in associating with an Indian'.[20] On another occasion he was advised to go to a college concert; broad hints were given that he should 'take an inconspicuous seat'.[21] Occasionally actions spoke louder than words, as when an English friend invited him to his room and proceeded to lock the door, thus (as Subbarao inferred) preventing anyone from seeing him. Any Englishman who was prepared to befriend an Indian would have to face the censure of his English friends. An example of this was related to Subbarao by his neighbour, who was told: 'I don't like to see niggers in your rooms.'[22]

One Indian student at Exeter College, Oxford, cited an instance 'in which an Indian candidate for office at the Union had met organised opposition'.[23] Deva Brata Muckerjea of Emmanuel College, Cambridge, attributed the discrimination experienced by Indians to three sources. Firstly, missionary lectures on topics such as the Indian *zenana*, which he believed portrayed an inaccurate and misleading picture of India as a bastion of backwardness and vice, secondly, the conduct of Indians themselves, by their lack of interest in sports and thirdly, the irresponsible conduct on the part of certain Indian students.[24]

The Secretary of the Edinburgh Indian Association, K. R. Iyengar, claimed colour prejudice was worse in Scotland than in the rest of the British Isles. Indians were made to feel unwelcome by unpleasant remarks at the union.[25] This view was supported by another Indian student in 1922 when he pointed to the segregation in seating arrangements between Indian and British undergraduates. Most Indian students complained of a want of cordiality in their reception, which was keenly felt and bitterly resented. The two areas where discrimination manifested itself most visibly were accommodation and admission into educational institutions.

ACCOMMODATION

Jaganath Luxman echoed the experience of many students when he relayed the case of an English landlady who told him: 'We don't have any blacks here.'[26] Fifteen years later K. G. M. Luke and R. N. Vaidya also testified to the colour prejudice they had encountered while trying to find lodgings. When Sheikh Abdul Kadir, a London law student, arrived in 1904 he had known newly arrived Indians seek vainly for lodgings. But he believed the situation had improved during his residence. He claimed that most students spent their first night in the hotel nearest the station. On this first night they would experience acute helplessness and fear, aggravated by the fact that stories of burglaries were common among Indian students. However, within a few days having obtained their remittances, they would settle down in lodgings with or near other Indians.[27] The prejudice of landladies posed a major problem and, as one Englishman observed, this irrational stance was a result of 'pure ignorance and not due to any unfortunate experience they may have had with Indians'.[28] The practice of excluding Indians was not always economically viable. It is significant that during college vacations, when the chance of procuring English boarders was lower, prejudice against Indians was no longer as prominent. In order to overcome hostility the guild of undergraduates at Birmingham University was forced to send their members to accompany Indian students when searching for rooms.[29]

One Indian student argued that Indians were denied admittance to boarding houses in Edinburgh, despite the fact that vacancies were abundant. Scottish students were able to exclude Indians by taking advantage of the electoral procedure that operated in these establishments.[30] Musharaful Haq observed that Indian students were especially apt to live together in houses 'where landladies made a point of cooking Indian dishes and where there were opportunities for studying together'. Students would usually answer advertisements in the *Scotsman*, being careful to choose lodgings near their place of study; for example, botanists would live in the north of the city, near the gardens, as they had classes early in the morning.[31] Edinburgh attempted to overcome this problem by the establishment of a residential college for Indians known as Portobello, founded by Dr C. F. Knight. Meals and classes were provided in the evenings and the university or medical school was attended during the day. The goal was international harmony and the ratio was five Indians to one Englishman. To aid intercourse between British and Indian residents, Indian vernaculars could be spoken only in bedrooms.[32]

Indian students experienced greater difficulty in securing

accommodation after the First World War. The post-war years saw an increase in the cost of living and a housing shortage. Demand was further swollen by an abundance of demobilised soldiers. In industrial areas the price of lodgings had increased as blue-collar workers found themselves able to afford to pay higher rents. N. C. Sen claimed that the so-called 'servant problem' (a shortage of domestics as a result of a movement into higher-status and more lucrative clerical jobs after the war) meant that 'the student had now to deal with a new and sometimes less friendly class of landlady, a class that was not so dependable as old'.[33]

OXFORD

Racial prejudice was particularly strong at Oxford. According to the Sri Lankan student Bandaranaike, few Indian students had managed to secure any prizes or scholarships:

> even when they would have otherwise been eligible, colour prejudice proves an effectual bar. It is an open secret that All Souls have decided never to violate the sacredness of their fellowship by admitting Easterners. Nothing can be more deprecated than this – that within the sphere of scholarship, the most learned and presumably, the most fair-minded of Oxford's sons finds it impossible to rise above the narrow prejudices, which are such a lamentable characteristic of the more ignorant and unthinking undergraduate.[34]

M. R. Jayakar experienced at first hand the restrictive policy operating at Oxford against Indian students. In 1902 Jayakar left India hoping to gain entrance to Balliol College. However, the Master, Dr Edward Caird, having read his certificates and testimonials responded: 'Our quota of Indian students is full and I can give you no admittance.'[35] When Caird offered him the prospect of entering as a non-collegiate student, Jayakar retorted: 'I have degrees galore behind me. I have not come here to gain one more degree, but to seek the benefit of the corporate life of a great university, which can be obtained only by residence and from full participation in the activities of the students.' His attempts to persuade the Master failed: 'I dropped the idea after revising my notions of India being an important member of the British Commonwealth.'[36] Jayakar's failure to gain a place at Balliol supports the suggestion that there was a quota system operating at all Oxford colleges. None admitted more than two Indians at any one time.

Jayakar also provides an interesting example of a student's encounter with intolerance. After the rebuff from Oxford he obtained a place in the legal chambers of Max Romer, the grandson of the proprietor of the magazine *Punch*. Jayakar had gained this privileged position, uncommon for an Indian student, through the help of his grandfather's friend Sir Lawrence Jenkins, the Chief Justice of Bombay, who had also been a junior there. His initial reception at the chambers was over-shadowed by racial prejudice. He wrote: 'My first reception in these chambers was hostile. I had three British colleagues, who had finished college education and were studying law. Their social connections were high with county families and they entertained a prejudice against Indians, then common in these quarters.'[37] Jayakar worked in close proximity with the three juniors in a small garret. He wrote:

> My companions began their teasing in various ways, so characteristic of vigorous young life … For the first few days, my companions were very surly and gruff and excluded me from sharing their tea. But when they found that this behaviour made no impression on me, their teasing increased, until one day I found an ink-spot split on my table, spoiling the books and papers lying there.

Jayakar decided to confront them. He said:

> If you fellows think that I have come here from 7,000 miles away to be frightened by these miserable tactics, you are jolly well mistaken. I am not proposing to take this quarrel to Mr Romer but will live it down and unless you make up your minds to put up with an Indian as colleague, life will be troublesome; for this game of teasing is one at which I can play equally well.[38]

After this remonstration Jayakar's victimisation gradually ceased.

N. B. Bonarjee described his experiences at Oxford after the war. He believed racial antagonism was simmering there under the surface of Indo-British relations. In the background was the magnitude of the Allied victory. It had enhanced and brought into sharper focus the more strident aspects of pre-war imperialism in Britain. He claimed: 'The most important factor determining the relations between Englishmen and Indians was the one that was kept well out of view – race.'[39] 'The racial factor', as he called it, 'though under the carpet at Oxford for the most part often pushed its way through. Events exacerbated it.' This racial animosity was clear by the fact that 'All coloured undergraduates were conveniently lumped together in the composite category of "wogs" or "nigger", derogatory terms both, carrying with them the stigma of inferiority.'[40] He believed the term to mean 'Westernised Oriental

Gentleman' and he recognised that there was some truth in this label: 'I know we were known as wogs. Nobody said, "you're a bloody wog" or anything … well they might have … but we were known as wogs.'[41] Furthermore 'There could be good "wogs" [an Indian who played a sport for his college for example] and bad "wogs", acceptable "wogs" and the reverse, but "wogs" all Indians were by virtue of their nature and colour.'[42]

SANDHURST

The first ten Indian cadets were admitted to the Royal Military Academy at Sandhurst in 1918; it was part of a broader policy of Indianisation of the army. Two of the young Indians who attended the Academy in the 1920s recounted the nature of racial prejudice they faced there. B. M. Kaul wrote of how he had purchased a straw hat in London, which was in vogue with the cadets. But an English officer destroyed the hat in front of his eyes, as in the officer's opinion the boater was to be worn only by English cadets. In another incident a British cadet chanted a childish rhyme about Gandhi. Although neither of these episodes was of a very serious nature, Kaul was deeply wounded by the last incident as he had been arrested for involvement with the nationalist movement.[43] M. R. A. Baig, who had attended public school in Britain, was surprised by his first exposure to racial prejudice at Sandhurst, which until then he had not experienced:

> We did not belong and were made to feel it. Sandhurst was full of the sons of retired or serving officers either of the Indian Army or of British regiments who had served in India, and Indian fellow-cadets were not only a social affront but a professional threat.[44]

Attempts were made to try and allay the fears of British cadets. Baig recalled how on his first day at the Academy an Indian army colonel told the assembled cadets: '[I]t has been decided to confine Indianisation only to two cavalry and six infantry regiments … so there will be no chance of you having to serve under Indians.' Baig concluded: 'Hardly words of encouragement for young Indians, who presumably were expected to be ready to die for the King-Emperor and the British Empire.'[45] The fact that Indianisation was seen as a 'dangerous experiment' by the British military authorities did little to improve relations between Indian and British cadets.

Thimayya, who also attended Sandhurst in the post-war years, argued that intolerance was closely related to the political situation in

India. 'During periods of political tranquillity in India, Indian cadets had earned "blue" in sports and rank in the cadet corps.'[46] However, when Thimayya attended Sandhurst (1924–26) India had recently been experiencing political upheaval. Consequently, 'the British tended to regard all Indians with suspicion'.[47] Despite his success on the sports field – he was used by the instructor to demonstrate hockey techniques – he was never asked to play for the college team. On one occasion Thimayya was promised his spurs (awarded for riding proficiency) earlier, as he had been able to jump a particularly difficult fence. Yet despite complaints to the authorities he was obliged to receive them with all the other cadets at the end of term, thereby foregoing any distinction. A contemporary of Thimayya suffered greater injustices at Sandhurst. Sant Singh was a gifted hockey player, a fact acknowledged by the local press who described him as 'the most brilliant player we have seen in years'.[48] He played in high-profile games outside Sandhurst, but he was never picked to play for Sandhurst against Oxford or Cambridge, which would have automatically earned him a 'blue'. The college authorities were not prepared to bestow such an honour on an Indian. These incidents of discrimination in collegiate sports are doubly significant as they refute allegations made by British officials and students about Indian reluctance to participate in or excel in sports. Racism on the sports field prevented students from becoming an integral part of collegiate life.

COLOUR BAR COMMITTEE

It was not just the victims of racial discrimination who complained about their treatment, the broader issue of the operation of a 'colour bar' in England also attracted the attention of British groups such as the Society of Friends (Quakers). On 22 October 1929, William. F. Nicholson chaired a meeting at the Quaker headquarters in London, Friends House, where the MP for St Pancras North, James Morley, gave an address on the 'Colour Bar Problem in England'. A great deal of interest was stimulated by the meeting and the Friends took the initiative of calling a conference to discover exactly what colour prejudice existed in Britain and how it could be removed. Of the 250 who attended, 80 were from Africa, India, Burma and the West Indies. The conference concluded that in the light of the evidence it had received 'of a colour bar … particularly on the part of hotels. It regards this racial discrimination and prejudice which causes it, as a great danger to peace and international understanding and as a reproach to our Christian civilisation.'[49] After the conference the Quakers formed a permanent 'Joint Council to promote understanding between white and coloured people in Great Britain'. The Council met to consider general and particular cases of discrimination against non-Europeans in Britain and the evidence it uncovered supported student testimony.

In the area of accommodation S. N. Mitra, a student of the Royal College of Science, brought the example of the Imperial College hostel's written request, that only applications from 'British students of European parentage'[50] would be considered, to the Council's notice. The President of the Joint Council, S. L. Polak, gave the following examples of discrimination in a letter to the editor of the *Spectator*. Of the 15 lodging houses visited in Bedford Place, Bloomsbury (London's university district) only one would take non-European students. The reason given was the objection raised by white lodgers. In nearby Brunswick Square it was believed that maintaining the Square's reputation depended on excluding non-whites, although one landlady had made allowances for 'a light-skinned lodger'. These distinctions over pigmentation also operated in hotels, where individuals with pale complexions (regardless of nationality) often benefited. However, hoteliers lost their racial scruples when wealthy non-Europeans agreed to pay for private suites. The uncertainty of the situation was illustrated by the Secretary of the Indian Student Hostel who knew of instances when rooms, booked in advance for well-known and distinguished Indians, became mysteriously unavailable on a 'flimsy excuse' when the visitor came to install himself at the hotel.[51]

University sport was another area of exclusion referred to earlier. At Edinburgh six Indian players were excluded from the university hockey team. They promptly joined the city club and helped to defeat the university team. In another incident at a lawn tennis tournament 'four Indians ... were purposely drawn in one half – so that there should not be an all-Indian final'.[52] Sometimes a problem could be resolved by the intervention of a student union official. In one case an official successfully advised female students to amend their behaviour when they refused to dance with Indian men. As this example demonstrates, the Joint Council's work was not of a 'spectacular nature' and, apart from removing the ban against black boxers imposed by the National Sporting Club, few major breakthroughs were made. Nevertheless, during its short existence it did seek, with some degree of success, to alleviate the discrimination suffered by non-Europeans in Britain. Finally in April 1935, overwhelmed by debt, the Executive Committee of the Society of Friends decided that the Joint Council was no longer viable as a separate body.

CLASS PREJUDICE

The prejudice Indian students suffered in Britain, throughout the late nineteenth and the early twentieth century, did not revolve solely around colour. British preoccupation with class also informed racial attitudes. As Christine Bolt has written: 'racial and class prejudice were so intertwined in Victorian times it is hard to separate them'.[53] This was also true of the early twentieth century. At one level class prejudice was infused with a metropolitan snobbery. Thimayya observed: 'It was based on an assumption that someone raised in the colonies could not have the refined standards of one brought up in England.'[54] Time and again class was used as an excuse to operate a 'closed shop' at educational establishments in Britain. This is summed up by the phrase 'not letting down one's side'. Thimayya articulated succinctly the coded meaning behind this popular British saying: 'it meant really that those with the same upper-class background stuck together to give each other rank and privilege'.[55] Thimayya believed that while it was possible for British cadets with unsuitable backgrounds to overcome class obstacles by sheer merit – indeed, his own company commander was a case in point – no amount of talent could make an Indian acceptable.

The importance of class for English undergraduates in the Edwardian period was illustrated by N. S. Subbarao, when he observed that they were divided into 'gentleman' and 'touts'. English students told him that their friendship would cease if he were seen associating with a tout. He felt that some touts were essentially gentlemen 'but they had some social failings which an Indian naturally found it difficult to detect or judge severely'.[56] What is interesting about Subbarao's case is that Indians could be accepted, albeit in a very tenuous and superficial way, if they behaved in a manner befitting a 'gentleman'. But, 'If Indian students adopted the manners, the speech and bearing of undesirable acquaintances or of a particular class of society, they were treated with reserve by other classes, whose members do not wish to be drawn into contact with the class in question', and as a result labelled 'touts'.[57] But at Sandhurst even attempts by Indians to conform were met by obduracy, accentuated by fears of a potential revolt against the British led by Indian officers.

ACCEPTANCE OF INDIAN PROFESSIONALS

While Indian students may have faced difficulty gaining acceptance, there is evidence to suggest that Indian professionals working in the United Kingdom, such as U. K. Dutt, gradually began to fare much

better. Jeffrey Green in his research into the Afro-Caribbean community
in early twentieth-century Britain has argued that 'The presence of Afro-
Caribbean medical practitioners in Britain ... indicates that perception
of class may have been more important than race.'[58] The same theory
could be applied to Indian doctors who settled in Britain in that period,
though it is important to be wary of class reductionism. Certainly, the
number of Indians practising in England increased after the First World
War. Dr Fram Gotla and Dr E. Nundy had large practices in London.
Outside the capital Dr Ram was health officer in Yorkshire and Dr
Chowry Muthu, an authority on tuberculosis, had a sanatorium in
Somerset. By 1919 17 Indian doctors were recorded, of these most were
practising in Derbyshire, Yorkshire and Durham. There were about six
Indian doctors working in Scotland by the turn of the century. Sir R.
Havelock Charles, Dean of the London School of Tropical Medicine,
noted: 'They were very popular with miners and other classes of
workmen and had established good practices, making as much as £2,000
a year.'[59] Some of these Indian doctors achieved a high measure of
popularity. Upendra Krishna Dutt overcame strong prejudice when he
took up practice in Cambridge and won the regard of his patients. Forty-
two years after his father's retirement Rajani Palme Dutt made a return
visit to Cambridge. He met a taxi driver who described Dr Dutt in the
most affectionate terms: 'He was our family doctor, the nicest, kindest,
finest doctor Cambridge has ever had.'[60]

These Indian doctors did not owe their popularity to a common class
background with their patients. Discrimination had forced them to
accept unprofitable practices in deprived areas. Indeed, Dutt's practice
was in such a poor part of Cambridge that hard-pressed patients could
hardly afford to pay for a doctor's services. Dutt would often be paid
in kind by gifts of food and flowers. In these desperate circumstances
racial qualms were abandoned in the face of health care needs. Thus it
was not so much their perception of class but their immediate difficulties
which made racial considerations secondary. The ability of Indian
doctors to build up thriving practices must also have been to a large
extent due to their own abilities and their rapport with patients. Another
factor, which would have greatly assisted them, was the fact that many
doctors who settled in Britain married English women, such as Dr
Sukhagar Datta of Bristol,[61] and there are parallels here, again, with contemporary West Indian doctors. This allowed them to be absorbed more
readily into the local community. The high esteem in which they were
held is testimony to the fact that, in Green's words, 'black professionals
could achieve a level of acceptance in Britain that largely ignored their
colour'.[62] Such a conclusion must be qualified. While Indian doctors may
have been accepted as private doctors, the British medical establishment

was less accommodating. No Indians were able to climb the hospital career structure in England and become consultants, which was not only more lucrative but commanded status and respect. Although some did quite well, such as Dr Mangaldas V. Mehta and Dr Jensha Jhirad (mentioned before), who both returned to India after building reputations in England. Perhaps the medical profession's association with scientific racial theories can explain the reluctance of medical colleges to admit Indians, despite the efforts of the authorities to confront the particularly entrenched prejudice that existed.[63]

THE CASE OF N. B. WAGLE

The story of N. B. Wagle, an Indian student from Bombay who apprenticed himself to a British factory, shows the enormous lengths one student went to in order to gain acceptance in the face of race and acute class prejudice. This case study is also useful in looking at an individual student's reaction to attempts to exclude him, a subject that will be discussed later. When Wagle arrived in London in February 1899 his object was to study the British glass industry by gaining an apprenticeship in a factory. He obtained the assistance of several influential friends in England, including Sir George Birdwood[64] and Sir Mancherjee Bhownagree.[65] Despite approaching numerous firms, all 32 declined on the grounds that the responsibility of taking on a foreigner was too great, except for one Yorkshire firm which agreed on condition that a hefty premium of £200 was paid in advance. Eventually Birdwood helped Wagle to gain an introduction to a factory in the city of London. But the workers immediately objected to his presence: 'I found that there was a feeling of jealousy in the mind of workmen, and a fear that my introduction to the factory would directly or indirectly interfere with the interests of their trade.'[66]

Wagle succeeded in persuading the factory owner, with the aid of Blue Books containing trade returns, that Austria was Britain's main rival in the glass trade and India posed no threat. The proprietor was convinced by the evidence and invited Wagle to commence work immediately. However, he had only been at the factory for half an hour, when 30 of the workforce threatened the proprietor with strike action. When Wagle apologised for any trouble he might have caused, he received this rather unexpected answer: 'My dear boy! Don't you look droopy and crying, for we don't strike just for you, but we hate all gents the same.' The man claimed that he would have taken the same course of action if Wagle had been an Englishman rather than an Indian.[67] In this case class appears to have taken precedence over race, as it was

Wagle's gentlemanly persona rather than his racial origins which repelled factory workers, or was this just a smokescreen for the foreman to hide his racial prejudice behind?

Wagle came across many instances of racial prejudice during his numerous attempts to gain an apprenticeship. He decided to ingratiate himself with the workmen rather than the factory owners, as this was usually where he faced the greatest opposition. Wagle visited several works every day, 'treated one or two of the principal workmen with drinks and drives on the tops of buses, tried all tactics and wits at each place, but with very little success'. 'Some flatly refused to hear me', he wrote. 'Some said they could not undertake the risk, some argued the want of any previous precedent, some directly declined the proposal and some ridiculed the idea in an unbearable way.'[68] The following are examples of some of the abuse he had to endure:

> Another man, when I made my request to him as I did to others, broke into an awful rage, and staring at me in such a furious manner, as if he was going to swallow the whole of me said 'Oh! these foreigners! We have too many of them here at present' and then without stopping there began to use the choicest language.[69]

The workers would invariably ask Wagle the following questions: 'Are they all men like you there?', 'What do they eat?', 'What do they drink?', 'Have you got houses like ours?', 'Have you any railways?'

> And when I answered the last question in the affirmative, they doubted it, and one of them asked me, 'Do you know what railways are?' ... I gave them enough information about tigers, snakes, and elephants to make them interested in me – at least as an Indian curiosity.[70]

It was only when he discovered the hatred harboured by workmen for gentlemen that he began to make any progress towards his goal. He noted:

> There is a great economic fight going on in this country between two men – the workman and the gentleman. The former is proud of his technical skill, imagines that he is the founder of the national wealth ... hates the latter as one who enjoys without the slightest claim, the fruit and credit of his hard labours. The gentleman, on the other hand, looks down upon the workman as a man who has accumulated skill only by instinct and practice, without possessing either the higher powers of the brain nor the feelings of the heart.[71]

Armed with this revelation he decided to approach the workmen, not in gentleman's clothes, as before, but as a fellow workman. He distressed his clothes for such a purpose, which in view of his increasing poverty was not very difficult. Eventually he obtained an apprenticeship, but the trade union threatened to take industrial action. When the proprietor of the factory refused to back down and gave Wagle his full support, the union decided not to pursue the matter any further.

In order to cultivate friendly relations with the workmen Wagle was obliged to imitate their lifestyle. He wrote: 'this could not be done in any other way or by any other methods, than by doing as they did, behaving as they did, talking, dressing and even swearing as they did'.[72] There was a strict set of rules to adhere to, which was seen as an alternative to gentlemanly conduct and any reference to what was 'gentlemanly' would receive severe rebuke and was considered 'bad form'. This shows how in turn-of-the-century Britain factory workers had developed their own distinct culture, one in direct opposition to middle-class codes of conduct. Furthermore, it demonstrates a clear distrust of middle-class values and standards. Instead, a celebration of 'working classdom' was actively promoted, although some of the scrupulous attention to detail may have been for Wagle's benefit.

Wagle described extensively what was regarded as acceptable and unacceptable conduct. Whenever he met workmen he had to shake their hands, 'in whatever condition their hands may be – dirty or worse!' He also became acquainted with the workers' home-life. Wagle gave advice to other Indians hoping to obtain an apprenticeship in Britain:

> Whenever you meet any of them, or when they go home, catch occasionally an opportunity to go as far as the man's house, and shake hands with his 'missus', or 'missie' and pick up the baby if there is one and say, 'How nice, exactly like the mother!' It does not matter if it is so or not! … If there is a boy or young girl drop a sixpence in their hand and you become a 'jolly good fellow'. The chief principle in all your conduct must be to treat them not only that you are their equal, but as belonging to the same creed.[73]

It was also important to avoid objectionable behaviour: 'never address anyone as "Mr", be moody and grave, but always singing and jolly. Never call yourself unlucky or unfortunate, for that lowers you in their eyes instantly.'[74]

These adjustments involved abandoning his Hindu caste scruples when drinking tea from a communal tin or glass blowing. However, he continued to abstain from eating meat, despite the furore it caused among some workmen. Wagle marvelled:

> All these little things had a marvellous effect in a short time. When I go now in the factory I am welcomed with the title 'old chap' or sometimes

'chappie' and one and all of them try their best to make me comfortable and easy ... none of them have any secret of the glass trade which they either have kept or have the wish to keep from me.[75]

Relations with the factory owner became so cordial that he left Wagle in sole charge of the factory when he took three weeks' holiday. Nevertheless, Wagle was required to pay a high price to get beyond the 'cloak of abusive language', in the form of outward assimilation. Nothing less was acceptable to the workmen. But the changes he adopted were cosmetic – a means to an end.

Wagle's decision to copy the rituals and behaviour of factory workers shows the way Bhabha's theory of mimicry[76] can be reworked to apply to a specific, historic moment. Wagle camouflaged his appropriation of imperial knowledge by adopting a mask of assimilation. But this time mimicry is relocated, away from the colonial periphery to the metropolitan centre, Britain, and the new class dimension causes Wagle (the colonised) to mimic British working-class, metropolitan culture rather than middle-class, colonial culture.

FINANCIAL DIFFICULTIES

The Indian student's experience of residence in Britain was blighted not only by racial and class prejudice but by the shadow of poverty. All three variables were deeply interwoven with each other, producing a knock-on effect. The complexity of the connection between them is shown clearly in the case of U. K. Dutt. Upendra's outsider status was reinforced not only by his colour but also by his lack of funds, which in turn jeopardised and confused his class status. His qualifications and his diverse cultural interests (he harmonised the thoughts of Tolstoy, his mentor, with whom he kept up a lifelong correspondence and the Indian philosophy of Vedantism) should have qualified him for a niche in middle-class society. But as R. P. Dutt wrote of his father: 'his poverty revealed he lacked their keen money-making sense and other doctors looked upon him as a "squatter", an infamous fellow with qualifications no doubt, but without the capital to have bought a practice in the proper way'.[77] Thus impoverishment led to class prejudice which also manifested itself in racial discrimination. Dutt's racial origins were exaggerated by poverty, which led to a low class status. Each variable served to reinforce his subordinate position in metropolitan society.

Although a student's life had by its nature always been a frugal one, Indian students in Britain suffered a more tenuous existence than most. One of the earliest examples of this was W. C. Bonnerjee. He had been awarded a scholarship to study in England, established by the wealthy Parsi Jamsetjee Jeejeebhai in 1864. But there was a delay and he did not receive the scholarship until 1866, two years after arriving in England, by which time he had turned 21. The staunch opposition of his father and the *kulin* community to his wishes to study in Britain had led him to have recourse to subterfuge. He ran away from his home in Calcutta during the *Bejoya* ceremony of *Durga Puja* and was assisted in his journey to London by an English lawyer, Cockerel Smith. The confusion concerning his departure from India led to the delay in funding. Even after 18 months in London his father still refused to provide financial assistance. Consequently he was forced to survive on the aid secretly sent by his mother and sister.

Bonnerjee's disagreement with his father distressed him deeply. He wrote to his cousin from England: 'Could I have reasonably, withstood such an opportunity? Could I have given up these chances for my father's crotchets, in a point in which we differed as widely as the North and South poles are different from each other?'[78] Relations were so strained that his father appears to have written to him only once during his whole time in England. Bonnerjee complained to his cousin:

> If you take into consideration my first letter to him about Randen [his creditor] was written in December 1864 and that his letter refusing me pecuniary assistance is dated in the beginning of this year [1866] you will see how very late he has been in putting me right as regards my position with him … I feel it very much indeed … It is very cool of him. Don't you think so? Well, I suppose I must submit.[79]

Forced economy caused him to walk the six miles every day to and from his home and Lincoln's Inn. He wrote: 'I seldom go about in cabs and do not often go in omnibuses.'[80] There is a small hint in a letter written on 2 August 1866 that he lived in a poor district of London: 'Asiatic cholera has made its appearance in London. In some poor localities it is raging very hard. Sanitary arrangements are being introduced and we are in a frightful state altogether.'[81] Bonnerjee's desperation was palpable when he wrote to his cousin: 'If you do not get my parents to assist me you will probably hear of my end having taken place from sheer starvation.'[82]

CAUSES OF DESTITUTION

The threat of destitution hung over many Indian students. The majority of them came to Britain in a private capacity, supported by remittances from their parents in India. Any unforeseen circumstances which prevented the arrival of the funds could suddenly plunge an otherwise financially secure student into debt and poverty. The Parliamentary Committee on Distressed Colonial and Indian Subjects reported:

> The death or sickness of the breadwinner, an unexpected lawsuit, or the failure of the monsoon, whereby tenants are unable to pay their usual rents – any one of these mishaps may prevent the family from forwarding the monthly or quarterly remittances and when this disaster occurs the Indian student with few acquaintances in this country and slender credit is brought to the verge of destitution.[83]

In some cases parents did not properly estimate the cost of educating a son in Britain. N. G. Ranga's father risked all his hard-earned savings to send his son to England and, although Ranga did not become destitute, his expenses were twice as much as his father had anticipated.[84]

Both Aurobindo Ghose and Manmohan Ghose, who completed their entire education in England in the last two decades of the nineteenth century, were constantly beset by debt and financial troubles. Dr K. D. Ghose brought all his four children, three boys and a girl, and his wife to England in 1879. He had himself been in Britain in 1869 pursuing medical studies. Eventually Ghose left his young sons in England to be educated and returned to India. Aurobindo Ghose described their unenviable position:

> I was sent to England when seven years age with my two brothers and for the last eight years we have been thrown on our own resources, without any English friend to help or advise us. Our father, Dr K. D. Ghose of Khulna, has been unable to provide the three of us with sufficient funds for the most necessary wants and we have long been in an embarrassed position.[85]

Aurobindo's university tutor testified to his impoverished condition:

> He has had a very hard and anxious time of it for the last two years. Supplies from home have almost entirely failed and he has had to keep his two brothers as well as himself ... I have several times written to his father on his behalf, but for the most part unsuccessfully. It is only lately that I managed to extract from him enough to pay some tradesmen, who would otherwise have put his son into the county court.[86]

Manmohan Ghose was constantly plagued by debts. He eventually decided to leave Oxford pleading pecuniary embarrassment. Although Christ Church did offer him a scholarship to allow him to finish his course, curiously he appears to have rejected it. The root of the brothers' financial difficulties lay with their father. Krishnadhan Ghose had become a very popular doctor in Khulna and a leading civic figure, responsible, according to his youngest son, for making Khulna free from malaria and introducing radical improvements to the city's infra- structure. However, his generosity meant that he frequently over- stretched his resources by trying to provide for a host of people. Bipin Chandra Pal wrote: 'Krishnadhan's purse was always open for his needy relations ... the poor, the widow and the orphan loved him for his selfless pity and soulful benevolence.'[87] The irregularity of remittances meant that his sons were often obliged to live at starvation level. Nevertheless, Manmohan at least did not reproach his father for his lack of resources. He wrote: 'I cannot but be proud with admiration at such dauntless self- sacrifice and heroic perseverance.'[88] Similarly, Gandhi's financial difficulties stemmed from the fact that his father had no savings:

> Though my father was the Prime Minister of more than one native state, he never hoarded money. He spent all that he had earned on charity and the education and marriages of his children. He said that his children represented his wealth, and if he hoarded much money he would spoil them.[89]

Some of the early members of the Indian student population who found themselves in financial straits would appeal to the India Office for assistance. When Jivan Singh requested money for a passage back to India his request was granted largely because he was supported by testimonials from missionaries, testifying to his conduct as a Christian.[90] However, L. Rahman was refused – the usual response in such cases – when he applied in 1886. Between 1887 and 1909 17 students applied to the India Office for relief or repatriation. In almost every case the student was in distressed circumstances due to a failure on the part of parents to forward remittances. In three of the 17 cases funds had been stopped when a son had been disowned for marrying an English woman.[91]

The Parliamentary Committee established to look into the whole question of distressed Indians in Britain was concerned that little provision was made by students in the event of pecuniary problems. K. Chowdhury, Assistant Secretary of the British Indian Seamen Institute, interviewed two students – one from Assam, the other from Calcutta – who had come to Britain under the auspices of the Calcutta Scientific Industrial Association:

> The Association found them passages and nothing more, they gave them two letters, one to the secretary of the YMCA and the second to the

manager of the British Indian shipping company ... I inquired about their means and they said that they might get some money from their parents.[92]

Chowdhury asked them what proof they gave the Association that they had made adequate provision for their maintenance in Britain. One of the students replied: 'because I happen to come from a district which has not yet sent any students, therefore the Association thought by sending me they would get some support from the district'.[93] The Committee was gravely concerned that a philanthropic body such as the Association was sending students to Britain without any means of support.

The situation was exacerbated by the impression that students could support themselves in England. As early as 1873 the National Indian Association reported the tragic case of 'A young man recently arrived in London from Calcutta with barely enough to support him, and provide clothes, books, college fees, etc. for three months and that little he was robbed of at the docks when landing.'[94] Not only did this illustrate the need for better information about the cost of living in England, but more significantly the young man had come under the assumption that he could maintain himself in England by teaching Bengali.

Figures for the number of students who did succeed in earning a living are not available. However, Chowdhury knew of three cases out of 13 or 14 within a twelve-month period (1909 to 1910) who 'had succeeded in getting employment or some sort of income in England'. He described these three men:

> One man is a language tutor. He goes to some of these schools of languages. He knows a little Hindustani and Arabic and he says he makes a few shillings that way. The other man is employed by Lipton's or some other tea company as a sort of showman. He is an educated man, an undergraduate, and he stands in front of one of their cafes as an advertisement. The third man is also an undergraduate. He has found employment in one of the music halls and he goes there in the evening for a couple of hours and gets some wages. Two of them once joined a polytechnic for a course of study in electricity and chemistry.[95]

The Committee believed such occupations were not suitable for educated men. It lamented: 'some of them have been driven to pitiable straits in their efforts to make a living'.[96]

In order to prevent the reoccurrence of this type of situation the report suggested several ways of correcting the misapprehensions students entertained about maintaining themselves in England. Chowdhury suggested two specific measures. First, the 'Government should publish in the provincial gazettes, the impossibility of obtaining employment in England and the danger which Indian students run of getting stranded in this country if they come here without sufficient funds'.[97] Local newspapers would also publish similar warnings. Secondly, it was also recommended that the newly created Student Advisory Committee in India should disperse information on destitute Indian students as widely as possible to act as a deterrent. However, in the meantime parents of destitute Indian students would at least be informed by telegram of their child's predicament.

It is significant that Chowdhury's attempts to persuade destitute students to return to India were often unsuccessful. They would rather starve than face the social ostracism that would follow were they to return and find themselves in no better position than most of their stay-at-home friends. N. B. Wagle reiterated this attitude when he wrote: 'Going back to India as an unsuccessful man was a thing I felt worse than death.'[98] It reveals why Wagle and others like him were so keen to persevere despite the numerous setbacks and disappointments they encountered in Britain.

There is evidence to suggest that students helped each other; for example, two destitute Indians were dispatched to America by fellow Indian students at Oxford.[99] One Oxford student suggested that a small exhibition of £20 to £50 per annum for the most deserving students should be introduced to alleviate the most serious cases of deprivation. He claimed that many Indian students in London lived on a meagre £150–£200 per year and the value of a government scholarship was £200, considerably less than a Rhodes scholarship at £300.[100] Seven years later, on the eve of the First World War, when Rajani Palme Dutt won a scholarship to Balliol, he was forced to stretch the £170 he had raised, £80 of which was the scholarship, to reach what was considered the minimum amount needed for subsistence at the time of £200. To make up the difference he was forced to live on a frugal diet of bread, cheese and biscuits, despite his overwhelming temptation to purchase a hot meal for 7d.[101]

Inadequate funds were also a major obstacle to maintaining good relations with English students – or for that matter any type of social life – as entertainment and participation in sports were costly. The need for economy put limitations on involvement in collegiate life. R. P. Dutt wrote: 'During the first term I participated in everything as far as extremely narrow financial limits allowed. I sought insatiably any kind of gathering formal or informal, conservative, liberal, socialist, Christian, oriental, empire builders or do-gooders provided it was free.'[102] This goes a long way in explaining why students had to abstain from college activities, provoking allegations of 'aloofness' by English officials and students. The Indian student J. Jaini reflected in his diary:

My residence in England has taught me the keenness of the teeth of poverty. Richer than millions here or elsewhere, still the deprivation of the wherewithal to procure what were bare necessities to me in my social life made me realise the infinite sufferings of the poor.[103]

Over a decade before the Committee reported in 1910 officials were attempting to arrest the tide of destitute Indians in England. The Secretary of State for India put forward the idea of identity certificates:

Advantage would be gained if some measures could be taken in India to ascertain particulars regarding persons contemplating such visits to England and report them to me. Inquiries could then be made in India as to the objects in view and the means of the travellers to carry out these objects. False impressions could be corrected and timely advice given. If the advice should be ignored the responsibility would rest on the parties themselves and it would be easy to dispose of any subsequent applicants for aid.[104]

Thus certificates were seen as a means to weed out individuals who could prove to be a financial burden. But the scheme was a failure as 'the majority of Indians neglected to provide themselves with certificates'.[105]

The difficulties presented by destitute Indians, not least British official concerns that such vulnerable individuals would become the tools of political agitators active in Britain as well as the lengthy amounts of time taken up by them, led T. W. Arnold, the Official Government Adviser to Indian Students, to consider the necessity of a separate organisation to deal with them. Consequently, in 1911, in the wake of the Committee on Distressed Colonial and Indian Subjects, the Distressed Indian Student Aid Committee was established to assist destitute students by providing loans. By 1918 the organisation had assisted 232 cases; of these 137 had repaid their loans fully and 22 partially.[106]

ANGLO-INDIAN RELATIONS

Interaction between Indian and British students and the development of social life were conducted within three separate arenas. These included, firstly, the collegiate setting for those who lived within university-controlled residences, such as Oxbridge students. Secondly, the arena of boarding houses and rented accommodation inhabited by all non-collegiate students as well as London law students, and, thirdly, associations formed for the benefit of Indians students.

Evidence from the Lee Warner Committee and the individual testimonies of British officials and students shows that Anglo-Indian student relations were strained during the early twentieth century. This is borne out by the experience of individual students at Oxford in the aftermath of the First World War. Few of them appear to have managed to acquire close friendships with English students. K. P. S. Menon was typical. He wrote in his memoirs: 'I made few English friends.'[107] He gave a detailed and illuminating account of the reasons for the poor relations, which is worth quoting in full:

> In my time the undergraduates fell into two categories, those who came up directly from school and those who returned to Oxford from the war. The former were younger than me and the latter were older, and, when you are 20, a difference of two or three years either way makes all the difference. Moreover, the ex-servicemen were a steady, hard-working lot, not over-anxious to make friends. I was temperamentally shy and felt tongue-tied in the presence of my fellow-students ... The playground was the best place for making friends but I was poor at games. I played a little tennis, which is hardly a companionable game ... Perhaps the real handicap from which I and most Indian students suffered was that we had a certain complex, resulting from the unnatural relationship between Great Britain and India, the ruler and the ruled. Whether it was an inferiority complex or a superiority complex I do not know, perhaps it was an inferiority complex, which, as it often does, took the form of a superiority complex. It was this, which created an invisible barrier in the way of any real friendship.[108]

Vishnu Sahay, at Oxford between 1923 and 1925, could not recall making many friendships with Englishmen, although he made friends with other colonials: 'I had friends but they were Rhodes scholars from America, Canada, Australia and the other victims of British tyranny, the Welshmen.'[109] He believed that the public and the non-public school divide was stronger than any other. S. H. Raza also became friendly with a Welsh student who felt out of place at Oxford. He reflected: 'This was the first time I learnt that the United Kingdom was not as united as appeared to us from a distance.'[110] C. S. Venkatachar came to England as an ICS probationer in 1920. He described his status as 'more an observer than a participant in university life'.[111] Like most Indian students he kept company with his fellow nationals. Thus although relations were 'cordial' a general basis for friendship between British and Indians did not exist.

Non-collegiate students or those who rented accommodation in London had even less opportunity of socialising with English students and, as the majority of the Indian student population were studying law at the Inns of Court, it is this experience which was most common at any given time. For London students their home-life revolved around an apartment or a boarding house. A. M. Dehlavi, who wrote an article about the different types of accommodation available to Indian students, pointed out that renting a flat was the least conducive for developing relations with the host community; but it was inexpensive as meals were not included. However, Dehlavi was a champion of the boarding house, where a cross-section of metropolitan society could be sampled. He described the one he had entered on first arriving in London as 'very satisfactory and the people praiseworthy',[112] especially conversation over dinner, which he had found highly entertaining with the views of all nations represented. Fazl-i-Husain agreed with Dehlavi; he believed boarding-house life was a schooling for English life. Before leaving for England he wrote in his diary of the principles which would guide him in England: one was 'to avoid popularity on principle'.[113] College experience had taught him that popularity could only be gained at the expense of time lost. Despite this rather puritanical adherence to his academic work, he managed to develop a cordial relationship with his Jewish landlady. However, the British authorities were concerned that it was this type of environment which would foster 'unsuitable' habits and acquaintances.

As already described, in 1871 an unofficial society, the National Indian Association, was formed to improve Indo-British relations in England. The problem of Indian student isolation was mentioned in the Association's council meeting of 6 May 1872: 'It having been reported that Indian students at Cambridge had few or no opportunities of association with English students and professors. It was resolved that enquiries should be made.'[114] Membership, which was open to Indians and English men and women, fluctuated greatly from year to year. One of its members, Sir Frederick Lely, estimated that nearly one-third of Indian members departed every year.[115] It is difficult to establish how successful the Association was in attracting Indian students. However, one student, Sukumar Ray, who lived at 21 Cromwell Road, the head-quarters of both the National Indian Association and the Northbrook Society – an organisation with similar aims to the NIA's – wrote to his mother in 1912 describing the party given by the National Indian Association as well-attended 'with a lot of singing and feasting – everyone felt happy'.[116]

The Victoria League, an organisation founded in 1901 to spread accurate information about the British dominions and to welcome colonial visitors, also considered offering hospitality to Indian visitors and students in 1907, in co-operation with the National Indian

Association and the Northbrook Society. The Victoria League, it was argued, would be of 'special value'[117] as it was more able to offer personal rather than the corporate hospitality already being offered by the Indian societies. But there was hostility among League members to this new departure in policy. One, R. N. Hordern, argued that the proposal 'was distinctly dangerous, and would lead to the League being involved in serious difficulties'. He urged that the matter be considered by an impartial committee 'of men not necessarily connected with India'.[118] But another member of the executive committee, Mrs Lyttleton, wanted to stop any further discussion of hospitality for Indians as she believed it was harming the League. She proposed that the resolution should be dropped, 'without pronouncing an opinion on the merits of the case ... owing to the widespread feeling against it, which exists among friends and well-wishers'.[119] Hordern and other members of the League felt that in the wake of the Lee Warner Committee and the generally bad publicity surrounding Indian students in Britain the question of offering hospitality to Indians was too controversial and as a result laden with potential problems. However, by 1930 the Victoria League's attitude to Indians had softened. Its Hospitality Committee agreed to find hosts for Indian cadets at Sandhurst.[120]

ICS probationers were not able to indulge in a vigorous social life as the rigorous academic work left little spare time, especially in comparison with the limited demands placed on students studying for the Bar. This is illustrated by R. C. Dutt in a letter to his brother: 'I need scarcely tell you that never before did we study so hard and so unremittingly as during the past year.'[121] Also membership of associations was, as some complained, a luxury they could ill afford. Thus for students who lacked the funds and opportunities to socialise, residence in Britain, especially in London, could be very lonely. Although some students did make lifelong friendships, and had both the cash and the inclination to seek entertainment at the theatre and other social attractions, they appear to have been the exception.

N. S. Subbarao was able to speak with authority on matters pertaining to Indian students. As president of the Cambridge Majlis he was able to maintain close relations with all Indians at the university. In addition he knew a number of Indians in London, where he admitted to spending 'considerable lengths of time'. Although his account of the life of an Indian student does have inherent shortcomings, largely connected to the fact that his generalisations about Cambridge students do not necessarily apply to Indian students in other parts of Britain. Nevertheless, his insights are still illuminating as may be seen from the following extract:

The average Indian when he comes to this country is able to express himself well in English and often has taken his degree at home and tackles his work with greater ease than the average English youth fresh from school … and freed from the restraints of home, revels in his liberty. He is as yet ignorant of the code of etiquette, a knowledge of which does not necessarily make one a gentleman, but an ignorance of which brands one as a 'tout'. But in the course of time he masters it. He also takes some time to get used to the relations of the sexes here, so different to what obtains at home. On the whole he gets on satisfactorily. He works well enough and finds enough company in his countrymen and in such Englishmen as chance throws in his way.[122]

He compared the lifestyles of the two groups of students: The Indian's life was 'work tempered by social relations and exercise of some sort or other', while the English student enjoyed, in contrast, a life of 'sports and society'.[123] Although he did not regret his stay in England, he had not found it 'enjoyable' and had made 'no real friends'. But most importantly of all his 'expectations of free comradeship with Englishmen had been disappointed'.[124] This echoed the sentiment of many Indian students; their stay was offset by a feeling of disillusionment which, according to Subbarao, set in on arrival in England. Many Indian students were admirers of English culture and others such as J. L. Sathe had been told by his school principal in India that he would be treated equally. Relations did not improve in the years that followed the Lee Warner Report; on the contrary as the nationalists gained more ground and student numbers increased animosity grew on both sides. The positive aspects of British life were tarnished for students who experienced racial and class prejudice, deprivation and limited contact with English life and people. All of which came as a particular blow in light of Indian students' high expectations.

So far I have focused almost exclusively on the experience of men; however, the experience of pioneering Indian women who came to study in Britain in the nineteenth century suggests that female students were subject to fewer difficulties and consequently reacted more positively to their residence. The main evidence for this comes from the papers of Cornelia Sorabji. Unlike her male counterparts, Sorabji's uniqueness and celebrity status allowed her to socialise within the upper echelons of British society, where she was feted. Her mentor and tutor, Benjamin Jowett, gave her access to a world debarred to most Indian male students. Cornelia, who came from a highly anglicised, Christian background faced little difficulty in adapting to college life. In fact, her sex may well have helped her in this respect, as she was shielded from the worst excesses of the crude and arrogant behaviour often experienced by Indian male students. British students would go out of their way to assist her. For example, other law students would give up books in the Codrington Library in All Souls College if the librarian hinted that Cornelia needed them.[125] She was frequently the object of other acts of kindness as well as privileges, such as having a permanent fire in her room during winter.[126] However, Cornelia did not always enjoy being singled out for special treatment in this way and complained: 'I wish he [Jowett] would treat me like a man and not make gallant speeches about my "intellect" and "quietness of perception".'[127]

While Cornelia may have been less critical than her contemporary Pandita Ramabai and some other women visitors, whom I shall discuss in the next chapter, the last remark shows that she too faced difficulties. Financial problems, the bane of many male students' lives, arose when the public fund established by Lady Hobhouse ran out and she was obliged to borrow. Cornelia was also targeted by missionaries who assumed that she was a 'heathen' and attempted to convert her (a pointless exercise, as she was already a Christian). Nevertheless, her writing seems to show a general satisfaction with her time in England. This is also true of her sister Alice, who was a medical student at the Great Ormond Street Hospital.[128] Mary Bhore, a student of Oxford University, was very impressed by the hospitality she received at Somerville College,[129] as was her devout fellow Christian Manorama Bose, who felt at ease within the religious environment of Britain.[130] As women and in Cornelia's case, an out-spoken supporter of British rule, they were not perceived by the British establishment as representing a challenge, whereas Indian male students (specially in the twentieth century) were regarded as both a sexual and a political threat.

Despite cases such as U. K. Dutt and Aurobindo Ghose, whose abiding memory of Britain was 'a struggle with hard realities – from hardships, starvation … and constant dangers and fierce difficulties',[131] the first generation of Indian students who came to Britain in the second half of the nineteenth century did receive a warmer reception than those who arrived in the twentieth century. J. R. McLane has stressed this point when he wrote:

> Many nationalists who went to London in the nineteenth century, before the numbers of Indians in England was large and before English-speaking Indians ceased to be a novelty, boarded with English families, continued to learn the ways of their rulers and returned with positive feelings about the English as individuals. R. C. Dutt, Surendranath Banerjea, Pherozeshah Mehta and Gandhi are examples.[132]

The fact that a few Indians gained entrance into 'polite' society and were well treated is another instance of this.

However, by the turn of the century the situation had deteriorated and restrictionist policies were being adopted against Indian students. D. A. Lorimar's argument about the hardening of racial attitudes in mid-nineteenth-century Britain[133] could be applied to Indian students in early twentieth-century Britain, who were faced with greater intolerance than the generation before them. The cult of the gentleman and the search for gentility had obtained a stranglehold over the English middle class. Whereas once differences of race had provoked curiosity, by the end of the century the English started to react adversely to differences of any sort and to exclude all those who did not match up to their ideal of a gentleman. By definition, gentlemen were leaders of society in ability, character and deportment. The hothouses of this new elite were the public schools, where attempts were made to instil pupils with manliness, athleticism, discipline and incorruptibility. The Hindu 'Babu' was regarded as the antithesis of this model: effeminate, complacent, easily led and treacherous. Consequently when English-educated Indians aspired to gentlemanly status they were ridiculed and stereotyped.

This chapter has investigated the interplay between race and class in British metropolitan society as experienced by Indians. The evidence illustrates the way in which poverty operated to exacerbate the racial and class inequalities faced by many students. This was also complicated by the mismatch in their class position. Although students came from middle-class families, once they left the colonial periphery and entered the metropolitan centre lack of funds and discrimination forced students, particularly in London, to take up lodgings in working-class districts. This change in circumstances inverted their class position, causing their position in Britain to be indeterminate, as well as confusing colonial hierarchies. Indian encounters with Britain were also affected by the political situation in India, gender, individual circumstances and the type of political and cultural baggage students brought with them.

NOTES

1 Gupta, *Life and Work of R. C. Dutt*, p. 19.
2 See J. Majeed, 'Putting God in his Place: Bradley, McTaggart and Muhammed Iqbal', *Journal of Islamic Studies*, 4, 2 (1993), pp. 208–36.
3 (IOL) MSS. Eur. F. 165/194, 7 November 1893, p. 3.
4 See Introduction.
5 (IOL) MSS. Eur. F. 165/2, 26 January 1890, pp. 44–5.
6 R. Ray, *My Reminiscences – Social Development during the Gandhian Era and After* (New Delhi: Allied Publishers, 1982), p. 35.
7 Gandhi, *Autobiography*, p. 87.

8 Ibid.
9 C. Dewey, 'The Education of a Ruling Caste: The Indian Civil Service in the Era of Competitive Examinations', *English Historical Review* (April 1973), pp. 279–80.
10 S. C. Bose, *An Indian Pilgrim: An Unfinished Autobiography and Collected Letters 1897–1921* (Calcutta: Netaji Research Bureau, 1965), p. 105.
11 D. Lelyveld, *Aligarh's First Generation – Muslim Solidarity in British India* (Princeton, NJ: Princeton University Press, 1978), p. 9.
12 M. Banton, *Race Relations* (London: Tavistock, 1967), p. 8.
13 British Communist Party Archives. R. P. Dutt Papers, File 23.
14 Ibid., p. 5.
15 Ibid.
16 *Indian Magazine*, No. 207 (March 1888), p. 218. In 1883 an Indian officer wrote to *The Times* (15 January) of the warm welcome he had received in England: 'Everywhere we were heartily cheered.'
17 (IOL) L/P&J/6/1120, 1911.
18 (IOL) L/P&J/6/845, p. 107.
19 Ibid., p. 200.
20 Ibid.
21 Ibid.
22 Ibid.
23 Ibid., Satya V. Muckerjea, pp. 252–3.
24 Ibid., p. 207.
25 Ibid., p. 288.
26 Ibid., p. 194. According to K. Chowdhury, even private families who received paying guests 'would have nothing to do with men of dusky complexion'. *Student Movement*, Vol. 12 (1910), p. 87.
27 Ibid., p. 65.
28 (IOL) W1757, p. 35.
29 Ibid., p. 45.
30 (IOL) L/P&J/6/845, p. 288.
31 Ibid., pp. 299–300.
32 Ibid., p. 282.
33 (IOL) W1757, p. 237. When the Indian Student Department was placed under the charge of Dr T. W. Arnold in 1916, his assistant of three years N. C. Sen took over responsibility for the Bureau of Information.
34 *Indus*, Vol. 4, No. 7 (April 1925), p. 123. Solomon West Ridgeway Dias Bandaranaike (1899–1959) became the fourth prime minister of Sri Lanka.
35 M. R. Jayakar, *The Story of My Life*, Vol. 1, *1873–1922* (New Delhi: Asia Publishing House, 1958), p. 38.
36 Ibid., p. 39.
37 Ibid., p. 40.
38 Ibid., p. 41.
39 N. B. Bonarjee, *Under Two Masters* (New Delhi: Oxford University Press, 1970), p. 73.
40 Ibid., p. 74.
41 (IOL) MSS. Eur. T. 81/2.
42 Bonarjee, *Under Two Masters*, p. 74.
43 B. M. Kaul, *The Untold Story* (Bombay: Allied Publishers, 1967), pp. 23–5.
44 M. R. A. Baig, *In Different Saddles* (Calcutta: Asia Publishing House, 1967), pp. 32–3.

45 Ibid., p. 33.
46 H. Evans, *Thimayya of India* (Dehra Dun: Natraj, 1988), p. 65.
47 Ibid.
48 Ibid., p. 64.
49 Friends House Papers, Colour Bar Committee 1929–31, Minutes of Committee for the Conference on Colour Bar, 27 November 1929, p. 1.
50 Ibid., p. 3.
51 *Spectator*, 14 February 1931.
52 Colour Bar Committee, 1929–31. I. Montague, 'Colour Bar in Sport', 1931, p. 7.
53 C. Bolt, 'Race and the Victorians', in C. C. Eldridge (ed.) *British Imperialism in the Nineteenth Century* (London: Macmillan, 1984), p. 142.
54 Evans, *Thimayya*, p. 65.
55 Ibid.
56 (IOL) L/P&J/6/845, p. 200.
57 Ibid.
58 J. P. Green, 'West Indian Doctors in London: John Alcindor (1873–1924) and James Jackson Brown (1882–1953)', *Journal of Caribbean History*, 20, 1 (June, 1986), p. 50.
59 (IOL) W1757, p. 309.
60 British Communist Party Archives. R. P. Dutt Papers, File 3.
61 R. Barrot, *Bristol and the Indian Independence Movement* (Bristol: Bristol Historical Association, 1988).
62 Green and Lotz, 'A Brown Alien in a White City', p. 71.
63 (IOL) L/P&J/6/1120, 1911. See remarks made by T. W. Arnold in Chapter 4.
64 Sir George Christopher Molesworth Birdwood (1832–1917) was a medical practitioner in Bombay and later joined the India Office. He was an orientalist and wrote extensively about Indian art.
65 Mancherjee Bhownagree (1851–1933) was elected Conservative MP for Bethnel Green in 1895. He was a prominent member of Britain's resident Indian and more particularly Parsi community, although his support of British rule in India marked him out from most of his Indian contemporaries in London.
66 N. B. Wagle, 'An Indian Student's Experience of English Factory Life', *Indian Magazine and Review*, No. 361 (1901), p. 14.
67 Ibid.
68 Ibid., p. 15.
69 Ibid.
70 Ibid., p. 17.
71 Ibid., pp. 15–6.
72 Ibid., p. 21.
73 Ibid. When quoting from primary sources I have tried to be faithful to the original, avoiding any grammatical or other alterations.
74 Ibid.
75 Ibid., p. 22.
76 See discussion of theory in the Preface.
77 British Communist Party Archives, R. P. Dutt Papers, File 23.
78 Muckerjee, *W. C. Bonerjee*, p. 11.
79 Ibid., p. 12.
80 Ibid., p. 9.
81 Ibid., p. 10.
82 Ibid., p. 14.

83 Committee on Distressed Colonial and Indian Subjects, Cd 5133 (London, 1910), p. 58.

84 N. G. Ranga, *Fight for Freedom* (Delhi: S. Chand, 1968), p. 8.

85 A. B. Purani, *Sri Aurobindo in England* (Pondicherry: Sri Aurobindo Ashram, 1956), pp. 9–10. On his return to India Aurobindo Ghose became involved in revolutionary politics. In 1907 he was arrested for publishing articles in *Bande Mataram*. He was rearrested in 1908 and spent a year in prison, during which time he became an aesthetic, withdrew from political activities and devoted himself entirely to literature and philosophy.

86 Ibid., p. 14.

87 L. Ghose, *Manmohan Ghose – Makers of Indian Literature* (New Delhi: Sahitya Akademi, 1975), p. 5.

88 Ibid.

89 *Indian Magazine and Review*, No. 248 (August 1891), p. 387.

90 (IOL)L/P&J/6/76, No. 1065, 24 June 1882.

91 (IOL)L/P&J/6/925, No. 830, 1909.

92 Committee on Distressed Colonial and Indian Subjects, Cd 5133, p. 158.

93 Ibid.

94 *Journal of the National Indian Association*, No. 25 (January 1873), p. 246.

95 Committee on Distressed Colonial and Indian Subjects, Cd 5133, p. 158.

96 Ibid.

97 Ibid.

98 Wagle, 'An Indian Student's Experience of English Factory Life', p. 14.

99 (IOL) L/P&J/6/845, S. V. Muckerjea, p. 253.

100 Ibid.

101 British Communist Party Archives, R. P. Dutt Papers, File 1, *Our History Journal*, 11 January 1987.

102 Ibid., File 1.

103 Jaini, *Fragments*, p. 180.

104 (IOL)L/P&J/6/483, No. 1231, 1898.

105 (IOL) L/P&J/6/647, No. 1972, 17 August 1903.

106 *Indian Magazine*, No. 572 (August 1882), p. 124.

107 Menon, *Many Worlds*, pp. 52–3.

108 Ibid.

109 (IOL) MSS. Eur. T. 122.

110 (IOL) MSS. Eur. F. 180/29a.

111 (IOL) MSS. Eur. F. 180/85.

112 *Indian Magazine and Review*, No. 269 (May 1893), p. 299.

113 (IOL) MSS. Eur. E. 352/2, 23 August 1898.

114 First Annual Report of the National Indian Association, 24 November 1871, p. 4.

115 Annual Meeting of National Indian Association, *Indian Magazine*, No. 511 (July 1913).

116 A. Robinson, 'Selected Letters of Sukumar Ray', *South Asia Research*, 7, 2 (1987), p. 207. Sukumar Ray (1887–1923), father of Satyajit Ray, the celebrated film-maker, became a gifted nonsense verse writer and illustrator.

117 Victoria League Papers, Minutes of the Executive Committee, 27 June 1907.

118 Ibid., 5 December 1907. I have not been able to find any more information about R. N. Hordern.

119 Ibid. Mrs (Dame) Edith Sophie Lyttleton was the wife of the Colonial Secretary (Alfred Lyttleton) and a member of the 'Souls' group. See J. Abdy and C. Gere, *The*

Souls (London: Sidgwick & Jackson, 1984).
120 Victoria League Papers, Minutes of Branches Committee, 12 March 1930.
121 Gupta, *Life and Work*, p. 19.
122 (IOL) L/P&J/6/845, p. 198.
123 Ibid., p. 197.
124 Ibid.
125 (IOL) MSS. Eur. F. 165/3, 9 November 1890, p. 273.
126 (IOL) MSS. Eur. F. 165/1.
127 (IOL) MSS. Eur. F. 165/6, 14 February 1892.
128 (IOL) MSS. Eur. F. 165/207.
129 *Indian Magazine and Review*, No. 360 (December 1900).
130 (IOL) MSS. Eur. F. 178/69.
131 Purani, *Sri Aurobindo*, p. 85.
132 J. R. McLane, *Indian Nationalism and the Early Congress* (Princeton, NJ: Princeton University Press, 1977), p. 53.
133 D. A. Lorimer, *Colour, Class and the Victorians: English Attitudes to the Negro in the Mid-Nineteenth Century* (Leicester: Leicester University Press, 1978).

3

Representations of Indians in Britain

T HE scholarship of the post-colonial cultural theorists Edward Said, Homi Bhabha, Robert Young, Gayatri Spivak and the historian John MacKenzie has revealed the importance of literature and popular culture as sites of colonial exchange. Cultural encounters through the media of the press, theatre and fiction constituted important 'contact zones'. Representations of colonial subjects in British popular culture are crucial in understanding how the host population and British policy-makers perceived students, as well as how this disproportionate or inappropriate attention affected the students' self-image and ultimately their experience of Britain. I also show that, while work on racial stereotypes in colonial literature on India has been prolific, the 'Indian student model' in Anglo-Indian fiction has not been utilised by commentators. Unlike Anglo-Indian novelists, who singled Indian students out for special attention, recent researchers have chosen to neglect Indians in Britain, focusing instead on more general depictions of India and Indians.

INDIA IN THE PRESS AND THE THEATRE

Before examining fictional accounts of Indians in Britain, I consider the representations of India found in the British press and theatre. A survey, at five-yearly intervals, of the January editions of *The Times* newspaper from 1880 to 1930 shows that although India attracted relatively little interest (at its lowest in 1896 with a total of 90 articles, and reaching a peak in 1920 of 992 articles on Indian-related subjects[1]), there was nevertheless an overwhelmingly negative tone to the topics which appeared on a regular basis. India and its inhabitants were often linked with violence and disorder. *The Times* gave particular attention to civil unrest of a communal or industrial nature, conspiracy bomb cases, sedition and murder. Indian National Congress activities were disparagingly reported and nationalist opinion was never sought. This was not surprising as *The Times*, mouthpiece of official government opinion, was always keen to play down Congress's demands, leading one Indian student in Britain to describe it as 'always zealously giving due weight to the opinions of Anglo-Indian officials on Indian matters'. There were also numerous references to India's trade and strategic importance. *The Times* also perpetuated a long-standing myth that India was a land of princes, with several articles on princely loyalty to the British. Lastly, British technological superiority was illustrated not only in discussion of railways, but in advertisements such as one for Lotus Waterproof Boots, in which a British officer describes the Indian reaction to his boots: 'You should have seen those coolies' faces, they thought it some devil that kept me dry. It was all I could do to keep them from kneeling down and offering up prayers to that blessed pair of Boots.'[2] The overall impression given to British readers was a negative one, of a country racked by famine, disease, fanaticism, lawlessness, superstition, cruelty and unrest of every conceivable type.

This distorted image of India transferred readily to a theatrical setting. The India Office's unpopular decision to stop a theatrical production entitled *Romance of India* from opening in 1913 provides an invaluable insight into how India was depicted in the popular theatre of the period. The play consisted of a prologue and six scenes. The prologue was tellingly entitled 'India's Darkest Age', subtitled 'The Worship of Siva Maha-Diva, the Great God Who Destroys' in which a ritual human sacrifice was presented in the most lurid terms. The spectacle was aimed at a working-class audience; consequently it pandered to popular tastes, deploying Brahmin priests 'chanting weird dirges', dancing nautch girls, fakirs and lepers. The basic symbolism of good, as represented by British rule conquering India's 'Evil Genius', took place within six tableaux chronicling major events in Indian history. This particular play was banned on the grounds that it would offend Indian religious feeling, with the India Office claiming that 'the antagonism between Hindu and Christian religion emanated from each scene and historically the scenario was full of anachronisms and grotesque misrepresentation of the facts'.[3] Nevertheless, similar productions on Indian themes had played in London for some time.

One of the earliest plays of this type was Dryden's Restoration play *Aurangzeb* (1676). Eleven plays with 'India' in the title were licensed between 1880 and 1930 including *Indian Prince* (1897), *My Friend from India* (1896) and *Prince of India* (1906). In total there were about 40 plays by British playwrights which had titles suggesting an Indian theme, such as *The Nautch Girl* (1891), *Behind the Veil* (1910) and *Jewels of the East* (1913).[4] But titles could be misleading: J. Clarke's *The Prince of India* was an historical drama set in Turkey, a measure of the ignorance surrounding India. Clearly India did not always correspond to a specific geographical area. Nevertheless, as J. M. MacKenzie has noted, India did not empty the theatre in the same way as it did the Commons. Indian productions often took the form of fairytale extravaganzas such as *Indian Pickle* (1919) and *When Fate is Kind* (1915), or a mystery like *The Eye of Siva* (1923), influenced by Wilkie Collins's *The Moonstone*. Plays and particularly musical comedies on Indian and more general eastern themes 'offered tremendous scope for oriental display' and had long runs.[5] *The Cingalee*, described by one regular theatre-going Indian student, M. R. Jayakar, as 'viciously parodying Indian life', ran for 365 performances.[6] Like *The Nautch Girl* it was unashamedly bawdy and titillating in its appeal, using stereotypical characters with ridiculous names and crude nonsense songs. *Chinese Honeymoon* ran for a record 1,075 performances from 1901,[7] illustrating the popularity of Asian backdrops and the disproportionate amount of attention received by the orient as a whole in the British theatre. The success of these productions set the tone for the type of material performed in theatres nationwide.

The fact that the *Daily Sketch* found official objections to the *Romance of India* extravaganza to be feeble suggests that Indian sensibilities had not been taken into consideration in the past.[8] In this case fears of inciting sedition among Indian students in London influenced the India Office's intervention. Also, coincidentally, the British Board of Censors was established in the same year, 1913, to regulate the film industry. Although only a small proportion of films were banned, objections were raised to 166 out of 7,488 films, of which 22 were actually prohibited in 1913. At least two of the offending categories created by the Board, 'native customs in foreign lands abhorrent to British ideas' and 'indecent dancing' (nautch girls) were directly applicable to films set in India.[9] These new regulatory powers may have affected the India Office's decision. By the 1920s plays set in Africa and India were enjoying a revival in the West End. Many were along the lines of *Prince Fazil*, based on a love affair between an Indian prince and an English woman which ends tragically. This kind of play was evidently familiar to the anonymous reviewer of the Indian student magazine *Indus*, who described it as a 'sheikh type' of play.[10] There was also an increase in the 1920s in the number of films set in India, such as *Shiraz* (1928) and *The Emerald of the East* (1929).

THE EDALJI CASE

While the total press coverage of Indian students in Britain may have been small, this group did nevertheless attract a disproportionately large amount of interest in relation to its size. 'From what had recently appeared in the English papers, both here and in India one might imagine that England was suffering from three calamities – the unemployed, the suffragettes and the Indian students',[11] exclaimed one Indian student in 1909. In reality the volume of coverage was not quite as great as Mr Tarapore believed, although the infamous Edalji case did stimulate interest in the first decade of the twentieth century.

This case, involving the criminal prosecution of an Anglo-Indian solicitor, was reported in English newspapers and received widespread publicity. The defendant, George Edalji, was the son of the Reverend Shapurji Edalji. It is unclear how Shapurji Edalji met his wife Miss Charlotte Stoneham. However, it was through his wife's uncle that this Parsi convert to Christianity was able to secure the living of Great Wyrley, a small village in Staffordshire 20 miles from Birmingham, in 1873.[12] For 18 years the vicar and his family were the subject of malicious anonymous letters, practical jokes and pranks. Matters came to a head in 1903 when George Edalji was arrested and imprisoned for seven years on a charge of animal maiming. Arthur Conan Doyle, creator of Sherlock Holmes and an amateur sleuth himself, decided to take up the case after he first read about George Edalji in 1906 in an obscure newspaper called the *Umpire*. It was only through Doyle's intervention that Edalji was eventually released, following three years' imprisonment.

Several peculiarities of the case interested Arthur Conan Doyle, who published his investigations in the *Daily Telegraph*. Firstly, the author remarked on Edalji's unusual background. Doyle felt that an Indian clergyman would inevitably excite animosity in an English village. He wrote: 'The experiment will not, I hope, be repeated, for though the vicar was an amiable and devoted man, the appearance of a coloured clergyman with a half-caste son in a rude, unrefined parish was bound to cause some regrettable situation.'[13] Secondly, the facts show that George Edalji's physique and character made him a very unlikely candidate for such crimes. 'If the whole land had been raked', Doyle reflected in his memoirs, 'I do not think it would have been possible to find a man who was so unlikely, and indeed so incapable, of committing such actions.'[14] Edalji's character was irreproachable. Both his old headmaster and the firm of solicitors where he worked gave him the most glowing references, testifying to 'his mild and tractable disposition'. But the most conclusive evidence in his favour was his severe myopia which prevented him from seeing beyond six yards, particularly at night. George even had an alibi: his father swore that he had never left the bedroom he shared with his son.

How was it then, that such a weak case, 'a thing of threads and patches' was successfully prosecuted? Edalji faced unequal odds. The police suppressed and fabricated forensic evidence and the Chief

Constable of Staffordshire, Captain George Anson, held a personal grudge against him. Doyle believed the Chief Constable's behaviour had infected the whole police force against the family. He accused the police, 'who should have been their natural protectors, of adopting from the beginning a harsh tone towards them and accusing them, beyond all sense and reason, of being the cause of their own troubles and of persecuting and maligning themselves'.[15]

At the root of Edalji's troubles was his colour. Although he played down the racial aspect of the case when he discussed his experiences in the *Umpire* on his release from prison: 'If any prejudice existed', wrote George, 'it is confined to a very small section of the community.'[16] Nevertheless, nearly two decades of persecution by locals demonstrates that this was, at least, an extremely vociferous section of the community. The racial motive of the real horse maimer, whose identity was soon discovered by Doyle, is evident from the following letter he wrote to Doyle on Edalji's release: 'The proof of what I tell you is in the writing he put in the paper when they loosed him out of prison where he ought to have been kept along with his dad and all black and yellow faced Jews.'[17]

The *Birmingham Express and Star* was keen to emphasis the savagery of the case and reported it in graphic detail. 'Many and wonderful', said one reporter, 'were the theories I heard propounded in the local ale-houses as to why Edalji had gone forth in the night to slay cattle, and a widely accepted idea was that he made nocturnal sacrifices to strange gods.'[18] This particular reporter was dissatisfied with the verdict in the Edalji case. He believed that local prejudice played a significant part in the conviction, claiming 'the average rustic can see no good in a foreigner and to him an Asiatic comes in the guise of an emissary of the devil'.[19] This view was supported by Doyle, who expected very little from villagers and agricultural labourers. As a result he had less difficulty excusing the behaviour of uneducated villagers towards 'the strange-looking Edalji' than the actions of the police force.

Doyle described the Edalji case as a kind of squalid Dreyfus case. 'In each affair you had a rising young professional man ruined by authority over a matter of forged handwriting. Captain Dreyfus, in France, had been made a scapegoat because he was a Jew. Edalji, in England, had been made a scapegoat because he was a Parsee.'[20] By alluding to Edalji's enviable professional status, Doyle had stumbled across the crux of the matter. Edalji was the epitome of a successful, self-made gentleman, the very model of propriety and respectability, qualifications deeply valued in Edwardian Britain. Yet herein lay the key to his downfall. It was not just his colour and his half-caste position which consigned him to the role of permanent outsider, but, as Doyle astutely, remarked: 'His very virtues made the young black man, with the goblin eyes seem far more terrible than his father.'[21] The *Daily Telegraph* journalist was also aware that it was Edalji's success which provoked greater intolerance and led to his fall from grace. He wrote: 'The fact that George Edalji was reserved and studious would heighten rather than dispel the antagonism of the countryside.'[22]

Edalji appears to have suspected that his rapid advance would soon be cut short. He allegedly told the police: 'I'm not surprised at this. I have been expecting it for some time.'[23] This was an ambiguous statement used by the police as evidence of a guilty conscience. Edalji's reaction on his arrest reveals that he was acutely aware of the enormous injustice of his situation:

> So, after 27 years of careful upbringing in an English vicarage, and after the expenditure of so much time and money upon my training to practice the honourable profession of the law, I am now, when standing upon the threshold of what was promised to be a highly successful career, seized as a felon, on a vile charge and cast into a hideous cell.[24]

It was not just what George Edalji represented, a person of colour (and, worse, a product of miscegenation), but more importantly what he aspired to be, a self-made professional man, which equally affronted and threatened his enemies.

Although Edalji received neither financial compensation nor public pardon on his release; his case and the wrongful conviction of Adolf Beck helped to establish the Court of Criminal Appeal in Britain. Furthermore, the case received widespread publicity as the non-copyright articles in the *Daily Telegraph*, the main national newspaper to cover the story, were copied and sold for a penny on street corners. This was a result of the development of high-speed presses and 'New Journalism', producing cheaper and more populist newspapers catering for a mass readership. It is clear that Britain's Indian community was watching the case when Dr Chowry Muthu wrote to the *Daily Telegraph* to thank Doyle for proclaiming Edalji's innocence, 'on behalf of England's Indian community'.[25] While the *Telegraph* launched a campaign to clear Edalji's name, most of the press coverage presented the young solicitor in a freakish and unsympathetic way, even his chief supporter Doyle was guilty of exaggerating the strangeness of his appearance. More importantly, Indian students were given a taste of how they could expect to be treated by the criminal justice system and the British press.[26]

The Edalji case is interesting on several levels. The *Daily Telegraph*'s reporting of the case was tinged with ambivalence; for while it was keen to stress that a miscarriage of justice had taken place and its tone was less blatantly racist than the local press, nevertheless Edalji presented a dilemma. The existence of an upright and talented Indian professional in England represented a confusion of categories for the press. Indians fell roughly into two camps: either the skilful but amoral Babu, or the honest but intellectually limited servant or soldier. Edalji did not fit into either of these pigeonholes; he possessed both integrity and professional status. This combination of attributes was deemed acceptable (or possible) only in an English gentleman, not an Indian; consequently even sympathetic reporting of the case was undercut by tension and resentment.

The Edalji case lies at the intersection of class, race, hybridity and identity. Racialised reporting of the case highlights the way in which the press exaggerated depictions of Edalji's appearance in order to emphasise his savage 'otherness'. But this conflicted with evidence which suggests that Edalji's dress, occupation and religion created the possibility of identification and recognition by the British public. Also Edalji's race and class position were out of kilter. Although subordinate by virtue of his racial origins, he was elevated by his middle-class status. Thus Edalji's racial and cultural hybridity suggested both 'resemblance and menace'.[27]

THE INDIAN RESPONSE TO THE BRITISH PRESS

How did Indians respond to their treatment in the British popular press? The British writer E. J. Thompson used his fictional creation Neogyi in his book *An Indian Day* to show how an Indian trained in England reacted to negative representations of Indians in the English press:

> As he sat down to dinner, his bearer handed him the *Asia Post*. There he read of a recent law-suit in London, in which an Indian of high position had played a part only less discreditable than that of the English men and women who had fleeced him, and made themselves rich out of his lechery. He read remarks of learned counsel on the extreme improbability that 'a black man' could have attracted a beautiful western woman, and statements that Orientals were naturally lustful and evil. His blood boiled, which was worse – the men who wrote these complacent leaders and asked these impudent questions, who said these things and arrogated this chastity to themselves and their race? Or the deogharias and zemindars of his own land?[28]

However, the real-life response of students to the press was much less ambiguous and in some cases more extreme. J. C. Chatterjee, a student at Trinity College, Cambridge, told the Lee Warner Committee in 1907 that Indian students' hatred of British rule was exacerbated during their stay in England by the tone and expressions found in the British press, which were believed to have currency in the India Office.[29] According to one witness, press reports also enraged Madan Lal Dhingra, the Indian student who assassinated the Political ADC, Sir William Curzon Wyllie, in London. H. K. Korgaonkar, a police informant at India House, the revolutionary Indian headquarters in Highgate, was well acquainted with Dhingra and observed:

> His hatred of Englishmen was intense. This was fed by articles against Indians that used to appear in English papers from time to time. He used to read over and over again articles like 'Coloured Men and English Women' which appeared in *London Opinion*, and 'Babu Black Sheep' which appeared in *Cassell's Weekly*.[30]

The article referred to by Korgaonkar in *London Opinion*, written by C. Hamilton McGuiness, was brimming with racial animosity. Indian students were depicted as devious, sexual predators, with designs on the unprotected female population of Britain. Although this was a common complaint, as articles in the *Daily Mail* and the *Spectator* warning English women and Indian students of the perils of interracial liaisons illustrate,[31] nevertheless, this article was particularly crude and racist. While the press was just one factor in Dhingra's complex motivation, his response, though extreme in its consequences, was not unique. When a moderate Indian student, Mr Israni, made a speech at India House denouncing extremist propaganda in favour of constitutional methods, his speech was derided by extremists, who recommended that he read the article in *London Opinion*.[32] Such articles caught the attention of Indian students who came across them and did little to improve Anglo-Indian relations in England.

While Jawaharlal Nehru was at Cambridge University he made sarcastic comments about the British press coverage of India; they were intended to provide an amusing postscript to a letter he had written to his father. Clearly, Nehru did not take press pronouncements as seriously as some of the students named earlier, ridiculing editorials against Indian Home Rule:

> The other day I saw in an evening paper that Indians were called 'invertebrates'. Rather good that, isn't it? The *Saturday Review*, by the by, made a very wise remark a few weeks ago. It said that Indians were bound to have self-government but – and herein lies the difficulty – not before a few aeons of geological time! This may mean anything between a few million years and a wholly incomprehensible period. The chief difficulty

was the want of education, and some million generations will be required
to educate them up to the colonial standard!!![33]

The 1924 Wembley Empire Exhibition provides a rare example of
favourable press coverage of India. One provincial newspaper wrote:
'The Indian pavilion is a place of endless variety and probably never
again will it be possible for the untravelled Englishmen to see and learn
so much of India ... as can be gathered in this alluring corner of the
great exhibition.'[34] Although the exhibition's main purpose was commercial, the Viceroy of India's speech, stating the aims of the Indian
section, showed the broader intention of giving the British public a
positive impression of the country:

> Indian exhibits will be viewed with the greatest interest by visitors from
> the United Kingdom and the Empire, and will demonstrate the great
> importance and variety of Indian achievements in the domains of Arts,
> Crafts, Science, Industry and Production and the vast wealth of her natural
> resources and raw materials.[35]

Many of the Indian representatives at Wembley felt that the exhibition
had fulfilled its goal of promoting India in Britain. The Bihar and Orrisa
representative noted 'the keenness with which the public availed themselves of the opportunity of acquiring a better knowledge of India.
Thousands were brought into personal touch with the representatives
of provinces and states and thus learnt something of the personality
and character of the Indian gentlemen.'[36]

Earlier in the century Jawaharlal Nehru had informed his father about
the opening of the Franco-British exhibition in Shepherd's Bush. But
unlike the Indian representatives at Wembley in 1924, he feared that the
1908 exhibition would present India in a stereotypical way, as a crude
and backward country. Nehru wrote:

> The daily papers, specially the halfpenny ones, are chanting its praises
> every day. It will be one of the finest ever held on earth, if one were to
> believe them. There is, by the by, going to be a 'Typical Indian Village' in
> it. I shudder to think what that will be like. A congregation of half-naked
> people, I should imagine.[37]

While the India Office gave its approval to an Indian section at the
Wembley exhibition, it did not at any time actively promote a whole-
some image of India in Britain. At best it would intervene out of political
expediency, as in the case of the *Romance of India* extravaganza.[38]
However, although India's image may have been a low priority, official
concern was often voiced about the need to present Indian students in
Britain with a favourable impression of English life.[39]

INDIANS IN ANGLO-INDIAN FICTION

Another area of British popular culture was popular fiction, specifically Anglo-Indian fiction. Writers of this genre were usually women such as F. E. F. Penny, Flora Annie Steel, E. W. Savi and Maud Diver who started their writing careers after returning from India. However, some novelists such as I. A. R. Wyllie had never set foot there. She was inspired to write on this unfamiliar topic by an Anglo-Indian girl she had met at Cheltenham Ladies College: 'At the end of my first year Esme rejoined her parents in India but she left behind her enough sahibs, memsahibs, Bo-trees, ayahs and compounds to furnish me with all the necessary ingredients for an Anglo-Indian novel, when I was twenty-one.'[40]

Most of the authors who wrote about Indian students or princes studying in Britain had never met such individuals. John Eyton, author of *Mr Ram*, the story of an Indian student at Oxford, admitted that the story was completely fabricated and not modelled on any particular student he had ever met, even though he does refer to 'the memory of a certain dusky countenance, passed on a certain staircase, of an invitation, delivered in halting English, to a coffee party and of belated regrets and self-reproaching to which the rejection of that invitation gave rise'.[41] Edmund Chandler, however, had known Indian students in England and described them pejoratively as the 'hybrid mimetic product of English university'.[42] But it was on board the ship taking him to India that he first became aware of the difficulties western-educated Indian students faced. He described how this 'mysterious and complex' young man seemed unaware that the English passengers ostracised him as he moved among them 'detached and self-contained'. Chandler wrote: 'Here was a clean, self-respecting, unobtrusive young man, responsive to courtesy, who read Shelley and Herbert Spencer, and yet he was shut out of the world we had educated him to admire by our senseless barriers.'[43] The sympathy displayed in Chandler's autobiography is not present in his novel *Siri Ram: Revolutionist*, where the England-returned is a sinister character.

Popular Anglo-Indian fiction was often crude and sensationalist, containing romance, action, adventure and political intrigue. This cocktail of ingredients attracted a broad readership, ranging from working-class women, who could identify with the heroines of the novels, to Viceroys of India. A. E. W. Mason's book *The Broken Road* influenced Lord Minto's thinking on western-educated Indians. He wrote to Lord Morley on 22 January 1908:

> I wonder if you have read a novel called 'The Broken Road' by Mason. I am reading it by fits and starts, when I can snatch a moment to myself,

generally after I go to bed. There is much in it that is very true. We shall have to deal with the possibility of offering careers to young Indian gentlemen.[44]

It is more difficult, however, to gauge whether Indian students in England read these books and the impact it may have had on them. Interestingly, the working-class female readers of these novels were often the very people Indians who lived in rented accommodation, especially in London, had most contact with during their residence in England. Therefore even if the Indians had no personal exposure to this fiction they may have been recipients of attitudes and perceptions engendered by Anglo-Indian literature (which was often translated into plays and films[45]) in the minds of the English people they came across in everyday life.

The typology of Indian characters in English fiction during 1880–1930 has been explored extensively by Benita Parry, A. J. Greenberger and more recently by David Dabydeen and Francis Mannsakar. All these commentators have noted that Indian characters fitted into indexes of preference, whereby certain criteria made characters more or less appealing. Both Parry and Greenberger have observed that Muslims, Sikhs, Rajputs and peasants were always portrayed more sympathetically than middle-class Hindus, who were usually cast as villains. Mannsaker divides Indian characters according to how closely they resemble the English gentleman.[46] In the world of Anglo-Indian fiction Indians were type-cast as 'oleaginous Babus', 'half-naked fakirs', 'black-holers', 'faithful retainers', 'child-like peasants' or 'westernised princes'. These categories were rigid. Any character who tried to deviate or break free from these groupings was doomed to meet a tragic end.

According to R. B. Singh, Indians educated in England were 'seldom even mentioned in Anglo-Indian literature'.[47] However, a closer inspection of these novels reveals that many British authors placed Indian characters within a British location, usually as students. In the remainder of this chapter I show the several ways in which Indians in Britain were depicted in Anglo-Indian novels.

THE BABU

Probably the most potent and abiding image of the western-educated Indian was the stereotypical Babu. In literature the 'Babu' was usually, but not exclusively Bengali and trained in England. Christine Baxter has shown how the term 'Babu' developed from a title of respect, defined in the *Indian Journal* of 1823 (for the benefit of the British) as 'the name of the native Hindoo gentlemen answering to our esquire', into an abusive and derogatory term employed by both Indians and English. Baxter traced the term to the nineteenth-century social satirist Bhabanicharan Bannerji.[48] Yule and Burnell's Anglo-Indian dictionary, *Hobson-Jobson*, published in 1886, provided another definition of Babu; it was not just a Bengali equivalent for the term Esquire or Mr, or a word for a 'superficially anglicised Bengali … Babu also came to be used to indicate a Bengali clerk who wrote English, a Bengali, who managed the pecuniary affairs of the British'.

However, the satirical figure of the Bengali Babu came to greatest prominence in English literature at the end of the nineteenth century when T. A. Guthrie, under the pseudonym F. Anstey, published a series of articles in the magazine *Punch*, which were converted into a book in 1897 entitled *Baboo Hurry Bungsho Jabberjee, BA London*. Guthrie had no personal knowledge of Indians. He relied solely on his collection of Anglo-Indian literature and anecdotes from friends who had lived in India. His main purpose was to write a story using 'Babu English'. Some protest was voiced when his work was serialised on the grounds that it would cause ill-feeling among middle-class Indians. Guthrie dismissed any criticism and replied cynically: 'I doubt whether they were, or are, accustomed to regard the Bengali Babu with such veneration as all that.'[49]

Guthrie's fictional creation Baboo Bungsho Jabberjee, an Indian student in Britain, exhibited all the features commonly associated with a stereotypical Bengali Babu. The character has a ludicrously inflated view of himself and his mastery of the English language. As his name implies, he speaks in a tongue, derisively known as 'Babu English',[50] a phrase used by the British to describe what they viewed as the excessively ornate and somewhat unidiomatic English of a western-educated Indian – an Indian who had learnt the language principally from books. In the first chapter of the parody, Jabberjee offers his services as a contributor to *Punch*, complaining that the journal's literary standards had dropped; only he could provide English 'pure and undefiled'. But the book written in the first person (by Jabberjee) is saturated with errors, involving the misuse of words, Latin phrases and clichés, as the following string of malapropisms illustrates:

> I will take the cow by the horns after preliminary course of instruction at Government Art School, all expenses etc., to be defrayed on the nail out of your purse of fortunates, seeing that esteemed correspondent is so hard up between two stools, that he is reduced to a choice of Hodson's Horse![51]

This was designed to show Jabberjee's misplaced pride in his own prowess and allow the reader to laugh at his expense.

Guthrie demonstrates another recognisable Babu trait, cowardice, when Jabberjee is confronted by a pack of dogs in a railway compartment. On another occasion he agrees to attend a boxing match 'from a safe distance'. Jabberjee continues: 'for I am sufficiently a lover of sportfulness to appreciate highly the sight of courage and science in third parties'.[52] Paradoxically, the author also uses the boxing match to show Jabberjee's blood lust and barbarism: he was very disappointed to find the match 'totally devoid of bloodshed or any danger to life and limb of the performers'.[53] The law student's lack of athleticism is apparent in another chapter when he gives his landlady's daughter a lesson in bicycling with disastrous consequences.

Most of Jabberjee's difficulties stem from his ignorance and lack of understanding of British society, its structure, code of conduct and language. The book is littered with examples of this. For instance, when visiting the theatre he has difficulty comprehending the plot, which is explained to him by an English woman. At the boxing match his comments reflect a misunderstanding of British notions of sportsmanship. At a practical level the superficiality of his knowledge results in his losing all his money to a confidence trickster and an unwanted engagement to his landlady's daughter, followed by a court case for breach of promise when Jabberjee attempts to extricate himself from pending matrimony. There is a slight hint that Jabberjee's landlady, believing him to be a prince, has deliberately set out to ensnare her tenant into marriage with her daughter. Finally, Jabberjee loses the court case, which is turned into a fiasco when he conducts his own defence.

In his second 'Babu' story, *A Bayard from Bengal* published in 1902, Guthrie's main protagonist is Chunder Bindabun Bhosh, an undergraduate of Cambridge University. This time the action takes place in a rural location and Bhosh is found socialising in aristocratic circles, specifically the country seat of his best friend and fellow student Lord Jack Jolly. The ridiculous and convoluted plot originates from Bhosh's unknowing ability to, in the words of the author, 'fascinate' two ladies of the British nobility – Lord Jolly's fiancée and a duchess. The latter decides to seek revenge and plots Bhosh's downfall when he spurns her advances. But her scheming comes to nothing and after several escapades and numerous misunderstandings between Bhosh, Lord Jolly and his fiancée, order is restored when Lord Jolly marries his betrothed (who is no longer besotted by Bhosh). The dastardly duchess is defeated and Bhosh returns to India.

These books show that not only was the 'Babu' a figure of derision, a pretentious prig and poseur, but he was regarded as even more contemptible because he had the impertinence to imitate traits which British ethnology had assigned exclusively to the English gentlemen, producing disharmony. It is significant that both Guthrie's fictional Babus appear to cause disruption and discord wherever they go, a reflection of their internal anomalous condition. The fact that Jabberjee was a London law student had particular ramifications for Indian students in Britain. Westernised Indians provided a rich seam of humour for British satirists, as the popularity of these comic novels and musical comedies demonstrates. However, the targets of these crude tirades, Indian students, were less amused by the parodies. The pejorative treatment of an Indian student in a play called *Tilly of Bloomsbury* by Ian Hay caused G. K. Chettur, a student at Oxford, to leave the theatre. When the Vice-Chancellor was informed about the play he reluctantly had the offending scene removed.[54]

DISCONTENTED REVOLUTIONARY

Discontented Indian revolutionaries, trained in Britain, often assumed the role of villain in Anglo-Indian novels. This particular representation was closely related to the Babu stereotype, as the 'Babu' was also characterised as treacherous and disloyal, two of the main features ascribed to fictional Indian characters, conspiring to bring about the demise of the British Raj. Several authors used their novels to show a link between English education and Indian sedition. F. E. F. Penny referred to the 'overproduction of BAs who instead of feeling grateful for their education and enlightenment are idle and discontented'.[55] However, it was Indians educated in England who were most commonly dubbed 'potential sedition mongers',[56] such as Bahadur Gobind, a barrister with a BA from Cambridge, described in Mason's book *The Broken Road* as the 'most seditious man in the city'.[57]

Hatred of the British and a corresponding growth in nationalist sympathy within these novels, usually taking the form of a bomb conspiracy, often stemmed from a personal incident which had occurred during the Indian character's residence in England, to which the characteristically 'touchy' Indian takes disproportionate offence and overreacts. A good example of this phenomenon is the revolutionary nationalist leader Swami Narasimha in Edmund Chandler's novel, *Siri Ram, Revolutionalist: A Transcript from Life 1907–1910*. The swami is traumatised when a 'country bumpkin, in cap and gown who had brushed up rudely against him … at Cambridge and called him "a dammed nigger"'.[58] The insult is profoundly felt since before the incident the swami had been especially well received, even lionised in the West, as the following extract illustrates: 'He addressed societies and sipped tea in fashionable boudoirs, romantic hostesses felt he brought more of the mystery and repose of the East into their drawing-rooms than a shelf-full of bronze Buddhas ... At Cambridge he lectured on Sanskrit and Indian philosophy ... He was a figure in the West.'[59]

Another fictional creation, Ali Mirza Habibullah, also takes up revolutionary politics in India after a bad experience in England as a student. Like Swami Narasimha his ill-treatment has a greater impact because it contrasts starkly with the previous success he has enjoyed in England. The author, Wilfred David, shows that it is Habibullah's extravagant lifestyle which especially provokes jealousy: 'it was the most heinous crime, the utterly unforgivable sin to be an Indian highbrow'.[60] The theme of Indian cleverness combined with a lack of judgement is a common one. Habibullah experiences the double humiliation of being beaten by a Tory candidate for the post of president of the student union, as well as being beaten by a gang of drunken marauding students, who

> dragged the hapless Habibullah out of the infuriatingly smart car down from London, mauled and mishandled him vigorously and dropped him unconscious into the street drain in front of the college. There they left him. 'Bloody aesthetic! Filthy nig!' They had heard about his strangely decorated room. He had become to them a legendary, evil, spidery figure.[61]

F. E. F. Penny provides a slight variation on this theme in her book *The Inevitable Law* by showing how academic failure in Britain attracts a student to the nationalist cause. The character Desika, described as a 'mere wind-bag', having failed in an examination in England, turns 'congress-wallah'.[62]

The device of an Indian directing seditionary activity from Britain, under the guise of a student, is frequently used. It is evident in the book *The Unlucky Mark* when conspirator Dharma Govinda escapes to England, where he settles in a southern suburb of London and runs a boarding house for his fellow countrymen, under the name of 'Hindu Retreat'.[63] He also produces a newspaper, ironically titled *The Moderate Mind* (a pseudonym for the radical Indian newspaper *Indian Sociologist*). In another one of Penny's works *The Daughter of Brahma* a whole chapter is dedicated to describing a similar hostel for Indian law students, this time named 'Indra House'.[64] It is used in the novel as a headquarters for armed rebellion against the British, where weapons could be stored before being sent to India. Both accounts are thinly veiled descriptions of the real-life haunt of revolutionary Indian students in London, India House. As Benita Parry has shown, both the 'Hindu Retreat' and 'Indra House' closely resemble references found in Sir Valentine Chirol's influential work 'India Unrest'.[65]

CULTURAL HYBRID

Representations of Indians in British fiction in the early twentieth century often revolved around the notion of a 'denationalised hybrid'. In *Abdullah and His Two Strings* an Indian student at Edinburgh University is warned against aping English ways: 'Stick to your own countrywomen ... keep your own virtues, don't drop them to make room for our vices and carry these vices home. It's not fair to your fatherland, and it is not fair to us, for your ignorant people may judge us by what you take away.' He concludes: 'In all things be an Indian. Don't try to be more European than a European, for in that case you'll be nothing at all.'[66] The perils of denationalisation are the core concern of Mason's book *The Broken Road* which shows the folly of sending princes to England for education. Shere Ali, the only son of a maharaja, is sent to England at the age of 14 to attend Eton and Oxford. In the ten years Shere Ali spends in England he becomes thoroughly anglicised. The process is completed when he tells himself he has become one of the white men.[67] Residence in England and the consequent westernisation turn Shere Ali into what was commonly termed in Anglo-Indian fiction as a 'hybrid'. Mason, however, treats this subject in a much more serious way. The deracinated Indian is no longer merely a figure of fun; the character Shere Ali actually presents a threat to British hegemony, as the title *The Broken Road* implies. The eponymous road through Chilistan in the North-West Province is a symbol of British rule.

The story starts with a veteran British officer prophesying, on his deathbed, the tragedy that will unfold if the newly born son of the region's maharaja is educated in Britain. Luffe describes training in the West for rule in the East as 'sheer lunacy', resulting in a 'hybrid mixture of East and West'.[68]

> You take these boys, you give them Oxford, a season in London ... You give them opportunities of enjoyment, such as no other age, no other place affords – has ever afforded. You give them, for a short while, a life of colour, of swift crowded hours of pleasure, and then you send them back, to settle down in their native states, and obey the orders of the Resident ... Do you think they will have their heart in their work, in their humdrum life, in their elaborate ceremonies?[69]

The officer's prediction comes true. On returning to India the displaced and dispossessed prince suffers an identity crisis: 'Do I belong here?', he asks, 'or do I belong to Chilistan? It is neither in England nor in Chilistan. I am a citizen of no country. I have no place anywhere at all.'[70] Finally Shere Ali vents his anger at the British by leading an unsuccessful rebellion.

British official attitudes towards princes, the subject of the next chapter, were influenced by Anglo-Indian fiction. Lord Minto, Viceroy of India, described the son of the Maharaja of Cooch Behar as 'somewhat of a "Broken Road" case – a boy who might have done well in a good regiment, if properly looked after, but for whom there was no opening for any employment under our administration'.[71] Clearly there were parallels between the real-life prince and his fictional counterpart. Both spent many years of their youth in England, at public school and university. Minto wrote to Morley: 'I am sorry to read what you say about young Cooch Behar. He is not naturally a blackguard at all, but terribly weak. He was at Eton, has many old Eton friends here and is popular in English society.'[72] But, like Shere Ali, Minto believed 'Raji', as the prince was known, had been irreparably spoilt by his stay in England. It later emerged that the character of Shere Ali had actually been based on this particular prince.

Brian Street has shown in his book *The Savage in Literature* how the British revolted against any concept of hybridity or eclecticism.[73] This is evident in John Eyton's characterisation of an Indian student as

> the product of an age of doubt; he has learned enough to laugh at his forefathers, but not enough to discriminate between the genuine and the tawdry elements of the new age. Stripped naked of tradition he asks for a sign and the gaudier it is the more likely is he to accept it.[74]

F. E. F. Penny's sarcasm is clear when she shows an Indian father's reaction to his western-educated son's newly acquired western dress and habits:

> The old man watched his son's display of European manners, just as the owner of a clever dog might watch its tricks. He had paid a high price for these tricks when he sent his son to England. It was as well he should gain some amusement and gratification from their exhibition. He was proud of his boy and firmly believed he was equal to the Viceroy himself in style and behaviour.[75]

Both Penny and her readers were confident in their belief that no Indian could ever claim parity with the Viceroy, a true-born Englishman. Edmund Chandler mocks the westernised Indian in his story *The General Plan*: 'The assistant magistrate was a young Bengali of the hybrid Cambridge type, with the veneer fast wearing off – a prig, prematurely fat and a bundle of touchiness. He welcomed Dick with disconcerting familiarity, adopting the spurious pseudo-jolly-good-well-met air which sits as well on men of his type as clothes on a scarecrow.' The thoroughly British hero of the novel is repulsed by him: 'Dick drew back dismayed and the Bengali's pose veered instantly into one of injured aloofness.'[76]

Greenberger has argued convincingly that the westernised Indian was a threat to the British image of India: 'This image, based as it is on the separation of the races, cannot allow for any group which might stand in an intermediate position either racially or culturally.'[77] This view was supported by W. G. A. Ormsby Gore, Parliamentary Under-Secretary of State for the Colonies. He believed that 'The Englishman has an instinctive dislike of "assimilation". We like to keep our life distinct from other races whether European or not. The more other people acquire our culture, our outlook, our social habits, very often the wider the gulf between us.'[78]

Kipling's use of the term 'mule' to describe English-university-trained Indians who tried to break through the niche reserved for them by the British exposes the quasi-scientific origin of the term 'hybrid'. Cultural hybridity was equally as heinous in the minds of British writers as biological hybridity. The British 'half-caste pathology' is applicable to culture as well as race.[79] The author Maud Diver illustrates this in her strikingly similar descriptions of first, a Eurasian: 'the pathetic half and half who seemed to inhabit a racial no-man's land'[80] and, secondly, within the same book, the English-university-educated Dyan Singh, as 'half-savage, half-chivalrous gentleman, idealist in the grain, lover of England and India'.[81] Brian Street went one step further when he wrote: 'It is bad enough to be born between racial groups ... but actually to choose to reject one's background and adopt another is more disastrous.'[82]

Characters who attempted to transcend their background and racial characteristics by taking on the lifestyle of another group engaged the attention of popular writers. However, while British characters were able to move between the West and the East without impunity, Indian characters were not so fortunate; no amount of education could conceal their racial heritage. For example, Kipling's Huree Chunder Mookerjee, with his western dress and flowery speech, is unsuccessful in his imitation of the British; whereas the Irish hero of the novel *Kim*, in comparison, is a master of disguise and can adopt the appearance of an Indian whenever he chooses, without discovery. As Edward Said has observed: 'He can pass from one dialect, one set of values and beliefs to another.'[83] Although the English spy in Arthur Wallis's *Slipped Moorings* is not as adept as 'the little friend of all the world' (and in this respect *Kim* is unique), nevertheless, he is able to adopt the garb of an Indian without exciting suspicion from either the British or Indians, as his appearance before the novel's hero shows:

A meagre decrepit Oriental, turbaned and shabbily robed, shambled into the room. For a moment he paused without speaking and then made an obeisance so cringing, so mingled with distrust and covert hate, that Edgar rose instinctively and gathered his scattered papers … The Indian turned his yellow eyeballs slowly round the apartment as if loth to lose a single detail of his surroundings. Cunning was deep-written in every line of his withered countenance. [Having removed his disguise the English spy says:] 'I thought you should judge for yourself whether I am competent to go among the Bengalis.'[84]

The swing door between the orient and the occident was closed to Indians. The British, however, were able to pass through it in both directions superficially unscathed, retaining their instinctive English-ness. Indians, on the other hand, who adopted European vices, such as the unfeeling, vain drunk Mr Sen in Jane Hukk's novel *Abdullah and His Two Strings*[85] were always exposed as frauds. But there were exceptions to the rule. A character in one of Kipling's short stories is not shown to be sullied by his exposure to the West. Peroo, the metaphorical and actual 'bridge-builder' of the title, a lascar, returns from Britain having acquired western training, without abandoning Indian customs. He provides a foil for the local maharaja in 'tweed shooting-suit and seven-hued turban', described by Kipling 'as a walking perversion of what the West can offer the East'.[86] The rajah has taken on the superficial trappings of the West, but is ill at ease with what Kipling sees as the West's greatest gift to the East, its technology. For his creator, Peroo represents the 'true India', but a successful fusion of East and West has only been possible because Peroo has not tried to ape western ways or demand equality and self-rule.

SLAVE TO HEREDITY

Indian characters who attempted to be absorbed into the West were frequently presented in Anglo-Indian literature within the context of the much repeated theme of interracial union or 'mixed marriages', as they were commonly known. Even Indians who were depicted in a sympathetic light by authors succumbed to the inevitable and reverted to racial type by the end of the novel. Numerous examples may be deployed to illustrate this phenomenon. Mr Ram, a non-collegiate Oxford student in the book of the same name, tries unsuccessfully to become part of collegiate life, but instead he faces a series of rejections and snubs. Finally, Ram is sent down after being caught in a compro-mising situation with the housemaid Miss Steptoe, the story's narrator.

It is when he returns to India that his true nature is revealed. Miss Steptoe is reluctant to believe Jita Ram has changed and travels to India to marry him. On board the ship a missionary advises her against such a course of action: 'he'll take advantage, it's in his nature. He can't help it … His mind works differently from yours – so different that it would be impossible for you or even me, to follow it … there is a point beyond which you can't trust them … even the very best.'[87]

On her arrival Steptoe discovers that Ram is a fraud; his conversion to Christianity, his deadly illness and the house he was building are all untrue. When she sees Ram in his natural village setting, stripped of all his gentlemanly accoutrements, he loses all his previous appeal. A British officer, Brewley, explains Ram's motives to his mystified fiancée: 'Partly to impress the neighbourhood, it magnifies him to have one of the ruling race at his beck and call. Partly because, no doubt you made him comfortable. And partly because of the alternative, which is marriage with an illiterate nincompoop.'[88] Brewley believed that while the British judged Indians by the same standards that they would themselves, they would continue to face disappointment: 'You can't depend on them in that way. After thirty years' experience I have to admit it. They haven't that sort of conscience … Their minds work differently from ours. They tend to tell lies in their cradles. He wouldn't think anything about it … it wouldn't occur to him that it was wrong.'[89] A reviewer described the novel as a 'clever book' and believed the portrayal of the Indian student to be accurate: 'His passive attitude is Indian all right, and as the best Indians do not marry landladies' daughters … presumably it is all fairly put.'[90]

Location was important in Anglo-Indian novels. In England the Indian character is able to mask his nature and assume the outward appearance of an English gentleman, but it is impossible to continue this pretence in India. One contemporary reviewer observed that in Claude Bray's indictment of interracial marriage *Chattel or Wife* the heroine's disenchantment begins from the moment of meeting Molah Bux (her Indian husband) on his own ground.[91] Benita Parry describes the same process in *The Rajah*. The plot is based on a romance between a young Indian prince attending a university in Britain and an English girl, Delphine. The spell surrounding Delphine is broken when 'she sees him in his natural Indian surrounding where his regression to eastern taste and habits repels her'.[92] Authors also appear to have been influenced by the setting of a chapter. As long as the writer John Eyton keeps his Indian character Jita Ram in England he retains his detachment and sense of perspective. But when Jita Ram returns to India, Eyton's imagination seems to be adversely affected and he loses touch with the humanity in Ram, who becomes a lifeless symbol of all that is bad in the

Indian character – insincere, vulgar, indolent, without conscience or scruple.

In F. E. F. Penny's book *A Mixed Marriage* the Indian prince is presented as a model English gentleman in terms of colour (conveniently pale), education, refinement and even religion. In this case, however, Penny does not move the prince into a more conducive Indian location in order to show that he is far from gentle. He reveals his 'true racial instinct by decapitating a sheep while out riding'.[93] This incident is intended to demonstrate the prince's innate cruelty and barbarity and prove to the reader, as well as his fiancée, that he is not a real gentleman. Racial instincts also triumph in the *Unlucky Mark*. In many ways the book is similar to Penny's *A Mixed Marriage*. Firstly, both the Indian prince and Major Adam Udin are virtually indistinguishable from Englishmen; so much so that the novel's heroine mistakes Udin for an Englishman. Secondly, in both books the Indian character gives himself away by an act of uncontrolled violence. In the *Unlucky Mark* Udin nearly kills the anarchist who has planted a bomb, endangering the life of the heroine Miss Lawrence. But this story is exceptional, as not only does the Indian character transgress the bounds of accepted behaviour, his English rival also harbours a guilty secret – he has fathered an illegitimate child and abandoned the Muslim mother.

The aristocratic heroines of Anglo-Indian fiction are 'in love with the idea of life with a prince in India'.[94] Their working-class fictional counter-parts have more to gain. They are usually attracted to Indian students by their gentlemanly demeanour, wealth (sometimes confusing students with princes) and above all the prospects of social elevation. In *Abdullah and His Two Strings* the author is unequivocal about the motives of the landlady's daughter: 'She had asked for a life of ease, a home of her own, a husband who looked a gentleman. She had got them and was content.'[95] The female protagonist's motivation is also discussed in Savi's *The Daughter in Law*: 'in her blindness she judged him a gentleman by European standard and married', wrote Savi, 'as she believed him to be one of aristocratic, if not noble parentage, of recognised social status and unlimited wealth'. But on returning to India he again acquires the customs 'to which he had been born and bred' that of a Bengali Babu.[96] Class prejudices are also apparent as working-class heroines have particular difficulty in identifying a gentleman and are more likely to be duped.

Not even the most 'tolerant, enlightened Hindu',[97] the phrase used to describe Rama Rao, an Indian doctor, who marries a music hall actress while studying in Britain in the detective story *The Burqa*, is able to resist his racial destiny. At the beginning of the book Rao is concerned with social uplift and alleviating the lot of the peasantry. However, after his death he is revealed to be a quarrelsome, violent and a 'madly jealous man'. The Jekyll and Hyde transformation familiar in Anglo-Indian novels concerning Indian students and princes educated in Britain usually occurs after marriage. Hukk's moderate Hindu vanishes, Rama now possesses 'an ardent impulsive nature, his soaring ideas breaking violently away from every shackle of caste, tradition, rushing into a "western" marriage only to find himself held inexorably in chains, not only of heredity, but of the limitations imposed by his earlier upbring-ing'.[98] Biology transforms a calm, westernised idealist such as Rama into a kind of Othello figure, imprisoned by birth and breeding, driven by passion not reason. Not only is Rama shown to be false in his private life, but the author also suggests that he leads a double life as a drug trafficker.

The importance given to biological determinism in this type of literature, especially when an Indian character's environment changes, was a legacy of Darwinian theories and the scientific racism of nineteenth-century anthropologists such as De Gobineau and Hunt. Furthermore, the hackneyed device whereby Indian characters always reverted to racial type was part of the all-pervasive ideology of essentialism that informed all race thinking, as shown in the Preface. Ronald Inden defines essentialism as 'the idea that humans and human institutions … are governed by determinate natures that inhere in them in the same way that they are supposed to inhere in the entities of the natural world'.[99] In these novels the West is shown to be a liberating environment for Indians, containing rational choice and freedom, whereas in India they are enslaved, unable to exercise free will. Identity is inviolate in this literature, at least for Indians. Any attempt to challenge essentialism by defying rigidly imposed categories produces discord and ultimately tragedy.

DISILLUSIONED ENGLAND-RETURNED

Popular writers often portrayed Indian students as confronting prob-lems in adjusting to their environment; firstly, in England as students and, secondly, when they returned to India. As I have shown, Indian fictional characters who became embroiled in revolutionary activities were often attracted to nationalism by bad experiences in Britain. Several authors take this theme of discontent further and explore the difficulties faced by students in adjusting to life in England. Jane Hukk's eponymous character Abdullah, a medical student, faces great difficulty in settling in Edinburgh. Above all he suffers from acute loneliness, which is compounded by high expectations before his arrival. Hukk wrote 'Loneliness instead of society had been his lot.'[100] It is his isolation that makes him vulnerable to his landlady's daughter.

John Eyton's protagonist, Mr Ram, is also disillusioned by his new life in England. He becomes progressively weighed down by a series of disappointments. For example, he does not get an opportunity to play when he joins his Oxford college hockey team, despite his experience in India. He feels snubbed when he is not invited to take coffee by the other undergraduates after dining in college. Ram voices his disillusionment in the following speech: 'It will always be the same ... They are of the West – white. I am dark-skinned. They have their *bhaibundi* – their castehood – their common interests of sports and society and so on. I am outside that charmed circle ... Me, they do not notice, any more than they would notice some shadow.'[101]

The other aspect of this theme of disillusionment is the more common problem of the alienated England-returned, linked either with an 'unsuitable' marriage or general displacement. Dealing first with marriage, Susanne Howe in *Novels of Empire* viewed 'England always as a husband of India'.[102] This analogy works well in Maud Diver's book *Lilamani* and its sequel *Far to Seek*, which show the successful marriage between a Rajput princess and a British aristocrat in England,[103] but this does not hold true for the majority of novels concerned with interracial unions. India is more commonly represented as a student or prince studying in Britain, and England by his European and often working-class wife. Perhaps it is this inversion of the power relations between India and England, reflected in male/female relations, which contributes to dysfunction in these novels. Only in Diver's two books where India is represented by a dependent woman is a successful marriage possible. The mismatch in class and race positions, when a middle-class Indian student marries a working-class white woman thus subverting the colonial power structure, represented an insoluble tension which had to be discouraged.

Even if the fictional England-returned did not return to India with an English bride, difficulties still awaited him. A favourite concern of F. E. F. Penny's was the plight of the England-returned forced to marry an Indian girl, depicted as his social inferior, uneducated and ignorant. Penny claimed that: 'Educated Indian men have imbibed the spirit of western ideas of companionship and love in marriage while Indian women have not changed.'[104] This problem is resolved in one of her stories by a stint in England for the Indian bride. In the *Two Brides*, loosely based on Shaw's *Pygmalion*, the England-returned Narisimha marries, in Penny's words, 'a wild thing out of the jungle'. Her husband sends her to Britain and, after being subjected to a process of domestication, she returns to India a model wife. Again England acts as an allegedly 'civilising' force, subduing the sensual and uncontrollable aspects of the Indian character.

Popular writers attributed the alienation of Indians trained in England to their cultural hybridity. E. M. Thompson, in his book *An Indian Day*, describes his Bengali character Kamalakanta Neogyi, the Oxford-educated magistrate of Vishnugram, as a 'displaced person, without a country or an ethos'.[105] Characters such as Penny's Narisimha, who attends public school in England and studies for the ICS at Oxford, is shown to have problems reconciling an English childhood with life in India:

> As soon as he arrived he was expected to cast off all his western habits and to resume the old customs ... He hated it all and could not reconcile himself to the life ... He missed the orderly daily routine. The various little refinements ... which he had faithfully observed ever since, were entirely absent ... Their manners jarred on him to the point of irritation, but he had to bear it all in silence.[106]

Savi's *The Daughter in Law* contains a classic exposition of this well-worn theme. Here the England-returned is presented as an outsider, in a permanent state of limbo, doomed to inhabit a no-man's-land between East and West: 'in many things I am like most Englishmen ... Yet there are times when I feel it a relief to throw off European customs and return to those of my country ... In spite of my education I shall never be received by white men as a man and a brother. I am of the East and between the East and West is a division that will never be bridged.' He contrasted his position in London and India:

> In London everything is for us on a very different footing. There I feel I have some claims to fellowship with the western world. The Englishman who has never been in India is indifferent to the prejudice which exists and can afford to be magnanimous. He is ever 'mine host' to the foreigner, whatever be his nationality – so long as he is not a native of Africa! But, here, in my own country, I am an 'outsider' in British circles.[107]

Torrick Ameer Ali, a real-life England-returned, believed that the internal and external 'revulsion' which characterised Indians trained in England within Anglo-Indian literature was exaggerated and mis-leading. Mason's *The Broken Road* was singled out as a particularly 'dangerous delusion'.[108] Although he found such literature entertaining, his own successful marriage in India to his headmaster's niece, whom he had met while studying in England, had not ended in disaster as soon as he returned to India, as prescribed in the Anglo-Indian popular fiction formula.

CASE STUDY: MRS THEODORE PENNEL

It is useful to compare the work of Mrs Theodore Pennel with that of contemporary authors writing in the same genre. The main way in which she differed from her peers was her background. She was the sister of Cornelia Sorabji. Alice had also studied medicine in England.[109] She married a British officer serving in India, Theodore Pennel, and lived a rather perilous existence on the north-western frontier.[110] Her most popular story, *Doorways to the East*, reflects her Indian background. The novel revolves around the lives of a brother and sister, Rama Ditta, Shanti and Rama's wife Kamala, all of whom study in Britain at some point in the novel. Mrs Pennel's own education equipped her to describe the life of an Indian woman student in England. The character Shanti is a mixture of herself and her sister Cornelia. Shanti is intelligent, attractive, humorous and can adapt to any environment. Above all she knows her place in the world, reflecting the author's conservative, pro-British sympathies. Although Shanti is highly educated and determined to serve her country through social reform (like Cornelia Sorabji), when motherhood comes she places her duties as wife and mother before personal ambition. Shanti's attitude is conditioned by the fact that her mother neglected her brother and herself when campaigning for Congress.

Mrs Pennel contrasts the treatment Shanti and her brother receive at Cambridge University. Although Rama has been educated in Britain since the age of 10, it is he who faces more difficulties at university than his sister, who is unaccustomed to England. Both Indian students and the equally exclusive English students reject him. In contrast, Shanti is assimilated into her Cambridge college immediately. Pennel attributes this to three dubious generalisations. Firstly, educated English women were less race-conscious than men. Secondly, Indian women were less likely to take offence than men. Thirdly, women of another race were always more acceptable than the men.[111] All three explanations seem highly tenuous. In the second half of the novel Rama Ditta returns to India to marry Kamala, in order to satisfy his dying grandmother's wishes. Kamala's experience of Britain is in stark contrast to Shanti's. Kamala does not enjoy camaraderie with the other women students. Pennel tries to show that women who take on a radical nationalist stance are unable to adapt to collegiate life. Two other Indian women characters at Cambridge are depicted as vehemently anti-British, over-sensitive and aloof.[112] Kamala becomes involved with a Punjabi student organisation in London and in terrorist activities. She is eventually fatally wounded by a bomb she has planted in India.

One critic described Kamala as Mrs Pennel's *bête noire*: 'Kamala has no balance and is entirely swayed by vanity. Mrs Pennel intends to show that a girl having no background, religion or family training must end badly.'[113] Clearly, there is a warning for women not to place public life, especially politics, before domestic responsibilities. A political message is also evident. Nationalists are portrayed as individuals consumed by illogical hatred, blind to the benefits of British rule. Only in the character of Shanti are East and West successfully accommodated. For the other characters contact with the West leads to varying degrees of misery and alienation. As Mrs Pennel was a supporter of British rule and an opponent of the women's movement, characters involved with anti-British activities, especially women, come off badly; nevertheless, there is still a greater sophistication in the handling of issues such as identity, influenced no doubt by her own chequered background. While there is crudity in her one-sided depiction of Kamala, her work is subtler than that of many of her British contemporaries.

DIVERSITY OF VIEWS

Not all writing on India adhered to the negative assertions present within popular fiction, the theatre and the press. For example, the image of the Babu as a *bête noire*, discussed earlier, was in sharp contrast to the Sadler Committee's references to Bengali students possessing 'keen intelligence', 'a retentive memory', as well as being gifted in music, poetry and metaphysics.[114] While satirists ridiculed the Indian's grasp of the English language, the Sadler Committee praised the Babu's aptitude for linguistics: 'In no part of the continent of Europe are there so many men and women who speak the English language with faultless accuracy ... as among the highly educated Indian communities.'[115] Sympathetic views ranged from anti-colonial literature on the left to more moderate critiques. The theosophist movement glorified India's spiritualism and the orientalist Max Müller spread knowledge of India in the West. After his death B. G. Tilak wrote of the enormous influence Professor Müller had exerted 'in making British people regard the Indian people with far greater respect than they would have done otherwise'.[116]

British supporters of the Indian National Congress, Sir William Wedderburn and William Digby, were equally keen to alert the British public's attention to India's economic condition. But it was Gilbert Murray, Governor of New Guinea, who voiced the concerns of a number of liberals about the effects of derogatory perceptions of India and Indians. In his speech 'Empire and Subject Races' to a conference in 1910 he censured Rudyard Kipling for stirring up 'in the minds of hundreds of thousands of Englishmen a blind and savage contempt for the Bengali'. 'Year after year', he continued, 'clever natives of India come over to England at great sacrifice of money and trouble, to our universities and satisfy our tests for obtaining positions in their own countries ... And year after year they have found in our greatest newspapers caricatures of themselves ... You cannot govern the man and insult him too.'[117] Keir Hardie, leader of the Labour Party, also sought to highlight the essential similarities between the British and Indians: 'Take a gathering of Indians. Remove their graceful picturesque costumes, and clothe them in coat and trousers, wash the sun out of their skins and then a stranger suddenly let down in the midst of them would have difficulty in saying whether he was in Manchester or Madras.'[118]

Sympathetic opinions were apparent within the enormous number of books published on the subject of India between 1880 and 1930. The popular book *New India*, by the civil servant (and member of the Lee Warner Committee) Sir Henry Cotton, first published in 1885 was already in its fourth edition by 1909. He devoted a chapter to British racial prejudice and concluded: 'The security of our Raj in India depends more on the existence of sympathy and goodwill than on British bayonets.' Cotton took a balanced approach, in contrast to the Anglo-Indian prejudices of Sir John Strachey's official history of India, entitled *India – Its Administration and Progress*, which described Indian social customs as 'horrid and cruel'.[119] Some books were written with the object of refuting common misconceptions about India. According to C. F. Andrews's introduction to H. G. Alexander's book *Indian Ferment* (1929), this was intended as a rebuke to Mayo's controversial *Mother India* (1927). Monier Williams also acknowledged that the historian Mill had done much to blacken India's reputation.[120] Even the Conservative MP A. D. Rees agreed that India was misrepresented, and particularly Indian women, who he argued were not all subject to purdah or prohibited from remarriage: 'By no means ... are Hindoo women miserable. Their lives are made of light and shade, like those of other races, nor have they less light.'[121] Sidney Low claimed that the 'habitual timidity' of the Bengali Babu had been exaggerated and that it was unfair to lampoon his mode of speech: 'If English boys had to read Chinese classics at school and learn Chinese from masters who had never been nearer China than Dover beach, I daresay their literary style would cause amusement in Peking.'[122] Treating the anglicised Indian with contempt, it was argued, only served to heighten his anger. All these authors stressed the need to counteract the totally negative perception of India by testifying to the Indians 'as courteous and intelligent people as any in the world, kind to their children, respectful to their parents, charitable, honest and industrious, and with such vices as are common to human nature'.[123]

Other books had the modest but laudable aim of providing the reader with an accurate and balanced account of Indian history, devoid of 'national or racial bias'. These included *A Brief History of Indian Peoples* by Sir William Hunter, *Rise and Fulfilment of British Rule* by Garret and Thompson, *Modern India: A Co-operative Survey*, edited by Sir John Cummings and *Indian Scene* by J. A. Spender, described by the Indian press as 'fair', 'temperate' and 'sensible'. Hunter endeavoured to present the history of India in an attractive way: 'to show how an early gifted race … created a language, a literature and a religion of rare stateliness and beauty' and thereby move away from what he viewed as the tendencies of presenting Indian history 'as nothing but a dreary record of disunion and subjugation'.[124] It is significant that none of these writers were straightforward apologists, defending India from attack, by replacing common misconceptions with flattering epithets. They were anxious to enlighten the reading public with a dispassionate and even-handed presentation of the country. Within this setting Indians were 'neither angelic nor demoniacal'.[125] However, these works were not ones Indian students would have noticed as keenly as those which were derogatory, and even these 'sympathetic' works contained stereotypes and assumed British superiority.

While the so-called 'high literature' of Rudyard Kipling and Joseph Conrad was far from revolutionary, Andrea White[126] and Zohreh Sullivan[127] have argued that both authors have a subversive element in their work which breaks away from the traditions of popular fiction. It is difficult to compare the complex and sophisticated writing of Kipling and Conrad with the crude, one-dimensional, formula-driven fiction of Anglo-Indian novelists I have discussed. Kipling may have surveyed the 'Indian scene delighting in its variety and copiousness and responding to the individuality of its people'.[128] Nevertheless, despite his undoubted aesthetic vision and enormous knowledge of Indian life, he does not always contradict the prejudices in popular fiction. In *Kim* the character of Hurree Chunder Mookerjee reinforces British stereotypes of the Bengali Babu, a foil for Mahbub Ali, a typically athletic, Afghan horse-dealer. Kipling's personal dislike of western-educated Indians went beyond the realm of his writing. One incident in particular demonstrates the strength of his animosity. The executive committee of the Victoria League reported in autumn of 1907: 'Mr Rudyard Kipling, having been invited to become a Vice-President, had written to say that should the League undertake to offer hospitality to young Asiatics residing in England he could not except any connection with the League.'[129] In addition, the competing voices present in Kipling and Conrad were frequently not perceived by their readers. It is possible to conclude that, while an alternative view of India existed, its influence was limited. Negative images of India and Indians found in British popular culture dominated the colonial discourse.

Finally, why did popular English writers choose to represent Indians in Britain as either ridiculous Babus, monstrous hybrids, discontented villainous nationalists or disillusioned individuals? Several commentators, including Philip Curtin[130] and S. H. Alatas, have argued that negative and distorted images of Africa and south-east Asia were determined by events in the West in order to meet imperial needs. In *The Myth of the Lazy Native*, Alatas has shown how the image of the indolent native in Malaysia, the Philippines and Java, although not completely devoid of truth, had a function in colonial ideology.[131] Similarly, the unflattering characteristics assigned to western-educated Indians served an imperial purpose. To present the English-educated Indian as a travesty of the English gentleman, inept, incompetent and above all ineffectual, neutralised any perceived threat. How could a race of effete writers and babblers pose any danger to British rule? The disillusioned England-returned, at war with himself, torn between his eastern and western halves, was, as a result, emasculated and rendered useless. In the same way, by belittling the Babu's intellectual accomplishments, the British reduced the Indian's claim to be taken seriously. If the Indian were allowed to match the British in speech, dress and education it would be difficult to avoid his claim to equal footing. Utilising negative stereotypes to mock and misrepresent, and marginalising this group by excluding its claim to the term 'true' or 'real' India, were all devices for concealing insecurity.

Indians in Britain were not only presented as outsiders, in conflict with their environment, even if it was not always initially apparent; they were also represented as something much more sinister. By endeavouring to emulate English gentlemen they took on the role of impostor, attempting to deceive the reader and themselves, provoking disharmony and disorder in the plots of novels by disturbing the natural balance of 'them' and 'us' – East and West. As a product of colonial synthesis, the English-trained Indian was portrayed as an incongruous, monstrous aberration. In Singh's words: 'The Indian who spoke English was therefore a sort of Frankenstein – the coloniser created him and then began to fear him.'[132] The closer the Indian began to resemble the Englishman in appearance, manners and above all professional and university education, the more alarming he became.[133]

NOTES

1 *The Times*, Index 1880–1930.
2 *The Times*, 11 January 1905.

3 (IOL) L/P&J/6/1290, No. 4644, 1913.
4 Lord Chamberlain Plays, British Library Manuscripts (LCP).
5 MacKenzie, *Propaganda and Empire*, p. 49.
6 Jayakar, *Story of My Life*, p. 44.
7 MacKenzie, *Propaganda and Empire*, p. 53.
8 *Daily Sketch*, 29 November 1913.
9 R. Low, *History of the British Film 1900–1914* (London: Allen & Unwin, 1949), p. 91. See list of categories.
10 *Indus*, Vol. 5, No. 8 (May 1926).
11 (IOL) MSS. Eur. F. 147, *Proceedings of East India Association*, January 1909, p. 17.
12 *Daily Telegraph*, 11 January 1907, p. 5. For an extended version of this section see the present author's article entitled 'Uncovering Britain's South Asian Past: The Case of George Edalji', *Immigrants and Minorities*, 17, 3 (1998).
13 A. C. Doyle, *Memoirs and Adventures* (London: John Murray, 1930), pp. 251–2.
14 Ibid., p. 253.
15 Ibid., p. 254.
16 *Umpire*, 11 December 1906, p. 2.
17 J. D. Carr, *Life of Sir Arthur Conan Doyle* (London: John Murray, 1959), p. 230.
18 *Daily Telegraph*, 17 January 1907, p. 10.
19 Ibid.
20 Carr, *Life of Sir Arthur Conan Doyle*, p. 228. Edalji was actually a Christian.
21 Ibid., p. 220.
22 *Daily Telegraph*, 17 January 1907.
23 Carr, *Life of Sir Arthur Conan Doyle*, p. 223.
24 *Umpire*, 18 November 1906, p. 2.
25 *Daily Telegraph*, 15 December 1907.
26 Nehru commented on the case in a letter to his father. Gopal, *Selected Works*, p. 16, 18 January 1907: 'I suppose you have heard about the Edalji case and the new phase it has taken here. Whole pages are devoted to it in some of the papers and you know what a page of a newspaper is here. The poor chap must have been quite innocent and I am sure he was convicted simply and solely because he was an Indian.'
27 H. Bhabha, 'Of Mimicry and Men – The Ambivalence of Colonial Discourse', in F. Cooper and A. L. Stoler (eds), *Tensions of Empire: Colonial Cultures in a Bourgeois World* (London: University of California Press, 1997), pp. 152–60.
28 E. J. Thompson, *An Indian Day* (London: Knopf, 1927), p. 44. Deogharias and zemindars refer to Indian landowners.
29 (IOL) L/P&J/6/845, 1908.
30 (IOL) L/P&J/6/986, No. 349, 1910.
31 This will be discussed in greater depth in the next chapter.
32 (IOL) L/P&J/6/986, No. 349, 1910.
33 Gopal, *Selected Works*, p. 58, 4 June 1908.
34 *Report by the Commissioner for India of the British Empire Exhibition* (Calcutta, 1925), p. 66. Indian villages, forming the backdrop to working demonstrations by Indian craftsmen, became a common sight at exhibitions held all over Europe during the period. The Indian pavilion in the 1924 British Empire Exhibition at Wembley was manned by 27 Indians. Most of the assistants were drawn from Indian students, who had completed their courses in London. English women usually filled the secretarial and sales posts, but in the case of one state (UP) Indian women were brought over especially for this purpose. The majority of Indian artisans, bandsmen

and catering staff employed at the restaurant were from north India. Although a south Indian snake-charmer and his wife from Madras attracted such large audiences that additional attendants had to be drafted in to prevent overcrowding. The exhibition also proved popular with Indian visitors, an estimated 5,000 attended.

35 Ibid., p. 34.
36 Ibid., p. 66.
37 Gopal, *Selected Works*, p. 53, 7 May 1908. Exhibitions had been taking place in Britain from as early as the middle of the nineteenth century. Forty-five Indian artisans, both men and women, exhibited their skills in various crafts, including stone carving and weaving during the colonial and Indian exhibition held in 1886. (See *Report of the Royal Commission for Colonial and Indian Exhibition*, London, 1887.) These crafts-men attracted large crowds of people and were invited to visit Queen Victoria at Windsor. (Professor J. M. MacKenzie has informed me that there is an entire corridor at Osborne, the Queen's residence on the Isle of Wight, devoted to portraits of them.) A year after the exhibition in 1887, Queen Victoria employed Indian servants. One, Abdul Karim, was elevated to the post of 'Indian Secretary' and taught the Queen Hindustani. Her correspondence and Journals show her fondness for this man, whom she sided with against the advice of her household staff. [C. Hibbert, *Queen Victoria in Her Letters and Journals* (London: Murray, 1984)].
38 This is the only evidence I have of the India Office's reacting to a potentially damaging representation of India.
39 (IOL) W1757, p. 85. Indian Student Department 1912–13.
40 I. A. R. Wyllie, *My Life with George* (London, 1940), p. 129.
41 J. Eyton, *Mr Ram – A Story of Oxford and India* (London: Arrowsmith, 1929), p. 7.
42 E. Chandler, *Youth and the East: An Unconventional Autobiography* (Edinburgh: Blackwood, 1924), p. 61.
43 Ibid., p. 64.
44 (IOL) MSS Eur. D. 573/4, 22 January 1908.
45 A. E. W. Mason's book *The Broken Road* (London: Smith Elder, 1907) was made into a film in the 1920s.
46 F. Mannsakar, 'The Dog that Didn't Bark: The Subject Races in Imperial Fiction at the Turn of the Century', in D. Dabydeen (ed.), *Black Presence in English Literature* (Manchester: Manchester University Press, 1985), p. 119.
47 R. B. Singh, *The Imperishable Empire: A Study of British Fiction on India* (Washington, DC: Three Continents Press, 1986), p. 139.
48 C. Baxter, 'The Genesis of the Babu, Bhabanicharan Bannerji and Kalikata Kamalalam', in P. Robb and D. Taylor (eds), *Rule, Protest and Identity: Aspects of Modern South Asia* (London: Curzon Press, 1978), p. 203.
49 T. A. Guthrie, *A Long Retrospective* (London: Oxford University Press, 1936), pp. 323–3.
50 'Babus' or 'Westernised oriental gentlemen' were also present in British musical comedies, such as the character Chamboodhy in *The Cingalee* (1904). 'Babu English' was put to music in nonsense songs, such as 'What's the matter with Cham?' MacKenzie, *Propaganda and Empire*, p. 54. The character of Chamboodhy can clearly trace his ancestry to Anstey's Baboo Hurry Bungsho Jabberjee, whom he resembled very closely, from his mixed metaphors to his appearance.
51 F. Anstey, *Baboo Bungsho Jabberjee, BA London* (London: J. M. Dent, 1897), p. xvi; Anstey is better known as the author of *Vice Versa*.
52 Ibid., p. 75.

53 Ibid., p. 79.
54 G. K. Chettur, *The Last Enchantment: Recollections of Oxford* (Mangalore, 1934), p. 161. Unfortunately only a revised copy of the play exists; consequently it is difficult to judge exactly what Chettur found offensive. But even after revision the character of the law student Mehta Ram is shown during his extremely brief appearance in the play to be petty, cowardly and his dialogue is exclusively in 'Babu English'.
55 B. Singh, *A Survey of Anglo-Indian Fiction* (London: Oxford University Press, 1934), p. 205.
56 Ibid., Mrs Kenneth Coombe.
57 A. E. W. Mason, *Broken Road*, p. 292. Mason is best known as the author of *The Four Feathers*.
58 E. Chandler, *Siri Ram Revolutionist: A Transcript from Life 1907–1910* (London: Constable, 1912), p. 139.
59 Ibid., pp. 137–8.
60 W. David, *Monsoon – A Novel* (London: Hamish Hamilton, 1913), p. 159.
61 Ibid., pp. 159–60.
62 Singh, *Survey*, p. 201.
63 F. E. F. Penny, *The Unlucky Mark* (London: Chatto & Windus, 1908), p. 349.
64 F. E. F. Penny, *The Daughter of Brahma* (London, 1911), p. 253.
65 B. Parry, *Delusions and Discoveries: Studies on India in the British Imagination 1880–1930* (London: Allen Lane, 1972), p. 86.
66 J. Hukk, *Abdullah and his Two Strings* (London: Hurst & Blackett, 1927) p. 106.
67 A. E. W. Mason, *Broken Road*, p. 59.
68 Ibid., pp. 30–1.
69 Ibid., p. 32.
70 Ibid., p. 137.
71 (IOL) MSS. Eur. D. 573/20, Minto to Morley, 10 June 1909.
72 Ibid.
73 B. V. Street, *The Savage in Literature: Representations of Primitive Society in English Fiction 1858–1920* (London: Routledge & Kegan Paul, 1975), pp. 104–19.
74 J. Eyton, *The Dancing Fakir* (London: Longman, 1922), p. 137.
75 Penny, *Unlucky Mark*, p. 165.
76 E. Chandler, *The General Plan* (London: Blackwood, 1911), pp. 23–4.
77 A. J. Greenberger, *The British Image of India: A Study in the Literature of Imperialism 1880–1960* (London: Oxford University Press, 1969), p. 66.
78 Ibid., p. 24.
79 P. B. Rich, *Race and Empire in British Politics* (Cambridge: Cambridge University Press, 1990), p. 120.
80 M. Diver, *Far to Seek* (London: Blackwood, 1921), p. 298.
81 Ibid., p. 78.
82 Street, *Savage in Literature*, p. 104.
83 Said, *Culture and Imperialism*, p. 191.
84 A. F. Wallis, *Slipped Moorings* (London: E. J. Larby, 1910), p. 85.
85 See Hukk, *Abdullah*, pp. 109, 121–4.
86 R. Kipling, 'The Bridge Builders', in *The Day's Work* (New York: Doubleday & McClure, 1898), p. 43.
87 J. Eyton, *Mr Ram*, p. 236.
88 Ibid., p. 313.
89 Ibid., p. 309.

90 *Times Literary Supplement*, 30 May 1929, p. 437.
91 *Indian Magazine*, No. 349 (January 1900), pp. 9–10.
92 Parry, *Delusions and Discoveries*, p. 79.
93 F. E. F. Penny, *A Mixed Marriage* (London: Methuen, 1903), p. 30.
94 Ibid., p. 106.
95 Hukk, *Abdullah*, p. 245.
96 E. W. Savi, *The Daughter in Law* (London: Hurst & Blackett, 1913), p. 24.
97 H. Campbell, *The Burqa – A Detective Story* (London: John Long, 1930), p. 45.
98 Ibid., p. 154.
99 Inden, *Imagining India*, p. 2.
100 Hukk, *Abdullah*, p. 66.
101 Eyton, *Mr Ram*, pp. 64–5.
102 S. Howe, *Novels of Empire* (New York: Columbia University Press, 1949), p. 9.
103 The loyalty of an Indian wife to her English husband is shown in Percey Davidson's play *Jewel of the East*. LCP 1913/9.
104 Singh, *Survey*, p. 290.
105 Thompson, *Indian Day*, p. 91.
106 F. E. F. Penny, *The Two Brides* (London: Hodder & Stoughton, 1929), p. 44.
107 Savi, *Daughter in Law*, pp. 372–3.
108 (IOL) MSS. Eur. C. 336/3, Ch. 16.
109 (IOL) MSS. Eur. F. 165/207.
110 Interview with Professor Richard Sorabji, 21 March 94.
111 Mrs Theodore Pennel, *Doorways of the East: An Indian Novel* (London: John Murray, 1930), p. 92.
112 Ibid., pp. 102–3.
113 Singh, *Survey*.
114 Calcutta University Commission Report 1917–19, Vol. 1, Ch. 5 (Calcutta, 1919), pp. 105–15.
115 Ibid., p. 113.
116 J. H. Voight, *Max Müller: The Man and His Ideas* (Calcutta: Mukhopadhyay, 1981) p. 49.
117 R. Symonds, *Oxford and Empire: The Last Lost Cause?* (London: Macmillan, 1986), pp. 92–3. Max Müller also devoted many lectures to defending the Indian character from attack. The Sanskrit scholar R. G. Bhandarkar wrote: 'The character of all us Indians had been greatly traduced in Europe. We were described as men given habitually to lying, of no substance or worth in us, possessing no self-respect and incapable of any great effort. Max Müller combated this view.' N. C. Chaudhuri, *Scholar Extraordinary – Life of Professor the Rt Hon Friedrich Max Müller* (London: Chatto & Windus, 1974), p. 305.
118 J. Keir Hardie, *India: Impressions and Suggestions* (London: Independent Labour Party, 1909), p. 102.
119 J. Strachey, *India – Its Administration and Progress* (London: Macmillan, 1911), p. 540.
120 M. Monier Williams, *Modern India and Indians* (London: Trubner, 1891), p. 358. Sir Monier Williams was Professor of Sanskrit at Oxford University.
121 J. D. Rees, *Real India* (London: Methuen, 1908), p. 275. Rees also served on the Lee Warner Committee.
122 S. Low, *A Vision of India* (London: Smith Elder, 1906), p. 226.
123 Rees, *Real India*, p. 275.

124 W. Hunter, *A Brief History of Indian Peoples* (Oxford: Clarendon Press, 1897), p. 8.

125 Monier Williams, *Modern India*, p. 360.

126 A. White, *Joseph Conrad and the Adventure Tradition: Constructing and Deconstructing the Imperial Subject* (Cambridge: Cambridge University Press, 1993).

127 Z. T. Sullivan, *Narratives of Empire: The Fictions of Rudyard Kipling* (Cambridge: Cambridge University Press, 1993).

128 T. Pinney (ed.), *Kipling's India: Uncollected Sketches 1884–88* (London: Macmillan, 1988), p. 22.

129 Victoria League Papers. Minutes of the Executive Committee, 1907, p. 17a.

130 P. D. Curtin, *Image of Africa: British Ideas and Action, 1780–1850*, 2 Vols. (Madison: University of Wisconsin, 1964).

131 S. H. Alatas, *The Myth of the Lazy Native: A Study of the Image of Malays, Filipinos and Javanese from the Sixteenth to the Twentieth Century and its Function in the Ideology of Colonial Capitalism* (London: Frank Cass, 1977).

132 Singh, *Imperishable Empire*, p. 133.

133 R. J. C. Young, *White Mythologies: Writing History and the West* (London: Routledge, 1990), p. 147: 'the coloniser sees a grotesquely displayed image of himself ... the imitation subverts the identity of that which is being represented'. Again ambivalence is reflected in 'resemblance and menace'. See note 27.

4

Characteristics of British Policy:
Dynamics of Reciprocity and Control

B RITISH policy towards Indian students in Britain was characterised
on the one hand by fears of political and sexual threats presented
by students, coloured by the political situation in India and racial and
cultural stereotyping; and on the other by strategies evolved to overcome these perceived threats in the form of surveillance, control and
restriction, executed under the cloak of paternalism and protection.
Interwoven in these processes are the themes of reciprocity and
ambivalence.

THE POLITICAL SITUATION IN INDIA

In order to appreciate fully British official concern for Indian students
in Britain, it is crucial to understand the close connection between British
official attitudes and the political situation in India. By the turn of the
century signs of political unrest were beginning to emerge throughout
India. The new radical direction of Indian nationalism in the Edwardian
period is demonstrated by the rise of the extremist wing of the Indian
National Congress, spearheaded by Balgangadhar Tilak, the boycott
of British goods during the Swadeshi Era in reaction to the Partition
of Bengal in 1905, Hindu revivalism and the growth of revolutionary
terrorism.
    The insecurity and anxiety felt by the British was reflected in the
repressive measures taken to stamp out this new strand of militancy. In
India security was tightened up by the establishment of a Criminal
Intelligence Department to deal with political crimes. An Official Secrets
Act was also put on the statute book in 1904 and there was a clampdown
on the press and political activity in general. In 1907, the year of the Lee
Warner Committee, established to investigate Indian students in Britain,
seditious newspapers could be shut down in India. There was a ban on
freedom of association in Bengal and individuals found guilty of
terrorist acts could be deported. The measures taken to curb political
unrest in India echo the themes of British policy towards Indian students

in Britain – control, restriction and surveillance. British policy on higher education in India paralleled official attitudes in Britain. The colonial government was also concerned about the politicisation of students in India. Calcutta University was viewed as a breeding-ground of political agitation. The 1904 University Act restricted access by increasing fees and introduced new controls on affiliation and grants. This was implemented more strictly after 1905 to stem student radicalism.[1]

Clearly, British anxiety about Indian students in Britain, reflected by an increasingly interventionist stance, was, at least in part, symptomatic of wider fears concerning political unrest in India. These fears, stemming from the periphery, worked themselves out on the metropolitan stage by an increased racial consciousness among British officials in England.

CULTURAL AND RACIAL STEREOTYPING

Even before the Lee Warner Committee discussed the issue of Indian students in 1907 *The Times* had already coined the phrase the 'Indian student problem'. While Indian princes visiting Britain had for some time, particularly during Lord Curzon's viceroyalty, vexed the government, the term 'problem' was not used to stigmatise them in the way that it was applied to students. Government and university officials presented Indian students as a problem on several levels. They were morally weak, especially with regard to English women; they attracted undesirable acquaintances; they exhibited separatist tendencies; they were reluctant to take part in sports; and, to a lesser degree, were financially untrustworthy. As I have shown, these criticisms were based on preconceived, racial and cultural assumptions fostered by racial theorists, popular literature, the press and the theatre.

British witnesses to the Lee Warner Committee were concerned about the susceptibility of Indian students to so-called 'immoral influences'. The report concluded: 'We have received evidence which convinces us that an appreciable proportion of Indian students in London do succumb to the temptations to which they are exposed.'[2] But it was not specific about what percentage these students were in relation to the whole Indian student population. The portrayal of Indians as lacking in moral fibre was common before the twentieth century. For instance, a contributor to the *Indian Magazine and Review* described in some detail the inadequacy of the Indian character, in comparison with the English: 'There is a certain limpness about the Oriental character, a want of pluck and backbone, and a general ignorance of what is expressed by the word "honour".'[3] While English schoolboys were truthful and upright, the oriental mind, in comparison, delighted 'naturally in crooked ways'. According to Mary A. Pinhey, 'To conduct a difficult piece of scheming through many tortuous and deceitful passages to a successful issue, would be regarded as evidence of cleverness.'[4] Pinhey attributed this lack of honesty to the fact that Indians 'were never taught as children, that a lie was wrong in itself without regard to its consequences, and the idea that it was dishonest and disgraceful to obtain any wished for advantage by what we call bribery would never enter their heads'.[5] Consequently, they lacked a 'moral sense'.

British criticisms of Indian students all stemmed from what was perceived to be an essential deficiency of character, which was inherent in Indians and entirely attributable to their racial make-up. The Master of Emmanuel College, Cambridge, could not find a single example of an Indian student's breaching discipline or morality; on the contrary, he found the Indian student to be 'submissive and amenable to any suggestion or hints from the authorities'.[6] Nevertheless, he still believed certain characteristics were more common in orientals. Virtually replicating Mrs Pinhey, he wrote: 'They have not the high sense of honour, or the strict regard for truthfulness, which we expect from the best class of English students.'[7] This example shows how even when experience refuted their prejudices many would still continue to ignore the evidence.

British opinion of industrial students was also influenced by racial stereotyping. Professor F. W. Burstall of Birmingham University was convinced that the attitudes of different races towards engineering were affected by 'national character'. He believed the British had a natural aptitude for anything practical; while Indians, in contrast, preferred abstraction – not a good quality for engineers.[8] Dr J. Gordon Parkes, principal of a technical college in Bermondsey, also compared the 'English mind ... bred and cultured in commercial thought for generations' with 'the Indian mind ... incapable of realising the necessity for detail and exacting methods'.[9]

Sir Edward Candy, Deputy Reader in Indian Law, Cambridge, was also quick to jump to conclusions concerning Indian students. He classified the three ICS probationers he knew as shy, resentful of anything that could be construed as patronising and naturally reserved. However, T. F. C. Huddleston, censor of non-collegiate students at Cambridge, found them 'very pushy and inclined to take every sort of advantage'. As censor, he was in close contact with non-collegiate Indian students, but they were 'generally a source of difficulty to himself', and although he was responsible for them he had become in his own words 'gradually estranged from them as a class'.[10] Only Professor D. J. Cunningham, Dean of the Medical Faculty of Edinburgh, was pleased with the Indian element at his university. They were 'industrious, well-behaved and very amenable to discipline'.[11]

A common complaint against the students was that they held aloof from collegiate life and indulged in clannish behaviour. The Master of Emmanuel College observed that Indians at Emmanuel were insular, mixing only with each other and Indians outside the college. He noted a particularly wide gulf in the case of Bengalis, in comparison with other Indians.[12] As Sir William Wedderburn had pointed out, many Bengali students resented the partition of 1905. Several explanations were given for this insularity. A. S. Ramsay of Magdalene College, Cambridge, believed that Indian reserve was due to natural timidity and shyness.[13] A resident at the Inns of Court believed that Indians had by 1909 found it easier to seek the company of their fellow countrymen, as 'native students, instead of being in a minority, as in former years, had now become an enormous majority, and that instead of dining at the same table, they almost invariably dined apart'.[14] Sir William Lee Warner, member of the Council of India, was one of the few Englishmen to appreciate that the cost of having a vigorous social life was an inhibiting factor. In 1906 – a year before he chaired the Committee into Indian students – he suggested several ways of combating this problem. Firstly, Indian students should be encouraged to take up residence in colleges rather than in lodgings. Secondly, the distribution of Indians in small numbers throughout the college would force them to mix with English fellow students and prevent the formation of purely Indian clubs. Thirdly, social gatherings to encourage Anglo-Indian intercourse should exclude political agitators.

British criticism about Indian 'aloofness' was connected to the broader theme of Indian failure to participate in the corporate life of universities or the Inns of Court. One of the key avenues to social acceptance was on the sports field. It was believed that greater sympathy could be created between students if Indians paid more attention to sports. Edward Dicey wrote dismissively:

> The rough games in which British lads ... take delight are distasteful to ordinary Hindus and, even if they understood the attraction possessed for their English fellow-students by such games as cricket and football, the expenses attaching to these games are sufficiently large to prohibit their pursuit even by the small native minority who understood their attraction.[15]

However, on this rare occasion, an English student, K. E. Kirk, defended the Indian student's reputation in his response to Dicey's article. He argued that the Indian student was, as a rule, acquainted with both the meaning and fascination of athletics … [T]he Hindu, whose theory denies the possibility of a personality expressing itself in physical activity and condemns the cult of the body, is yet instinctively an admirer of the athlete, and takes to games with the zeal of a schoolboy. It is certainly true that a large proportion of the Indians who visit England play cricket, tennis and golf with a skill not far, if at all, below the English average.[16]

To illustrate his point, Kirk gave the example of a group of Indian students at Glasgow who beat the university team at hockey. But notions of racial superiority led the Lytton Committee in 1922 to conclude that 'Indians were handicapped in sports because they were physically weaker.'[17] Indians were regarded as effeminate, lacking the essential manliness associated with physical exercise. Notions of the 'effete East' were especially strong at Oxford and Cambridge, strongholds of 'muscular Christianity' as well as English public schools, where the classical Greek tradition of twinning a healthy mind with a healthy body was strongly adhered to.

Complaints about the non-payment of bills were voiced at both Oxford and Cambridge. As a result Indian students had acquired a bad reputation in this matter. St John's College, Oxford had taken precautions against any financial irregularities by admitting only government scholars, thereby ensuring the payment of fees, as scholarships were paid direct through the college. The college had contemplated increasing the 'caution money' (deposit), as it was known, for Indians. Sidney Ball, a tutor, had received complaints from lodging-house keepers about Indians who were in arrears. Several colleges at Cambridge had also been alerted by tradesmen about the outstanding debts of students who had returned to India.[18]

Interestingly, Indian students were often compared unfavourably with other groups of Asian students. T. F. C. Huddleston, the censor of non-collegiate students at Cambridge, claimed that Japanese students were perceived to be admirable undergraduates, 'being quick to assimilate, gentlemanly and amiable'. In contrast, Indians 'behaved insolently to inferiors such as lodging-house keepers, and often left without paying their bills'. He concluded that 'If Indians behaved in the same way as the Japanese, Englishmen would respond at once.'[19] Other members of the university staff had also noticed that 'Japanese, Siamese and Chinese students were much better received than Indians.' H. Jackson claimed this was because 'The latter were regarded as "black men" and the others merely as "yellow men".'[20] Oscar Browning of King's College, Cambridge, echoed this view. He also linked the greater acceptance of other Asian students, notably the Japanese, to their English public school background.

THE PROBLEM OF WOMEN

The perception of the Indian student as a sexual predator threw up another racial stereotype, deeply embedded in British popular culture. K. Ballhatchet, in his book *Race, Sex and Class under the Raj*, has argued that 'the British in India were peculiarly prone to the jealousy felt by men of a dominant elite at the possibility of sexual relations between women of the elite and men of subordinate groups'.[21] The powerful stereotype of the lascivious Indian, the product of child marriage and polygamy was, he claimed, essential for the preservation of British hegemony in India. By bridging the social distance between ruler and ruled interracial sexual relations threatened this imperial power structure. Ronald Hyam has shown the hypocrisy of the British stance: while non-Europeans were required to exercise restraint in relations with white women, the British 'imposed no parallel self-denying ordinance on themselves in their relations with black women'.[22]

The subject provoked ambiguous feelings among officials, resulting in defensive and protective posturings, both of which were key features of British attitudes towards Indian students. Miscegenation was a form of hybridity that not only worried the British in India but also caused considerable consternation when it occurred in Britain. J. B. Douthwaite testified:

> Socially the worst evil that I know is the tendency of these students to marry English women. Usually (but not always) the wife is a young girl of no social standing, who has been deceived by tales of the affluent life she will lead in India. Sometimes I think that the student is himself enticed (or threatened) into marriage. There have been other cases in my knowledge where the wife has been of good social standing – sometimes of mature age. I need not say what great misery always follows on these marriages.[23]

The steward of Gray's Inn gave the example of a Muslim student who in 1906 had charges brought against him by a Welsh waitress, with whom he had been living, for taking all her savings and valuables and leaving her destitute when she lost her job. He was saved when he married a Scottish boarding-house keeper, who paid his debts. Douthwaite concluded: 'In his whole five years he had passed no exams and lived off women the whole time.'

Dr Knight at Edinburgh University had also observed that, while students in general were often pursued 'by shop girls and women of that class', Indians in particular were singled out more than other students. He attributed this to the fact that Indian students were often regarded as princes. With the rise in the number of Indian students residing in private lodging houses, and not at the residential hostel, Portobello, 'mishaps', as he called them, were more frequent. Knight noted: 'The landlady's daughter was often a snare, and certain drapery establishments where they could flirt with attendants, had great attractions for Indians.'[24] He knew of cases where Indian students had married such girls and either settled in India or alternatively taken up practice in mining areas of Britain such as Durham or Wales. The Reverend Gibson, Chaplain of Balliol College, claimed that Indians in India were 'accustomed to an abundance of female society, whereas in England they were excluded from all except the lowest'. He felt that they were quicker to seek out low society than were English under-graduates.[25]

Concern about interracial marriages became so great in official circles that in 1913 the India Office distributed a circular to all registry offices in Britain, 'to explain to British women contemplating marriage with Hindus, Mohamedans and other subjects or citizens of countries where polygamy is legal, the risks attendant on such marriages'.[26] The *Daily Mail* published the circular, restating its purpose: 'It cannot be too frequently pointed out that a white woman marrying a coloured man becomes subject to the law of his country, laws which may encourage polygamy and make divorce easy.'[27] It was no coincidence that the article was placed next to a story called 'The Rescue of an English Girl from a Harem', which conveniently served to reinforce the message. As we have seen, the problems of interracial marriages were a favourite theme of popular fiction on India, consequently *Daily Mail* readers were probably already aware of the dangers alluded to in the article, having come across more titillating expositions of the subject in novels. Before the publication of the memorandum the *Spectator* magazine made it clear that marriages between Indians and English women were not welcome, when it reported the London weddings of two members of the ICS – a Hindu and a Muslim – to Indian women educated in England. The magazine suggested that Indians in Britain should take notice of the weddings, advising them 'to seek brides within their own community'.[28]

Although the *Spectator* was targeting Indian readers in this instance, all non-European men in England were a potential threat. A. Gordon Ingram, Inspector of the Public Security Division, Alexandria, felt that the National Vigilance Association, an organisation devoting itself to the emotive topic of the 'white slave traffic', should interest itself in the question of British women marrying Egyptian students, who risked losing their citizenship if they were divorced in Egypt. But this was deemed to be beyond the remit of the Association. The Student Christian Movement, an organisation interested in the welfare of all foreign students, concluded that fears about the prospects of friendship between British women and foreign students, especially orientals and Africans, were based on 'the vague but very common suspicion that the moral standards of foreigners as a whole are lower than our own'.[29] It is clear from the India Office's circular that it shared some of these attitudes. Hence the obsession of novelists with 'mixed marriages' and hybridity was reflected in official policy towards Indian students.

THE POLITICAL DIMENSION

Official British thinking on Indian students was overshadowed by the spectre of a 'discontented revolutionary' plotting the violent demise of the Raj in the capital city of the empire. This representation of the Indian student was also already familiar to the reading public. India House, a building in Highgate, was the headquarters of a group of revolutionary Indian students under the leadership of Shyamji Krishnavarma. He had started a scholarship scheme for Indian students and edited a journal called the *Indian Sociologist*, in which he stated that the group's aim was: 'to frustrate in every way possible the efforts of those enemies of our country who are bent upon weaning the young Indian student community in England from the nationalist movement'. To further this cause among Indian students in England, India House accommodated 'a few political Missionaries ... to preach the nationalist Cause'.[30] Krishnavarma's emissaries would meet students as they arrived fresh off the mail trains at Victoria or Charing Cross. The turnover of students at India House was rumoured to be high; this seems probable as the hostel had only 24 beds.[31]

The 1907 government committee established to investigate the 'Indian student problem' came to two main conclusions. Firstly, 'A majority of students are imbued before leaving India with the political opinions of the advanced section of the Indian opposition and are animated by a feeling of discontent with British rule.' Secondly, 'these political opinions and this discontent are usually strengthened by their residence in England'.[32]

Dr Tanner of St John's College, Cambridge, attributed further radicalisation of students in Britain to the impact of political ideas, imbibed freely at the union debates, in societies, conversation and as part of their studies. He believed that English political thought was so influential that it mentally 'threw them [the students] off their balance and profoundly affected their views about government'. Indian students were quick to use examples from history and apply them to India. Consequently, it was inferred that 'the mental atmosphere of England itself' acted as a potent force on suggestible students. Party politics was the commonest subject of conversation, debated with vigour in public and private. Behind Tanner's words was the tacit assumption that European political theory and culture were superior to eastern traditions and that contact with such ideas would overwhelm students. In Tanner's words: 'The abler the man the quicker he felt it all.'[33] The most academic students were able to see clear contradictions between theories of democracy, equality, civil rights and notions of the nation-state – all essential parts of the classical education received by Indians in India and Britain – and the realities of imperialism in India. The only way it was possible to justify limiting the application of principles of universal enlightenment was to claim that the racial inferiority of non-Europeans was an effective bar to the introduction of such principles.

The Lee Warner Committee acknowledged the politicising role of the British press: the Indian student 'dwells upon phrases and sentences used by politicians and by the party press, and believes they embody an official policy and accepted line of action'.[34] Also the presence of extremists in the metropolis, with effective recruitment techniques, provided centres for students. Sir Charles Elliott[35] compared how in the past his open Saturday invitation for Indian students to visit him had been taken up and attendance was constant. However, he had noticed, over the period 1906–07, that numbers had fallen, most notably among Bengalis. Elliott regarded this as an illustration of the suspicion that was building up within the student population. T. F. C. Huddleston was aware that disaffection was to a degree normal among students, who were by nature vulnerable to the sway of opinion. Nevertheless, he made a distinction between the disaffection of the English student and his Indian counterpart: 'their hostility to British Rule was much deeper and more abiding than the crudely "advanced" views often held by young Englishmen'. He concluded: 'The Indian had lost all illusions as to the supposed superiority of the "White Man".'[36] Huddleston's position was complex because, while he admitted to disliking Indians, he was clearly not a diehard imperialist because he used terms such as 'illusions' and 'supposed superiority'.

Some British officials were concerned about open displays of disloyalty. Curzon Wyllie wrote to Sir Charles Lyall on 5 November 1908 with reference to a meeting at Caxton Hall at which Indian students expressed their distrust of the India Office and stated their claim to an equal footing with Englishmen in regard to liberty of action and freedom of speech. Curzon Wyllie wrote of his fears: 'There can be no doubt that the feeling of disloyalty among Indian students is growing day by day and the majority of the students in London are neither afraid nor ashamed to openly manifest their disloyalty.'[37] Sir Raymond West, Reader in Indian Law at Cambridge, argued that Indian students should have it impressed on them that they must show active, not passive, loyalty and support for the government. Dr Tanner felt: 'The spirit of disloyalty ... lay very deep.' He felt the 'best of them (in other respects) were the most disloyal'.[38] The most studious students – who read widely, took part in college debates and, on the surface, appeared to be the most anglicised and settled students, satisfying British academic and social requirements – were the first to realise the conflict between their position as colonised people and the European political philosophy which they were studying at universities and the Inns of Court. British officials had long been aware that contact with radical European thought provided Indians with an intellectual stick with which to beat them, such as Naoroji's book on 'un-British rule'. However, the Lee Warner Report was more keen to show the volume of disaffection among Indians in Britain.

Another witness to the Lee Warner Committee, J. W. Neill, found that he was less familiar with Indian students than in former times as a result of a greater tendency on the part of students 'to talk bitterly on political matters to the exclusion of other topics, which made their society less pleasant than formerly ... [S]tudents had read "advanced" papers and imbibed extreme ideas from barristers, friends and others of extreme views.'[39] He believed there was a widespread distrust of Englishmen who had first-hand knowledge of India. Indeed, Indians preferred those with whom they could 'lay down the law on matters connected with India'. He saw Muslims in a better light; they were more willing to mix with Englishmen and help each other. But he felt that they too had become more politicised along Congress lines. *The Times* reported a 'demonstration of disloyalty' where Indian students had booed and hissed at the mention of the King's name while attending an East Indian Association meeting. Sir Henry Cotton, on the other hand, believed student hostility was anti-official rather than anti-British. Dr Tanner agreed that animosity was directed at the government not the British people. He was keen to point out that relations with the college authorities were 'sometimes very cordial'.[40]

All this evidence highlights the deep concern in official circles that discontented and alienated students in Britain would take refuge in 'extremist' politics. This view was supported by two Indian students, Sheikh Abdul Kadir and Charu Ghose. Both believed the influence of

India House was growing. Kadir pointed to the increasing boycott of positions in government service; he personally knew Indian ICS candidates who had been dissuaded from competing. With his journalist connections, Ghose was aware that the *Indian Sociologist* had attracted serious notice in the newspaper world. Its openly disloyal character was preferred to the veiled sedition of Congress newspapers. Ghose attributed India House's popularity to the opposition provoked by Curzon's partition of Bengal.

However, the Reverend S. D. Bhabha, President of the Indian Christian Union, took a contrary view. He claimed that India House's authority was limited, arguing that the *Indian Sociologist*'s circulation was small even among students. His opinion was strengthened by the fact that, unlike the others, he had actually met Krishnavarma when attending the inaugural meeting of India House. He described Krishnavarma as a man whose 'bark was worse than his bite'.[41] Some of Krishnavarma's 'scholars' had lived with Bhabha and spoke respectfully about Krishnavarma; nevertheless, Bhabha believed that he had little personal hold over them. The same could not be said of Vinayak Damodar Savarkar, who took over the leadership of India House after Krishnavarma. One youth, Rafik Muhammed Khan Nabha, under the direction of Savarkar wrote an open letter to his father repudiating all parental control.[42] D. Garnett, an Englishman who attended a meeting of India House and was later involved in assisting Savarkar in an unsuccessful escape from police custody, noted Savarkar's 'extraordinary personal magnetism'.[43]

Despite India House's notoriety as a haunt of extremists and revolutionaries, students of moderate political persuasion could be found residing there. In a newspaper article Pandit Bhagwadin Dube, a member of the Student Advisory Committee, described how he arrived in London in 1907 friendless and homeless: 'I went to India House, where I understood all Indians were welcome. I spent two or three weeks there. There were a number of students who entertained a variety of opinions on political questions. Residence in the house certainly does not imply agreement with any political creed.'[44] H. K. Korgaonkar (government informant) also noted the presence of some moderates at Highgate. Nevertheless, he believed most were what the British regarded as rank extremists.[45]

Even students not involved in politics were attracted to revolutionary ideas or their proponents. The Cambridge government scholar Panna Lall claimed that, although he was entirely opposed to Krishnavarma on political grounds, when he met him to ask about a scholarship for a friend, he was struck by the 'great sincerity, honesty and conviction' by which he had expressed himself.[46] J. Jaini, a London law student, was not attached to any political party, yet he commented on the appeal of extremist propaganda: 'so gloriously patriotic and so irresistibly logical. The policy of the British is so stupidly short-sighted, and drives us against our will, at least tends to drive us, to become Extremists.'[47]

As discussed earlier, the political aspect of the Indian presence in England had a wider significance in relation to India. Curzon Wyllie voiced his opinion categorically to Charles Lyall when he wrote: 'I have no hesitation in saying that the root of disaffection in India is to be found among Indian students in this country.'[48] On their return to India, ex-members of India House were reported by the Police Commissioner of Bombay to have talked of sedition during their voyage home and to be in possession of books on European revolution. In addition, several of the accused in the Manicktolla conspiracy case had remained attached to India House after returning to India.[49] The East India Association also felt that Indian students were likely to become 'centres of sedition when they returned to India'. In a memorandum the Association pointed to a meeting, commemorating 'the Martyrs' of the Indian Mutiny 'as proof that the state of feeling is even worse now than the Council described in the memorandum as constituting a serious danger to the state'.[50]

However, the authorities found that disciplinary action against students could prove problematic. For example, in 1909 the *Daily Mail* reported the decision to disbar two Indian law students, Harinam Singh and Savarkar. This decision was, in the words of the newspaper, 'the subject of acute discussion and professional opinion is not altogether favourable'. The article presented the difficulty as twofold. Firstly: 'The reasons that will justify disbarring have never been clearly stated. Generally they are supposed to be unprofessional conduct or criminal acts of which the barrister has been convicted.'[51] Secondly, the benchers' position was made more inconsistent by the fact that other 'disloyal' nationals had been called to the Bar – for example, Boers who had fought against the British and, going back further Americans who had fought in the War of Independence.

Bipin Chandra Pal told the *Daily News* on 8 June 1909 that, if members of India House were disbarred, 'it follows that every member of the Irish Land League should be treated in the same way'. As late as 1919 the Adviser to Indian students, T. W. Arnold, consulted the Oxford authorities as to whether it was possible to take disciplinary action against students with anti-British views. He was informed that any such action was only possible in the case of a violation of public order. In 1919 the whole matter was raised by the case of M. D. Bhat, who had spoken at the Majlis[52] – an association of Indian students founded at Cambridge University in 1907 – in a seditious manner. Bhat was mentioned in a letter sent by A. G. Shipley, Vice-Chancellor of Cambridge, to Lord Curzon, the Foreign Secretary. Mr Benians, who was in charge of Indian students at Oxford on behalf of the India Office, felt that there was 'no real malice' in Bhat's actions, just 'high spirits and thoughtlessness'. However, Rajani Palme Dutt (later to become a leading figure in the British Communist Party) and his brother Clemens were viewed in a different light. They were described as 'sinister characters'. Shipley continued: 'They are men of extraordinary ability and have quite got control of the socialist club here, though they never appear in public. In my opinion they ought to be very closely watched.'[53]

SURVEILLANCE

The problem of anti-British agitators proved serious enough to warrant Scotland Yard's surveillance of Indian students. Unfortunately, Metropolitan Police records are not available. But some documents have survived, such as a document entitled 'Indian Agitators Abroad'. It was a carefully compiled list of 102 individual reports, containing biographical information on political agitators. The derogatory tone used to describe them is striking. In the case of Madame Cama, her rejection of British rule was reduced to the fact that she was 'a quarrelsome woman' as she had 'been able to live in harmony neither with her own husband in Bombay nor with the small band of revolutionaries in Paris'. The report concluded: 'She is not a person of conspicuous ability.'[54]

It is interesting that most evidence on the top-secret world of surveillance is available as a result of police incompetence. Morley wrote to Minto on the subject in June 1908. He described the British police as 'wholly useless in the case of Indian conspirators, if such there be. They have no sort of agency able to distinguish Hindu from Mohammedan, or Verma from Varma.'[55] Nevertheless, he was reluctant to let the India Office take the lead in flushing out conspirators. Indian students were certainly aware that they were being watched. In one case Scotland Yard shadowed a student called Kunte. His landlady, Mrs East, who had been employed by Special Branch to spy on Kunte, reported that he was 'the most disloyal and anti-English of the number of Indian students she had staying at her house'. When East tactlessly harangued Kunte about the assassination of Curzon Wyllie, he left the house proclaiming: 'He could not live in a house where the movements of himself and his friends were being constantly communicated to the police.'[56]

When Munshi Ram Sagee, an engineering student, and his common-law English wife complained that they had been shadowed, the police's clandestine operations were exposed in the House of Commons by the Labour MP for Leeds East. He argued that, as a consequence of surveillance, students had been compelled to leave their lodgings, resulting in hardship and called for an end to shadowing. But the government was still reluctant to concede its involvement in espionage and passed all responsibility over to the police. The official parliamentary response read: 'This Department is not aware of the proceedings of the police, which have taken on their own responsibility for such reasons as they consider sufficient.'[57] However, the private correspondence of officials contradicts the public pronouncements. Sir James Dunlop-Smith wrote to his father, just after his appointment as Political ADC: 'I have a good deal to do with students … I am trying to learn something about the anarchists and have seen several suspected men.'[58] Additionally Lee Warner was in possession of a list of six extremist haunts in London.[59]

Mrs Katz, a German woman, wrote to the India Office requesting financial assistance to extend her dwelling, in order to establish a hostel for Indian students. It is clear from her letter that she was actually offering her services as a spy for the government. She had already furnished Scotland Yard with information about her Indian lodgers. By dealing with the India Office she hoped to extend her surveillance activities and put them on a more official footing. She wrote: 'Mr Arnold or any of your representatives could call and visit at liberty.'[60] However, she was rejected on the grounds that the India Office was not prepared to countenance any system of surveillance, especially 'subsidised espionage'. However, the Under-Secretary of State, Sir Herbert Risley, was tempted by her request. He admitted that Mrs Katz's position and popularity among Indians eminently qualified her to act as a government spy.

Another method of surveillance employed in India by the Director of Criminal Intelligence, C. J. Stevenson-Moore, was the interception of letters passing between known revolutionaries in London and India. In 1907 the Government of India, under the provisions of the Post Office Act, was able to intercept all postal articles arriving from abroad addressed to men of the Native Army. According to Stevenson-Moore, 'the loyalty of several regiments in the Native Army was very severely shaken'[61] by the activities of revolutionaries abroad. Intercepted letters were also used as evidence in conspiracy cases in India. For example, a letter sent by Lajpat Rai to an Indian student at Edinburgh University requesting books was used as evidence against the defendant, Ajit Singh, in the Lahore trial. Rai wrote:

> I shall feel very thankful if you can manage to send me one new book every month; it may be a revolutionary or political novel, or a history of some patriotic movement or the life of a nationalist. I am confident good literature, of the right sort, if supplied to boys will be productive of solid results.[62]

Links with India House were evident by Rai's reference to Shyamji Krishnavarma, whom he suggested 'might employ a little of his money in sending a number of such books on politics to the student community in India'.[63] William Wedderburn complained to the India Office when his mail was tampered with, by which time the order had already been cancelled as its continued implementation was regarded as pointless.

But sedition in India was still believed to have its roots in Britain. The Indian government had some measure of success in prohibiting the production of pamphlets in India. Minto stated that although bans had been placed on publications such as the *Indian Sociologist*, such measures had proved to be largely ineffective, as it was difficult to detect such literature in the post. He wrote: 'We earnestly ask your co-operation in putting an end to an evil which is now assuming grave proportions ... [It] is intolerable that the enemies of British rule in India should any longer be permitted to use the headquarters of the Empire, as the centre of a seditious and revolutionary campaign.'[64] Again this statement reinforces the connection between the political situation in India and policy towards Indians in Britain.

Despite the set-backs, in 1910 the Director of Criminal Intelligence reported that he was in the process of launching a conspiracy case against most members of India House. He wrote: 'The revolutionary aims and constitution of the India House society can be proved without difficulty.'[65] However, the evidence against the students involved was insufficient. He suggested that a police enquiry in London would strengthen the case. The Secretary to the Government of Bombay, J. H. DuBoulay, argued that the problem lay in the unsatisfactory nature of the evidence, based as it was overwhelmingly on the statement of former accomplices who had become police informants. Not only did the three accomplices' statements fail to corroborate each other, but crucially there was no independent corroboration of what took place at India House. Furthermore, there was the language difficulty: the informants could not be trusted to withstand cross-examination in court, where the jury would have to disentangle how much of their testimony was hearsay and how much was fact. Added to which none of the prosecution witnesses had managed to infiltrate the inner circle of the society. Consequently the British authorities were unable to act against India House.

CONTROL

Surveillance of students was connected to a much more fundamental feature of British policy towards Indian students in Britain: control. Attempts to exercise authority over students took place at several levels: at an institutional level guardianship was introduced and restrictive policies were intended to control the number and type of student.[66] Even unofficial bodies concerned with Indian student welfare[67] and student societies such as the Edinburgh Indian Association were not free from interference. These new forms of intervention during the Edwardian period were mirrored in the restrictive measures implemented towards higher education in India discussed earlier.

The British authorities' desire to control and superintend Indian students was the stimulus behind the reoccurring debate on the establishment of an official Indian student hostel in London. The question of a hostel was first raised by Henry Summermaine in 1868. Dr Leitner founded an oriental university to house Indian students according to strict religious convention. But the venture had patently failed when, even after three years, no students had enrolled.[68] The idea received a further airing in 1903, when the issue of an Indian hostel was simultaneously put forward by the steward of Gray's Inn in a letter to the India Office and, more publicly, by H. C. Richards, MP, in the journal *East and West*. It was debated by the Judicial and Public Committee in the India Office but was abandoned in the face of strong criticism until 1920, when an official hostel was eventually opened. However, what is particularly significant in this context is not that critics objected to a hostel in principle – on the contrary, many like Sir Henry Cotton viewed the absence of supervision and control as a real problem – but rather that a hostel would not be able to procure the desired object of increased control. Opponents of the hostel argued that similar plans to restrain the Indian student population had failed. Indian students would be reluctant to enter a hostel voluntarily, preferring instead their freedom away from official interference, while any compulsion would lead to a furore in India. Sir Charles Lyall believed the only way to bring any authority to bear over students was through their parents in India, who could operate financial sanctions.[69]

The hostel issue is interesting because it shows that, by the turn of the century, the British authorities were looking seriously for a means of containing the Indian student population, particularly in London. The fact that a hostel was not seen as a suitable mechanism for obtaining this goal does not diminish the underlying problem the hostel issue was trying to address – namely, that the majority of Indian students in London were not subject to any type of control.

GUARDIANSHIP

While the idea of a hostel was temporarily rejected, a loose system of guardianship had been in operation for some time. Indian students arriving in Britain in the nineteenth century were often left under the informal protection of family friends. For example, Dr K. D. Ghose left his three sons under the guardianship of the Reverend William Drewitt, a cousin of a family friend. In 1885 a scheme was suggested by Algernon Brown of the Northbrook Society for the guardianship of students over 14 at a cost of £200 per year. The topic was discussed for six months before its implementation; finally the first two students were accepted. In order to extend this aspect of its work an agent was appointed and a sub-committee of the Society was later formed to consider the matter further.[70] In the same year the National Indian Association also published a circular stating the terms of its superintendence. In essence this involved taking charge of the student's educational and welfare needs. In return, parents were required to pay a fee and ensure that the guardian's counsel and directions were adhered to, which it was hoped would minimise any opposition from students.[71]

British officials giving evidence to the Lee Warner Committee were acutely aware of the need to place some kind of restraint on Indian students, particularly non-collegiate ones; the system of guardianship was viewed as a useful method of achieving this goal. J. B. Douthwaite felt that it was essential for the guardian to be European. He believed that Indian students were more likely to try and defy the authority of an Indian guardian and assert their independence, whereas an English-man would command greater deference.[72] Austin Low, a financial guardian to Indian students, confided that he knew of Indians who had got into financial troubles; an unofficial guardian would, he felt, prevent them from overdrawing their accounts.[73]

With the establishment of an institutional framework in the wake of the Lee Warner Report, guardianship was no longer left to unofficial associations. The government-sponsored Bureau of Information became increasingly involved with this aspect of British policy. In the first three years after the Bureau was established there was a dramatic increase in the number of students under guardianship. The figures show that, while in June 1910 a mere 27 students were under direct government control, that number had tripled by March 1911, and by the time a report was written in 1912 the number was 137, exclusive of 46 government scholars and native state scholars.[74] The Bureau's main duties were arranging to meet students on arrival, finding accommodation for them, banking the students' remittances and providing their parents with half-yearly statements of accounts. Arguably its most important function was to provide a report on the conduct and progress of the students' studies.

Oxbridge students were virtually forced to accept guardianship, as admission would otherwise prove impossible. T. W. Arnold, adviser to Indian students, noted that parents often resorted to guardianship as a last resort. These were young men who had 'squandered large sums of money and exhausted the patience of their parents. Parents ask that such sons may be taken in hand and endeavours be made to reform them.'[75] However, Arnold reported that the Bureau had been uniformly unsuccessful in reforming individuals; instead they had been unceremoniously returned to India.

Arnold confessed that guardianship was in essence a means of exercising control over wayward young men. He demonstrated how control over their finances could enforce discipline on government scholars, which was not possible for the majority of independent students. For example, an undergraduate at Cambridge who had contracted debts was moved to London on the understanding that if he passed his law examination he could return to Cambridge and complete his degree. Another student under guardianship thwarted the authority of his guardian by going to Paris without obtaining permission first. In this case the power exercised over the student was absolute. Arnold wrote that he 'was brought back by the simple expedient of starving him out'.[76] Similarly, a student who had disobeyed his father by going to Edinburgh was brought back to London to continue his studies.

Guardianship was also seen as a means of offsetting seditious influences by deliberately directing students to accommodation that was, as far as feasible, beyond the reach of other Indians. Arnold wrote that 'In the case of such students as happen to be under guardianship, it has been found advantageous to place them in lodgings in a district not usually frequented by Indians, under conditions favourable to the formation of friendships with English persons.'[77] This is clear evidence of attempts to manipulate the movements and associations of students under government control and to stem the rising tide of extremism in the Indian student community.

By spring 1921 the Indian Student Department controlled £7,000 of student remittances,[78] and a year later when the Lytton Committee reported, one witness, J. E. Mackenzie, an adviser in Edinburgh, suggested an extension of the guardianship system: 'It would seem desirable that all students should be under some form of guardianship, of the lightest character so far as control goes, but with the power to report on idleness or bad conduct of any student.'[79] Ironically, control of private students under guardianship was tighter than the control over government scholars, since they were not required to account for how they spent their scholarships. There was also concern about the limitations on the supervisory aspect of the system, since there was no provision for visiting students once they were established, especially if they lived outside London. To remedy this it was suggested that one of the joint secretaries for the Department should tour the country visiting students.

RESTRICTIVE POLICIES

The restrictive policies adopted by universities and the Inns of Court allowed these institutions to exercise a much more fundamental form of control over the number and type of student permitted to study in Britain. By limiting access to knowledge, the British were able to thwart Indian ambitions. Attempts to limit the number of Indians entering the Inns of Court and the universities must be seen as part of a broader process taking place in British society. This involved restricting access to the professions. The professionalisation of all aspects of life in nineteenth-century England had a knock-on effect in India. It was no longer sufficient to get by on caste alone. Entry into the professions achieved through examination was the basis of status, illustrated by W. C. Bonnerjee while studying in London: 'My position as a Barrister, I thought would give me a better position in life than as a mere Brahmin.'[80] Of all the professions law was the most popular. In order to restrict entry Bar Councils were established, operating a closed shop similar to medieval guilds in Britain, to raise the status of law in relation to other professions. Just at a time when western-educated Indians sought to challenge the British monopoly in government service and the judiciary, one of the major avenues of entry into these prestigious careers, British universities, was undergoing revision, formalising services and tightening up admissions.

The increase in the number of Indian students had a direct effect on the admissions to Oxford and Cambridge. Dr Tanner, a tutor of St John's College, Cambridge, had been told that the college was 'overrun with Indians'. In response it restricted the admissions of Indians. Oscar Browning was aware that King's College also restricted entry on racial grounds. But this was not uniformly practised at Cambridge. Colleges such as Downing had an open admissions policy. The 1907 Lee Warner Report stated that 'the university is not able or willing to assimilate more than a limited number' of Indians.[81] But the larger Indian population at Cambridge, in comparison with Oxford, shows that the restrictive approach was not applied as rigorously as at Oxford.

Nevertheless, two years later a more strict limit on the admission of Indian students was advocated by an anonymous contributor to the *Cambridge Review*, the university journal: 'Absolute restriction as to numbers is a further safeguard, both as regards the university as a whole, and as regards the individual numbers at a college.'[82] Its author believed selection procedures were fallible and official certificates were of little value, as references from Indian colleges could not be trusted. In response, J. M. Keynes, the economist, who was a Fellow at King's College at the time, wrote to the *Review* stating that, although he was in favour of the recently established Student Advisory Committee's suggestion to redistribute Indians more evenly throughout the colleges, nevertheless he was anxious to avoid putting obstacles in the way of Indian ambitions in government service which would result from a total restriction on admissions.

Before the whole question of Indian students was raised in the 1909 *Cambridge Review*, Jawaharlal Nehru had received information about a meeting between Lord Morley and the college heads:

> Various resolutions were passed among which, I am told, was one to the effect that no other college should take in an Indian who had been forcibly made to leave his college. The Master of Downing was the only person who objected to this. He told them plainly that if an Indian was expelled through spite and without sufficient reason, from his college, he would take him in.[83]

Nehru later discovered through 'third-hand' sources (the meeting was private) that the number of Indian students would be limited to three per college, resulting in a total of 54. According to his information, 'Christ's mildly protested against this and Downing refused to have anything to do with it. The other colleges then retaliated by agreeing to take even fewer Indians if Downing took more than three, so that the final total should not exceed 54.' Nehru voiced his concerns about the implementation of such restrictions: 'At present there are about 90 Indians in Cambridge and over thirty of these are in Downing. I do not know how they propose to reduce these numbers.'[84] He was also aware of measures to introduce a guardianship scheme and certificates of loyalty.

The number of Indians at Oxford was less than half that at Cambridge. This was partly due to the compulsory Latin requirement. Sir William Markby said: 'I do not think the colleges much like taking Indian students. They would take them when they had room and from a sense of duty. All colleges in Oxford refused to take more than a handful of Indians, for fear of the undesirable consequences that they would form a set apart.'[85] The Warden of New College was especially anxious not to have any more Indians, as he already had two Egyptians and two Indians in residence. The figures for October 1907 show that no college had more than five Indian students. Dr E. J. Trevelyan, Reader in Indian Law at All Souls College, felt that Oxford had been generally successful in its bid to attract the intellectual cream of Indians. As part of this policy he wished to restrict entry to the following groups: '(1) Those who had been educated at an English school. (2) Those who had taken a degree with honours in India. (3) Men of high social position.'[86] Balliol College had one Indian student in October 1907. This had been facilitated by the fact that at Balliol 'about nine out of ten applicants were refused'.[87] A. L. Smith saw no prospect of a relaxation in this policy, even with the increase in pressure to admit Indians by the withdrawal of compulsory Latin.

St John's College is a particularly good example of Oxford's admissions policy. Sidney Ball, a tutor, explained how initially Indians had been well-received and their numbers were high. This was reflected in the 1907 figures, St John's still had the highest number of Indians of any Oxford college. But then a backlash set in and Indians became less popular. This reached a peak when English undergraduates approached Ball and stated categorically that they disliked Indians and had too many in their college.[88] This feeling was expressed by an English undergraduate, P. J. Lewis, when he said that English undergraduates felt that 'their college lost caste in the eyes of the undergraduate world by too free an admission of Indian members'.[89] Thus pressure from English undergraduates had forced the university authorities to take action and restrict admissions.

Thirteen years later, the secretary to the Commission on Oxford and Cambridge Universities reiterated the position of the Lee Warner Report showing that the exclusion of Indians was still practised. 'It seems clear', he claimed, 'that the authorities of Oxford and Cambridge do not like Indian students, and that, while they will arrange for the admission of a limited number on the above lines, the numbers admitted will, in practice, be severely restricted as hitherto.'[90] One Cambridge official went further, arguing: 'Some colleges do not want Indians at all, one admits Parsees freely but has to be pressed to take other Indians. The largest colleges take fewest Indians.'

The authorities at both London and Edinburgh also expressed fears about the damaging consequences of rising numbers. J. B. Forbes Watson at Edinburgh University felt that colour prejudice would increase if the numbers of Indians grew.[91] In London apprehension had grown that the high number of law students was diluting the general quality of Indian students and there was great fear that men of second-rate ability would enter Britain. Several recommendations concerning law students were advanced in 1907 by the Inns of Court in order to regulate the entry of Indians and pursue a policy of greater selectivity. These included the equalisation of privileges between *vakils* and advocates, the imposition of special examinations exclusively for Indian students, and certificates of good character from British officials in India. Although the first two suggestions were abandoned as unworkable, character certificates were taken up.

It is clear that political considerations were a major factor in determining whether a certificate would be granted. In 1922 the sub-treasurer of the Inner Temple argued that it was essential to investigate the applicant's loyalty, and if an applicant were found wanting in this respect a certificate was not given.[92] Consequently, the authorities were able to control the political complexion of students and weed out overtly anti-British elements. Another device used to halt the influx of Indian students was to raise the standard for admissions. As a result the Council of Legal Education revised its rules in 1911. A simple examination was adequate until the end of 1910, but after this date all colonial students required a degree.

In 1911 T. W. Arnold, Educational Adviser to Indian Students in Britain, reported: 'no success has attended the efforts made to break down the opposition shown in several medical colleges, to the admission of Indian students'.[93] Professor William Wright, Dean of the London Hospital Medical College, which admitted more Indian students than any other hospital in England, acknowledged that racial prejudice was particularly strong among medical students and staff. English students fell into two camps: those who supported Indian students and those who objected to the admission of any Indians. However, the two opposing factions managed to reach a compromise at a meeting of English students in the hospital and the following resolution was agreed: 'This meeting expresses its opinion that great care should be taken in the admission of oriental students to this hospital, both as regards type of men and number of men admitted, and it considers that the distribution of oriental students amongst the medical schools of the country should be readjusted.'[94] In some London hospitals Egyptian students were admitted more readily than Indians. St Mary's Hospital had eight Egyptians and three Indians, while King's College Medical School had five Egyptians and one Indian. Hospital authorities claimed that restrictions against Indians were due to the prejudice of staff, patients and other students.

CASE STUDY: EDINBURGH INDIAN ASSOCIATION

The litigation embarked upon by an Indian student body, the Edinburgh Indian Association (EIA), in 1911 in order to win independence from the university authorities resulted in confrontation.[95] The EIA was launched in 1883 by a handful of Indian students. Twenty years later in 1903 its membership had increased from six to 50. Its constitution stated three primary objectives. Firstly, 'affording every personal assistance to the natives of India coming to this country for study or business'; secondly, 'promoting social intercourse among the Indian residents in this country'; and thirdly, 'holding debates'.[96]

The idea of securing a permanent centre or 'local habitation' for Indian students at Edinburgh University dated back to 1903, when Sir William Lee Warner, one-time President of the Association and Honorary Secretary, petitioned the India Office for funds from the Indian revenues.[97] A few objections were voiced on the grounds that such a club would result in segregation, establishing an alternative forum to the students' union, one where Indian students would be free to voice anti-British views. Despite these objections, proponents of the scheme launched an appeal in 1907 to raise £5,000. This time the method adopted was an Indian fair. The trustees of the Habitation Committee elected by the EIA, who were all academics at Edinburgh University, published a circular advertising the fair and stating arguments in favour of a habitation. The trustees saw the habitation not only as a club, providing the usual facilities of lecture, reading and debating rooms, but as a centre 'for mutual co-operation and intellectual and social intercourse' between Indian and Scottish students.[98] Lastly, there was the question of equality of treatment. Other colonial and African students were provided for separately; Indian students, it was argued, should have access to equal facilities.

Despite the apparent goodwill that existed between the EIA and the trustees of the habitation fund, the EIA sued the trustees in October 1911 in order to retrieve the funds raised by the Indian fair. Although the case appears to have been shrouded in legal wrangling, at its heart was the question of who controlled the habitation, the students or the trustees? The trustees of the habitation fund were appointed by members of the EIA and the Association's constitution stated that a trust deed 'shall confer upon the Trustees such powers of administration of both capital and income of the funds'.[99] However, the EIA refused to recognise the provision of the deed or abide by it, arguing that the funds raised were the property of the EIA and not the habitation trustees. The defendants, on the other hand, claimed that the bazaar's success was based on the fact the contributors believed all funds would be administered by the trustees, or 'a body of gentlemen … connected with the University of Edinburgh', and it was on this assumption that contributions to the fund were made.

Isabelle Salvenson, convenor of the bazaar, shows clearly that the university authorities were not prepared to tolerate a completely independent, Indian student body, with power over its internal structure and nomination of trustees. She wrote: 'I cannot see how it would do to give the members of the habitation, or the association itself, an unqualified right to nominate a Trustee.'[100] She further argued that the empowering of Indian students in this way could lead to resignations, if 'objectionable' individuals were elected. Salvenson stressed that the habitation regulations were framed by the trustees and not decided by the rank-and-file members of the EIA. Similarly 'internal administration was not to be exclusively in the hands of students, but of "others interested in them"'.[101]

Why were the university authorities reluctant to let the EIA take complete control of the habitation? It is clear from earlier objections to it that there were fears regarding the political character of the EIA. One of the trustees, A. H. I. Barbour, wrote: 'the more conservative element is outside the association'.[102] His inquiries into the EIA had revealed that its membership represented only 30 to 40 per cent of the whole Indian student population in Edinburgh. He wrote: 'I wish to safeguard the interests of the other more than 60 per cent.'[103] Barbour wanted to draw attention to the fact that the money raised was for the benefit of all Indian students and not just Association members. Thus the authorities' concern for the habitation was connected to fears that once an Indian student attended the club he would be pressed into joining the EIA, where he would imbibe subversive dogma. But if the authorities were able to act as a vigilant and restraining force on the Association's activities, through the role of trustees, it would be able to curtail the EIA's influence.

However, the trustees' opinion of the EIA as an extremist body does not match an eye-witness account of the Association's 1906 annual dinner, reported in the journal *Indian Magazine*: 'Good fellowship and loyalty was sufficiently guaranteed by the sympathetic way in which the toasts of the King and Queen and Royal Family were honoured by the hearty singing of the National Anthem at the close.' At the dinner the students were warned 'to be on their guard against seeking to introduce too sudden and drastic change among their naturally conservative fellow countrymen'.[104] The impression given by the same journal of an EIA annual dinner held three years earlier is of an organisation concerned with developing good Anglo-Indian relations. Far from being the exclusive, unrepresentative body that officials feared, it was described by an anonymous guest as the body to which all the Indian students at Edinburgh belonged and in which all regions and faiths were represented. In addition, he observed that Indians present at the dinner were all dressed in western clothes and that, in order to encourage good Anglo-Indian relations, the seats were alternated between English and Indian guests.[105] J. R. Reid, late secretary to the Government of North-Western Provinces, characterised most members of the EIA as 'probably National Congress types', but argued that, although their discussion might sound disloyal, 'the sound is worse than the meaning'.[106] This view is supported by an examination of the subjects debated by the Association. Its 1908–09 list of 13 debates shows that only three were overtly political.[107]

Attempts to control the activities of the Edinburgh Indian Association were not just confined to welfare and politics. There is evidence to show that the question of gender also provoked the authorities to intervene in its administration. When it was discovered that women were also eligible for membership, the university authorities, as represented by the trustees, were alarmed and made the following response: 'They [the trustees] cannot agree to ladies using the habitation on the same footing as men. They would point out no mention was made of such arrangements in the appeal for funds, which was contributed on the tacit understanding the habitation was to be like the university, for men only.'[108] It is ironic that Indian men, often castigated by British reformist organisations for being reactionary on the issue of women, were regarded as too advanced by some of the university's most illustrious professors. Even though the action was dismissed by the Court of Sessions in Edinburgh and the students failed to win the case, the episode demonstrates how strongly the students felt about their right to the habitation fund and ultimately freedom from university control.

PROTECTION AND PATERNALISM

The role of the British authorities as the protector of Indian students was extremely ambiguous and was connected to another prominent feature of British policy: paternalism. The authorities were not entirely clear exactly from whom or what they were protecting the student: external forces or the student's own base instincts? This is especially true in the case of student relations with white women shown earlier. Officials adhered to a contradictory logic. On the one hand, the Indian student was a sexual predator, occupying the folk-devil niche of 'dark stranger', threatening the stability of the host population (and indirectly the Raj, as the virtue of British women was a cornerstone of the empire) by seducing and marrying British women, producing a 'moral panic' which was luridly presented in the press and the popular literature of the period. However, on the other, government officials often privately regarded Indians as victims in need of protection, duped by the machinations of conniving landladies' daughters and other unsavoury characters. Sir Owen Burne (ex-Political ADC), writing to Sir Curzon Wyllie in 1903, attempted to reconcile these contradictory stereotypes: 'in England white women rush at them and they are only too willing to become their victims. This is specially the case with women of the town.' Burne found this predilection absurd when he compared the attitude of 'Memsahibs' in India towards Indians: 'In India white women hate and despise the ordinary Bengali Baboos.'[109]

Only in confidential correspondence did British officials ever admit this unthinkable preference of some white women for Indians. When the subject was handled in the press a more conventional stance was predictably taken, presenting the student as a debauched individual. A newspaper article of January 1909 entitled 'White Women and Coloured Men' is a classic example of this. The author, C. Hamilton McGuiness, was in no doubt who needed to be shielded: the honour of white women against entrapment by Indian students. The author claimed to speak from experience; he had lived in a house with Indian students and observed their behaviour. The racial antagonism was palpable in the language and tone of the article. He wrote:

> The absolute prohibition of intercourse between our women and these crafty and cunning heathen cannot be too strongly urged ... It is positively nauseating to see them on the tops of buses, in the streets, at the theatres and almost everywhere one goes – coloured men and white women. These women have not the slightest idea of what grave risks they are running. Neither have they any knowledge of the cunning morals of the men with whom they are associating.[110]

He believed that the smart appearance and charming and gentlemanly manners of these men served as a veneer to mask 'a crafty and half-civilised nature'.

McGuiness argued that the root of the problem was education. Not only were 'some of these men ... far better educated than many white folk' but, in addition, he complained, 'It is because these people go to our universities, are treated there as gentlemen, and trusted accordingly that they get to know so many white women', and eventually 'accomplish the ruining of these white women through their plausible tales of eastern life'. He advocated police intervention in interracial liaisons and at the very least the ostracism of such couples 'by all decent English people'. In conclusion he wrote with some urgency: 'Now before the evil reaches any larger proportions is the time to insist on these Asiatics being placed in their proper positions. They should not be allowed to communicate with or go through any form of marriage with a white woman.'[111] The 1913 government circular, mentioned earlier, warning white women of the perils of interracial marriage at registry offices went some way to meeting this concern. In his article McGuiness combined the three elements necessary to create a 'moral panic': exaggeration of events, prediction of similar events and symbolisation.[112]

The ambivalence of British official thinking and the further divergence of public pronouncements and private conjecture on the issue of Indian students and white women illustrate the complexity of the subject. Nevertheless, it is clear that the authorities believed the Indian student was in urgent need of protection, whether from himself or others. The potential pitfalls were women, alcohol and the lodging-house culture in general, particularly in the metropolis, where undesirable habits could be quickly assimilated. These were all entrapments from which students needed rescuing. Several officials believed that their vulnerability was exacerbated by the fact that they arrived in Britain with large sums of money for their courses, making them magnets for unscrupulous individuals.

Without the necessary protection and supervision, the steward of Gray's Inn, J. B. Douthwaite, was convinced that many Indian students would meet a bad end. In his letter to the India Office in 1902, Douthwaite described the downward path to ruin taken by a typical Indian student. Having arrived in London he was befriended by another Indian and was taken to all the disreputable haunts. The student then went further into debt until he was penniless. The steward claimed such reprobates were apt to come to his notice when complaints were made by other students who had been defrauded of money. But, according to Douthwaite, the most dangerous period for a student was when he first arrived and the greatest source of danger was his own compatriots. Muslims in particular were singled out as the worst offenders. Although from his own study of the records of 74 Indian students only ten could be described as completely dissolute, he still concluded: 'If an Indian goes under he usually goes beyond hope of redemption ... The Indian seems to have no power of recovery.'[113]

The stakes were high; although the student population was small in size its influence on Indian opinion was disproportionately large. The importance of the England-returned was reflected in Lord Minto's correspondence:

> On their return to India they find that, in their own country, their social position is entirely changed. They are generally excluded from European clubs and there is no professional career open to them. We already face a rising generation of young men with ambitions, which we have ourselves encouraged, but which we deny any openings. The question to my mind is one of the most important which we have to deal with in India.[114]

Officials were well aware that the consequences of not shielding students from negative influences in Britain would make them 'centres of sedition'[115] when they returned to India. The Vice-Chancellor of Liverpool University believed that constant exposure to the 'lodging-house class or worse' would result in Indians returning to India with a misleading impression of British life. He wrote: 'they would be exposed to frequent affronts on account of their foreignness and would go back embittered … As a result, instead of their estimate of Great Britain and the British being raised, it would be very definitely lowered. Politically, we regard this as a most harmful state of affairs and are unwilling to encourage it.'[116]

The British view of Indian students as particularly susceptible to adverse influences was the result of a paternalistic attitude that was so insidious that it invaded every aspect of their thinking. All non-European subjects of the empire, by virtue of their dependent position and racial inheritance, were deemed to be essentially childlike. This was most visible in the concept of guardianship, when the guardian, who was quite often a representative of the British government, would act *in loco parentis* and thereby take the place of a parent, the very essence of paternalism. The language and tone deployed to describe Indian students in Britain was clearly paternalistic. For example, John Pollen wrote:

> [T]he Indian student has often been 'nobody's child' – the common care that no-one cared for. It may be that he himself does not care to be cared for, but nevertheless care is good for him … that he may return to India a broader-minded man and a better citizen in consequence of his stay amongst us.[117]

This paternalism is also reflected indirectly in the considerable weight given to the 'British home' within the parameters of the Indian student debate. This almost sacred institution was venerated and regarded as a panacea against society's vices. British officials believed contact with English family life would guard Indian students from potential dangers and temptations. One of the aims of the National Indian Association was to introduce Indians to private families through social gatherings. As early as 1875 the Association's journal expressed the following opinion: 'We believe that nothing gives to the Hindu gentlemen a higher appreciation of the English character and a greater desire to infuse its spirit into India, than residence with an English family.'[118] This emphasis on the British home as a solution to the Indian student problem was an extension of paternalism.

PARALLELS WITH OTHER GROUPS OF INDIANS

The persistence of these characteristics in British policy towards other groups of Indians in Britain in the late nineteenth and the early twentieth century shows that students were not unique in the treatment they received. The same fears and prejudices informed dealings with princes and soldiers. British policy towards princes set the precedent for the treatment of students. The parallels are numerous. In 1900 the Viceroy of India, Lord Curzon, issued a circular requiring all Indian nobles to request leave of absence from the Government of India before travelling to Europe. Although a circular system could not be implemented for students, as shown earlier, several devices were employed to restrict the student population in England. Just as the British authorities attempted to use the system of guardianship to manipulate and control student behaviour, for princes both these functions were partially fulfilled by political officers, who accompanied the princes during their trips to Europe.

Both groups were expected to avoid westernisation, while simultaneously imbibing western values from the British education system. In the case of the princes this involved remaining either Hindu or Muslim rather than converting to Christianity.[119] Princes were also urged to marry within their community, instead of following the example set by a few who chose to marry European women. The most notorious cases include the Maharaja of Patiala, the Rajah of Pudukottai, the Maharaja of Jind and the Maharaja of Kapurthala.[120] Lastly, Lord Curzon was keen that the princes should avoid foreign travel, remaining within the confines of their states and devoting themselves entirely to princely duties. These contradictory expectations reveal the competing demands of essentialism, on the one hand, represented by the fear of deracination and an emphasis on traditional Indian values, and hybridity on the other, which required Indian princes to adopt the English public school system of education provided at Rajkot College, with its emphasis on gentlemanly conduct and the absorption of British values and customs.

There was also confusion about the exact status of Indian princes in British society. As aristocrats they could expect a certain amount of homage, but their race and subordinate position in relation to the British undermined their position. The ambiguity surrounding the princes was further compounded by the fact that no precise precedence for the treatment of ruling princes in Britain had ever been established. However princes and students did differ in a fundamental way. Princes symbolised a conservative model of government and society, whereas students represented a bureaucratic and democratic element. Nevertheless, for the British it was crucial that neither group became alienated from their countrymen or British rule as both had important roles to play in ensuring the continuance of the Raj. Western education played a crucial role in creating and improving Indian allies.

Not only did Curzon do his utmost to limit princely visits to Britain, but he reacted in a similar fashion when it was suggested that the King proposed to keep Indian bodyguards in London. Unofficial newspaper reports were enough to make Curzon raise the matter with the Secretary of State for India, Lord Hamilton, in 1901: 'No body of Indian soldiers can be located for any length of time in England and least of all London, without being hopelessly demoralised and permanently spoiled.'[121] He suggested that the same precautions be taken with Indian troops as had been taken in Australia, where they had been housed outside the cities.

The isolation of soldiers was to ensure that relations with females of the host community be kept to a minimum. Just as with students, concern was as much for the protection of soldiers as for the honour of white women. Hamilton wrote to Curzon:

> There has always been such difficulty experienced in keeping low-class white women away from coloured soldiers, that on all previous occasions special precautions have had to be adopted, and I think that if any number of Indian troops do come over, we shall have to locate them in barracks, say at Woolwich.[122]

He noted:

> there is another very unpleasant characteristic which has developed itself during the last few years and that is the craze of white women for running after black men. Apparently it pervades all classes of society: the smartest peeresses were only too ready to make a fuss with Bikaner and other Indian chiefs, and as you go lower in the social scale, so does this tendency manifest itself more strongly, and in a way characteristic of the habits and lives of the respective classes of the community. At Hampton Court the great difficulty of officers was in keeping the white women away from our Native soldiers.[123]

Indian soldiers were not the only soldiers receiving female attention. African soldiers at Alexandra Palace attracted similar interest. Jealousy on the part of the Australian and New Zealand contingent nearly led to a fracas. Even when the question of Indian orderlies for the King was raised in the same year, 1901, the issue of English women repeatedly dominated discussions between Hamilton and Curzon. Hamilton wrote: 'If the men were carefully selected, they would, in all probability, be very fine specimens of humanity and women in this country might run after them.'[124] In response to the King's suggestion, Curzon replied that initially he felt the idea to be a feasible and good one; nevertheless he had familiar reservations:

> The 'woman' aspect of the question is rather a difficulty, since strange as it might seem, English women of the housemaid class and even higher, do

offer themselves to these Indian soldiers, attracted by their uniform, enamoured of their physique, and with a sort of idea that the warrior is also an oriental prince.[125]

Official concern about female sexuality reveals how gender and race were socially constructed and intersected in imperial Britain.

During the First World War when Indian soldiers were sent to hospitals in Britain concerns about women led to draconian restrictions on Indian soldiers' freedom of movement and association. The characteristics of the British policy towards princes and students – control, restriction, racial stereotyping and protection – were all evident in the extreme measures taken to prevent soldiers from leaving the hospitals unsupervised. Not only were no women permitted within hospital precincts, but a stringent system of passes was introduced. Those permitted to venture outside the confines of Kitchener Hospital in Brighton had to travel in groups accompanied by a British officer, 'to prevent communications and presents passing between the men and the outside public'.[126] Barbed wire and sentries further enhanced the impression of an impregnable fortress. Of the seven Indians who tried to escape, six were flogged and one was imprisoned for six weeks. No doubt it was hoped that such harsh penalties would act as a deterrent and, judging from the small numbers of escapees, the policy appeared to have been successful. Complaints about restrictions led to the establishment of a committee of enquiry. Predictably it concluded that the hospitals were homes-from-home for Indian soldiers, a part of India transferred to English soil, fulfilling all an Indian's wants and making frequent excursions unnecessary. Blatant infringements of civil liberties in this manner were easily accomplished in wartime in the defence of the realm; it would have been more difficult to detain students and princes in this manner during peacetime.

It was not just over the question of women that such approaches were adopted; the potentially damaging effects of residence in England overshadowed a great deal of official thinking on Indians in Britain. Paternalistic solutions show continuity of policy; for example, the system of guardianship established for students and the political officers attached to princes visiting Europe were both intended to provide guidance and protection from nefarious influences. British officials were united in the belief that residence in Britain had an unsettling effect on most groups of Indians. However, this manifested itself in different ways. In the case of the princes, officials were more concerned about denationalising tendencies, whereas students presented an immediate, political problem. Although the stereotype of the hybrid England-returned student, 'completely divorced in thought and feeling from the kindly family life and interests of their people', was also apparent in official discourse towards students.[127]

Here, too, it is possible to draw comparisons with the contradictory demands placed on the princes mentioned earlier. Students were also expected to assimilate British values while adhering to Indian orthodoxy. Indians who attempted to acquire a gentlemanly persona were lampooned in works such as *Baboo Jabberjee*, and those who did not conform to this prescribed code of conduct were rebuked for being aloof. Students were in an impossible position: acceptance into college life and British society at large required them to absorb gentlemanly values; but those that did so were accused by both the British and Indians of being denationalised. The ambiguity of the Indian princes' class position within the hierarchical structure of British society was also true of students. Students came mainly from middle-class backgrounds, yet in Britain the majority of students lived in boarding houses and rented accommodation, sometimes in an impoverished condition, exposed almost exclusively to working-class society, usually in the form of the landlady and her family. As a result their class position was confused and their threatening hybridity became more pronounced. Nevertheless, it was political discontent that provoked more immediate concern, as a result of which the British government watched the movements of students. Other groups of Indians do not seem to have been kept under surveillance. In this respect the policy towards students was unique.

In this chapter I have argued that there was a fundamental reciprocity in British relations with Indians, both in Britain and in India. Anxiety about Indian students was symptomatic of the paranoia and apprehension of the Edwardian period. On the domestic front Indians presented a political and sexual threat. These attitudes were influenced by racial and cultural stereotyping in Britain and more specifically by the new and radical direction taken by the Indian National Congress. This new radical nationalism caused British officials to move away from the non-interventionist policies of the nineteenth century and become more racially conscious in Britain, resulting in more repressive policies, characterised by control, restriction and exclusion. The hardening of British policy in turn produced greater radicalisation among students in Britain, which cascaded back into Indian nationalism when the students returned to India. Thus the effects of policy in the metropole, Britain, constantly fed back into the periphery, India, where they again stimulated policy in the metropole, producing a dynamic interplay between the centre and the periphery.

It is important to add that policy towards other groups of Indians – princes and soldiers – discussed above also reflected British concerns about India. British policy towards Indians in Britain was also marked by ambivalence, oscillating between incorporation and differentiation. Students faced contradictory demands of absorption into collegiate life, without compromising their 'essential otherness' and succumbing to hybridity.[128]

NOTES

1   For a general survey of the political situation in India during this period see S. Sarkar, *Modern India 1885–1947* (London: Macmillan, 1989), Chapter 4.
2   (IOL) L/P&J/6/845, p. 75.
3   M. A. Pinhey, 'England as a Training Ground for Young India', *Indian Magazine and Review*, No. 245 (1891), p. 228. I have not been able to find out more about Mary Pinhey.
4   Ibid.
5   Ibid., p. 229.
6   (IOL) L/P&J/6/845, p. 162.
7   Ibid.
8   (IOL) W1757, p. 50.
9   Ibid., p. 259.
10   Ibid., p. 175.
11   Ibid., p. 260.
12   Ibid., p. 284.
13   (IOL) W1757, p. 6.
14   E. Dicey, 'Hindu Students in England', *Nineteenth Century and After*, 66 (1909), p. 351.
15   Ibid., p. 356.
16   K. E. Kirk, 'Indian Students in England', *Nineteenth Century and After*, 66 (1909), p. 604.
17   (IOL) W1757, p. 1.
18   (IOL) L/P&J/6/845, p. 240.
19   Ibid., p. 175.
20   Ibid., p. 183. H. Jackson had been Senior Tutor at Downing College, Cambridge, for five years.
21   Ballhatchet, *Race, Sex and Class under the Raj*, p. 6.
22   R. Hyam, *Empire and Sexuality: The British Experience* (Manchester: Manchester University Press, 1990), p. 205.
23   (IOL) L/P&J/6/5845, p. 75.
24   Ibid., p. 283.
25   Ibid., p. 247.
26   (IOL) L/P&J/6/1225, 1913, No. 847.
27   *Daily Mail*, 1 May 1913.
28   *Indian Magazine*, No. 453 (September 1908), p. 245.
29   J. Green and R. Lotz, 'A Brown Alien in a White City', in R. Lotz and I. Pegg (eds), *Under the Imperial Carpet: Essays in Black History* (Crawley: Rabbit Press, 1986), p. 210.
30   (IOL) POS 8961, Indian Home Department, Political, Part B, No. 121, 22 May 1909.
31   (IOL) R/2 (33/312) Memo on Anti-British Agitation, p. 41.
32   (IOL) Appendix 4, p. 101.

33 (IOL) L/P&J/6/845, p. 179.
34 (IOL) Appendix 4, p. 102.
35 Sir Charles Alfred Elliott (1835–1911) served in the Indian Civil Service, rising to Lieutenant-Governor of Bengal, until he retired in 1895 and returned to Britain. Before becoming a member of the Lee Warner Committee, he had served on the London School Board and London County Council.
36 (IOL) L/P&J/6/845, p. 102.
37 (IOL) L/P&J/6/903, No. 4223, 1908. Sir Charles James Lyall (1844–1920) held various posts in the Indian Civil Service before joining the India Office in 1898. He also gave evidence to the Lee Warner Committee. Unlike Elliott, Lyall was an orientalist. He published several books on Hinduism and Arab poetry, took part in establishing the School of Oriental and African Studies and was active in the Royal Asiatic Society.
38 (IOL) L/P&J/6/845, p. 102.
39 Ibid., p. 179.
40 Ibid., p. 178.
41 (IOL) L/P&J/6/845, p. 108.
42 (IOL) R/2 (33/12), p. 40.
43 D. Garnett, *The Golden Echo* (London: Chatto & Windus, 1953), p. 149.
44 *Daily News*, 10 April 1909.
45 (IOL) L/P&J/ 6/939, No. 349, 1910.
46 (IOL) L/P&J/6/845, p. 212.
47 Jaini, *Fragments*, p. 185.
48 (IOL) L/P&J/6/903, No. 4223, 5 November 1908.
49 (IOL) POS 8962, Indian Home Department (Political), Part B, August 1909.
50 (IOL) L/P&J/6/881, No. 2627, 15 July 1908.
51 (IOL) L/P&J/6/939, No. 1849, 1909.
52 According to Rajani Palme Dutt, the name had its origins in the Persian revolution with the formation of a parliament or 'Majlis'. The Majlis were peculiar to Oxford and Cambridge. Both were formed at the beginning of the twentieth century and continued until Indian independence in 1947, and at Oxford to the present day. Meetings at Oxford were mainly attended by ICS probationers. Sri Lankan and Burmese students were also present at meetings. C. L. R. James regularly attended the Oxford Majlis. Symonds, *Oxford and Empire*.
53 Public Record Office, Kew: F.O. 371/4243.
54 (IOL) V/27/267/1, p. 27. Madam Bhikarji Cama (1861–1936) was born into a prosperous Parsi business family and married in 1885. She went into Europe in 1902 for medical treatment, where she became involved with Indian revolutionaries in London, Paris and Moscow. She served a three-and-a-half-year prison sentence in Paris for her political activities. When she was released, at the end of the First World War, she chose to reside in Paris before returning to India.
55 (IOL) MSS. Eur. D. 573/3.
56 (IOL) L/P&J/6/962, No. 3280, 16 August 1909.
57 L/P&J/6/ 924, No. 758, 1909.
58 MSS. Eur. F. 166/8.
59 MSS. Eur. F. 92/10.
60 (IOL) L/P&J/6/1061, No. 440, 7 February 1911.
61 (IOL) POS 5943, Indian Home Department (Political), Part A, April 1909.
62 *The Times*, 31 January 1910, p. 5.
63 Ibid.

64 (IOL) POS 5945, Indian Home Department (Political), Part A, No. 148, 4 March 1909.
65 Ibid., No. 133-35, May 1910.
66 Despite its lack of success, the implementation of identity certificates, which provided information on the financial and social status of Indian students at the beginning of the century, was another attempt to manipulate the types of student arriving in Britain. See Introduction.
67 In 1907 the India Office offered to fund half the costs needed to amalgamate the NIA, Northbrook Society and East India Association into one body, renamed the Northbrook Club. It was hoped that such a substantial investment 'would entitle the India Office to a large control over the management of the Northbrook Club'. But the amalgamation did not take place. (IOL) W1757, p. 92.
68 *Edinburgh Review*, Vol. 217, No. 443 (January 1913).
69 (IOL) L/P&J/6/642, No. 1638, 1903.
70 (IOL) MSS. Eur. F. 147/4.
71 *Journal of the National Indian Association*, No. 175 (July 1885).
72 (IOL) L/P&J/6/845, p. 87.
73 Ibid., p. 116.
74 (IOL) Report of the First Three Years of the Bureau of Information, L/P&J/6/1120, 1911, p. 55.
75 (IOL) L/P&J/6/1120, 1911, p. 60.
76 Ibid., p. 62.
77 Ibid., p. 47.
78 (IOL) Indian Student Department Report 1916–20, V/24/832, p. 26.
79 (IOL) W1757, p. 111.
80 Muckerjee, *W. C. Bonnerjee*, p. 2.
81 Appendix 4, p. 77.
82 *Cambridge Review*, Vol. 30, No. 756 (13 May 1909).
83 Gopal, *Selected Works*, p. 65, 12 March 1909.
84 Ibid., p. 66, 14 May 1909.
85 (IOL) L/P&J/6/845, p. 230.
86 Ibid., p. 236.
87 Ibid., p. 239.
88 Ibid., p. 240.
89 (IOL) Appendix 4, p. 77.
90 (IOL) L/P&J/6/1707, No. 6900, 1920.
91 (IOL) Appendix 4, p. 284.
92 (IOL) W1757, p. 160.
93 (IOL) W1757, p. 222.
94 (IOL) Report of the Indian Student Department, 1913–14.
95 In much the same way the issue arose of who would assume authority over a West African student hostel during the First World War. See H. Adi, 'West African Students in Britain (1900–60): Politics of Exile', *Immigrants and Minorities*, 12, 3 (1993), pp. 107–25.
96 Edinburgh University Library. Box Da 67 Ind, Folder 1, Constitution, Law and Regulations of the Edinburgh Indian Association, 1905, Chapter 1.
97 (IOL) L/P&J/6/625, No. 193, 1903.
98 Edinburgh University Library. Box Da 67 Ind, Folder 1.
99 Ibid., Constitution of EIA, 1905, Chapter 6, p. 25.

100 Edinburgh University Library. Box Da 67 Ind, Folder 3, 26 May 1911.
101 Ibid.
102 Edinburgh University Library. Box Da 67 Ind, Folder 1, 9 November 1910.
103 Ibid.
104 *Indian Magazine and Review*, No. 423 (March 1906), p. 64.
105 Ibid., No. 388 (April 1903).
106 (IOL) L/P&J/6/625, No. 193, 1903.
107 Edinburgh University Library. Box Da 67 Ind, Folder 1, Syllabus of Meetings 1908–09.
108 Ibid., Folder 3, n.d.
109 (IOL) L/P&J/6/642, No. 1638, 18 May 1903. Similarly at a contemporary exhibition at Earls Court called 'Savage South Africa' it was unclear who presented the greater danger, the Africans on display or the women who went to see them. This view was recorded in a newspaper at the time: 'The outcry was at first against the danger that these natives would run in a huge city and strange land. It looks as though, by the strange irony of fate, some of the "conquering race" require to be saved from themselves … it has become notorious that English women have petted and pampered these specimens of lower race in a manner which must sicken those who know the facts.' B. Shephard, 'Showbiz Imperialism – The Case of Peter Logengula', in J. M. MacKenzie (ed.), *Imperialism and Popular Culture* (Manchester: Manchester University Press, 1986) pp. 102–3.
110 *London Opinion*, 9 January 1909, p. 72. He was making particular reference to 'Hindoos and Japanese'. I have not been able to find out more about C. Hamilton McGuiness.
111 This hysterical reaction to interracial marriage is also reflected in the case of the African performer Peter Logengula when he attempted to marry an English woman. See Shephard, 'Showbiz Imperialism'.
112 See S. Cohen, *Folk Devils and Moral Panics* (London: MacGibbon & Kee, 1972).
113 (IOL) L/P&J/6/642, No. 1638, 1903.
114 MSS. Eur. D. 573/17, Minto to Morley, 2 September 1908.
115 MSS. Eur. F. 147/30, East India Association memorandum, 27 November 1908, p. 9.
116 W1757, Dr J. G. Adami, p. 85.
117 (IOL) L/P&J/6/903, No. 4223, p. 9. John Pollen (1848–1923) was Secretary of the East India Association, 1909–20; Orientalist (Linguist in Indian Languages), Collector and Magistrate in India and Political Officer for Indian Princes at Edward VII's coronation.
118 *Journal of the National Indian Association*, 1875, Fourth Annual Report, p. 4.
119 Some officials were concerned that lack of religious instruction would result in conversions. For a discussion of this and other issues concerning princes in Britain see S. Lahiri, 'British Policy towards Indian Princes in Late Nineteenth and Early Twentieth-Century Britain', *Immigrants and Minorities*, 15, 3 (1996), pp. 214–32
120 Ibid.
121 (IOL) MSS. Eur. F. 111/160, 8 May 1902, p. 130.
122 (IOL) Ibid., 25 September 1901.
123 (IOL) MSS. Eur. F. 111/161, 17 September 1902, p. 130. The interest shown by white women for the 'Savage Africa' exhibition at Earls Court, where Africans were on public display, caused the *Daily Mail* to campaign to close the area where Africans were housed. But instead the management of the exhibition banned women; 600 women a day were turned away. Shephard, 'Showbiz Imperialism'.

124 (IOL) MSS. Eur. F. 111/160, 23 October 1901.

125 Ibid., 15 November 1901.

126 (IOL) MSS. Eur. F. 143/82, A Report on the Kitchener Indian Hospital, Brighton by Colonel Sir Bruce Seton, p. 9.

127 (IOL) V/24/832, Indian Student Department Report 1929, T. Quayle, p. 19.

128 Thomas Metcalf has also argued that a tension existed 'between two ideals, one of similarity and the other of difference' which shaped strategies of British rule in India. One highlighted characteristics which Indians shared with the British, the other emphasised 'enduring qualities of Indian difference'. Thomas. R. Metcalf, *Ideologies of the Raj* (Cambridge: Cambridge University Press, 1995), p. x.

5

Indian Reactions:
Identification and Resistance

SOME of the best-documented sources of Indian reactions to residence in Britain are in the published accounts of individuals who visited Britain in the last quarter of the nineteenth century. While some, such as R. C. Dutt, came to study, most were either on government service or travelling for pleasure. Two of the most informative writers were women. Although these visitors may not have intended to take up academic studies in Britain, nevertheless they considered themselves to be students of European society, reflecting on all they observed. Their accounts encouraged more students to journey to England, breaking the taboo on foreign travel.[1] In this chapter I shall investigate general Indian responses to aspects of British life. This will be followed by a more detailed examination of specific student grievances, culminating in the politicisation of the student population.

ADMIRATION

A number of the early sojourners described the welcome they received in England. For example, in 1883 an Indian officer visiting England wrote to *The Times*: 'Everywhere we were heartily cheered.'[2] Many Indians were surprised to find themselves unmolested on the streets of London. It is clear that the first generation of arrivals were the beneficiaries of a unique status in British society, although the example of individuals such as U. P. Dutt shows that initial acceptance was not always easily won. Their curiosity value is demonstrated in the case of T. N. Mukharji, sent by the Government of India to attend the Colonial and Indian Exhibition in London. He noted that he and his companion received most patronage from women, who regarded them both as novelties and marvelled at their every movement. Mukharji took great pleasure in recounting false and outlandish tales of his exploits in India, which excited little suspicion from his gullible female audience. The two Indians subsequently became a feature of fashionable London society.

Mukharji and his contemporaries were struck by how Englishmen altered when they left England: 'The British people take a pride in being kind to strangers. The manners of an Englishman, however, undergo some change when he is outside his own country ... he is proud and somewhat disdainful.'[3] P. M. Chowdhury also observed in his book *British Experiences* 'the vast difference between the English at home and the English in India'.[4] Hafiz Ahmed Hassan, addressing a meeting of the Bristol branch of the National Indian Association, told his audience: 'The very affable and obliging manners of the English ladies and gentlemen "at home" ... are in full contrast to the blunt and cold manners they assume in India.'[5]

Certain aspects of British life impressed these nineteenth-century observers. Dwarkanath Tagore, who crossed the 'Kala Pani' (Black Waters) in 1842, wrote to his son Debendranath:

> After seeing everything on this continent I did not much expect that I should be so much taken by this little island; but really London is a wonderful city ... I do not think anyone could spend his life in a better climate. With operas and theatres I need not tell you how much I have been gratified. The beauty of the ladies in England puts me in mind of the fairy tales. What I read in my younger days in Persian tales, I begun to see in London. If a man has wealth this is the country to enjoy it.[6]

R. C. Dutt was also very partial to the theatre in England. He confessed: 'There is hardly any sort of amusement which gives me greater pleasure than going to theatres, if I had plenty of time at my disposal I should, I think, be at the theatre almost every evening.'[7] Sarat Chandra Bose (the brother of Subhas Chandra Bose) was also enthusiastic about the English theatre: 'What scenes! What acting! In our country, no one will dream that such things can take place. I think that people who come here should go to the theatre. One can learn many things.'[8] But he was wary of its addictive quality: 'If you go too much, then it gets to be a habit and I won't do that. I have been only four times, while others have gone forty times.'

Several Indians were impressed by the 'beauty' and 'nobility' of the English home.[9] The law student M. R. Jayakar admired British life, not in terms of cultural pursuits but in a more abstract sense:

> The clean brass doorplate, the call, the prim parlour-maid, Westminster Abbey, St Thomas's Hospital ... they are all linked together as an expression of the general sturdiness of community, its compactness, its love of method, dominant patriotism and a quiet desire for work and to make the best of life while it lasts.[10]

He felt that these aspects of British life were worthy of imitation in India. It was difficult for Indian visitors to ignore British technological advancement, although only a few of the early ones appear to have devoted much space to British scientific achievements within their accounts of England.[11] Lala Baijnath believed Europe was speeding ahead of India in the field of science and technology,[12] while P. J. Ragaviah described London as 'an immense tree which bears scientific fruits of every description'. The Wadia brothers, among the earliest Indian visitors to Britain, were fascinated by every aspect of British industry, including steam power and railway and tunnel technology.[13] Mukharji attributed the higher standard of living enjoyed in England, not to scientific prowess, but to 'love of comfort, combined with beauty. They know better than we do how to live well and how to secure the means to live well.'[14] This he argued was reflected in the proliferation of civic buildings, symbolising local pride. Books and verbal accounts of England could not sufficiently prepare newcomers for what they would encounter. It was the sheer difference between Indian and British society which overawed many Indians.

FREEDOM

One feature of British life referred to by visitors and students alike, from the late nineteenth to the early twentieth century, was the social and political freedom they witnessed and were able to enjoy. R. C. Dutt marvelled at the democratic rights available to British men and women. He noted the enormous interest taken at general elections:

> Every man in this country considering himself as a constituent part of a great and mighty nation, prides himself on the nationality and glory of the nation and therefore keeps a fixed eye on the welfare of his country … Such is England, a country where the people govern themselves – what wonder if such a people have secured for themselves an amount of political liberty which is nowhere else to be found on the face of the globe.[15]

No doubt the seeds of Dutt's nationalism were sown during his residence in Britain, where for the first time in his life he was able to witness a democracy in action. In addition he observed jealously, how such rights and liberties infused England with

> the spirit of independence and self-reliance which pervades every institution and every class of people … There are hardly any traces here of that baneful patriarchal system on which every institution in our country may be said to be based. Relative duties of different classes of people are determined here with an eye towards utility and not towards sentimental idealism.[16]

Lack of dependence was also noted in the treatment of children and domestics: 'Children in this country are not bondsmen to their parents nor are servants slaves. Possessed of a wonderful amount of self-respect, the servant and labouring classes of England deserve and receive a degree of good treatment from their masters, unheard of in oriental countries.'[17] P. J. Ragaviah also commented on the superior position occupied by British in comparison with Indian servants; but she was less certain of the propriety of English servants earning 'wages equal to that of a native clerk in government service'.[18]

Numerous students throughout the period commented on their newly acquired personal liberty, particularly those who attended Oxford. J. Jaini wrote at the beginning of the century: 'There is a freedom and spontaneity, real expression of life, an unrestrained (almost primitive) joy and enjoyment of fellow-feeling.'[19] In the post-war period N. G. Ranga noted the sense of liberation that came over Indian students within a few months at Oxford: 'We began to feel free from so many of the inhibitions of our Indian social environment.' He described 'the air of Europe' as 'politically, a liberating, intoxicating influence'.[20] Even Subhas Chandra Bose – not usually complimentary towards the British – was keen to stress how much he relished his freedom in Britain, in contrast to 'a police-ridden city like Calcutta, where every student was looked upon as a potential revolutionary and suspect'. He wrote: 'One can see here how man should treat his fellow man.'[21] The prospect of departure caused one student to experience nightmares and another to lament: 'An atmosphere of liberty and peace will be replaced by one of slavery and disquiet.'[22] However, this praise must be qualified. Emphasis on political freedom in Britain, regarded as commonplace after the First World War, was also a criticism of British rule. British freedom was a standard against which Indian subjugation was judged. Many students complained about government surveillance operations and other oppressive measures, as will be shown later, which further serves to reinforce the impression that the statements quoted earlier are partly rhetorical.

Women were one group of Indians who particularly savoured the relative latitude of life in Britain. After returning to India, Toru Dutt long cherished the hope of one day revisiting England. On 11 May 1874 she wrote to a friend in England: 'We all want so much to return to England. We miss the free life we led there, here we can hardly go out to the limits of our garden.'[23] Another woman, Krishnabhabani Das, of whom little appears to be known although she may have lived in Cambridge with her husband for 14 years,[24] wrote about the liberation she felt during her residence in England. A remarkable insight may be gained from the following:

There is a popular saying that even a slave becomes free as soon as he steps on the soil of England. I myself can feel very well that there has been a significant change in my attitudes and values since I started to breathe in the open air of England and to live with the free people of that country. I am unable to describe this change to the brothers and sisters of my country. I did not know anything of this while I was in India. I even did not think that the life of a person could be so different. I used to read about other countries – some independent, some under the rule of others, some democratic and some autocratic – but was unable to realise the significance of all these terms. I can now see that I used to imagine all other countries more or less like mine, because at that time, I was like a blind person to whom day and night had no difference.[25]

Krishnabhabini's perception of freedom in England was heightened by comparison with her previous existence within the confines of a *zenana*, which served to accentuate the difference between the two life-styles. Mary Bhore, who spent a year as a student at Somerville College, Oxford, was surprised at 'the freedom of life permitted women in England'.[26] Yet her description of the life of students at Somerville appears to contradict this opinion. According to Bhore, strict regulations put tight limits on the conduct and movement of women students. Contact between female and male students was prohibited and women students were constantly chaperoned.

Curtailment of freedom and attempts to exercise control over Indian students provoked bitter resentment and resulted in student suspicion and criticism. The following case studies are examples of students who came into direct confrontation with the British authorities over this issue. They were strikingly different individuals: Pandita Ramabai came to Britain in 1883 to study at Cheltenham Ladies College and Captain Thimayya enrolled at Sandhurst Royal Military Academy in 1924. Gender, background and some four decades separated them.

Pandita Ramabai was the product of an unconventional upbringing. Born in 1858 into a Marathi Brahmin family, she had accompanied her father and the rest of the family on pilgrimages around India.[27] Pandita's parents died when she was 16, by which time she was already fluent in Sanskrit, Marathi, Kanarese, Hindustani and Bengali, all taught to her by her mother, who had in turn been educated by her husband. Pandita and her brother travelled around India advocating female education. Six months after her brother died she married a Bengali, Bipin Bihari Medhavi, but he too died only two months after the birth of their daughter. She continued to lecture on female emancipation and in 1881 gave evidence to the Hunter Commission. Pandita decided to study medicine in England, believing it to be the only way she could effectively assist Indian women. The sisters of the community of St Mary the Virgin, Wantage, enabled her to travel to Britain. She perfected her English and eventually went to Cheltenham Ladies' College (having abandoned her plans to become a doctor), where she became Professor of Sanskrit and studied mathematics, natural science and English literature. During her three years as a student and teacher in England she converted to Christianity.[28]

Pandita's relationship with the missionary establishment in England was far from smooth. She was particularly sensitive to anything she believed constituted an infringement of her liberty. Her letters contain several examples of indignant outbursts whenever she disagreed with a decision which would compromise her personal freedom. She wrote one such angry letter to Dorothea Beale, the principal of the college and her personal tutor, on 8 May 1885, referring to a decision to prevent her teaching Sanskrit to boys in England. A matter over which she threatened to leave:

> They have no right to decide anything for me ... And I shall not allow anyone to lay a hand on my personal liberty ... I am poor and weak in body, but I have a mind strong enough to resist all these meaningless social customs which deprive a woman of her proper place in society. 'This decision', as Sister Geraldine names it, I consider a personal insult and I shall not act according to it.[29]

Pandita could not comprehend the church's objection to her teaching both sexes:

> It surprises me very much [she wrote] to think that neither my father nor my husband objected to my mother's or my teaching young men, while some English people are doing so ... Why do you say that to address mixed audiences is quite different from giving lessons to your Englishmen? I have not only addressed mixed audiences but most of them ... purely composed of men and have also given lessons to young men at different times.[30]

Pandita was surprised to find the stance adopted by the Anglican Church in England was more intransigent than the one she had seen in India.

The church felt that if news of Pandita's teaching English boys reached India, her proselytising influence would be weakened and she would be shunned by Indian society. Missionary concerns about Indian sensibilities appear to have acted as a cover for their own prejudices about the capacities of Indian women, their position in society and the intolerance of Indian men towards women in public life. These generalisations about the workings of Indian society compounded fears entertained by both the Bishop of Bombay and the Bishop of Lahore that Pandita was 'getting above herself' and would follow the bad example of other England-returned Christians. 'I am feeling a good deal of anxiety about the results of her being put forward in this way in England', wrote the Bishop of Bombay. 'All who have experience of native Christians know that it is the rarest thing possible for one of them to return to India from this country without having been completely spoilt and upset by the notice they have received here.'[31] The Bishop of Lahore suggested 'a less prominent position for a short time, with a humbler title such as teachership'. He believed that 'making no demonstration in any way would probably lessen the danger of elation of the mind very considerably' and, more importantly, make Pandita increasingly malleable and easier to manipulate.[32] The missionaries feared her growing independence would undermine their control over her activities when she returned to India.

Forty years later another Indian student also clashed with the British authorities over the issue of personal freedom. Thimayya, a cadet at Sandhurst, had long nursed a hatred for his official guardian and a confrontation was inevitable. Colonel Sturgess warned the Indian cadets of the perils of extravagance and association with British girls. Consequently, when he discovered that Thimayya was conducting a secret correspondence with a British girl he had met at a dance, he was appalled. Thimayya had broken two unwritten rules: Indians did not attend balls nor did they invite guests or dance. Thimayya quarrelled with the Colonel at what he viewed as an invasion of privacy. Sturgess, unaccustomed as he was 'to back talk from young Indians', threatened to inform the India Office and Thimayya's parents about his behaviour. But he was unperturbed, as he knew there was no written policy on relationships between Indians and English girls.[33] Many Indians seem to have appreciated the liberty they had in England. These two examples illustrate the high value some of them placed upon this experience.

ASSIMILATION

While certain students and visitors believed Britain to be an open and welcoming society, particularly in the nineteenth century, some still felt that imitation of British customs and assimilation would help them to be more readily accepted. A notorious example of this is Gandhi's attempt at 'Playing the Gentleman', the title of Chapter 15 of his autobiography. This involved taking dancing, piano, violin and elocution lessons.[34] Gandhi also passed himself off as a bachelor, even though he was a married man. He did so, along with many other Indian students, in order to fit in, as most English students of the same age were unmarried. Gandhi revealed that such pretence often had an ulterior motive. It allowed Indians to flirt with young women. However, he soon discovered the dangers of such a deception when a young lady assumed that she was engaged to him. He was obliged to tell her the truth.[35] Clearly this was a popular pastime for young Indians, as the two other key figures in twentieth-century Indian politics, Muhammad Ali Jinnah and Jawaharlal Nehru, both tried to ape 'the man about town' during their student days in London.[36]

Rabid anti-Semitism and the segregation of Jewish boys into separate accommodation at his boarding school, Clifton, taught M. R. A. Baig his first lesson in 'the penalties of minority-status, of the vices of segregation and the virtues of assimilation'. Baig remarked: 'Boys denied uniformity and anything out of pattern invites either their ridicule or hostility.'[37] His experiences suggest that, given the apparent depth of anti-Semitism in Edwardian Britain, Indian boys fitted more closely the model of Englishness constructed at the time than Jewish boys did. N. B. Bonarjee, who also attended school in Britain, commented on how his family was absorbed into British suburbia, infamous for its narrow-minded parochialism. The Bonarjees invited their neighbours to their home. This 'at home' functioned as an initiation ceremony. Bonarjee reflected: 'This pleasantly innocuous ritual rather than Christianity as such helped us as Indians to be acceptable to the neighbourhood. We had been vetted and had passed the test.'[38]

When K. P. S. Menon attended Oxford in the early 1920s it was still helpful to assume the garb and manner of an English gentleman in order to penetrate the exclusive world of collegiate Oxford. He wrote:

> I also strove to acquire the airs and graces of an Oxford man ... I wore nothing but grey flannels and tweed coat and I shunned hats ... I learnt that lectures were meant to be cut ... I sedulously cultivated the Oxford slang though not the Oxford accent ... I developed a healthy contempt for women.[39]

For many Indian students cultivating the 'cuff and collar cult',[40] as it was known, was a kind of survival technique which enabled them to cope with a potentially hostile environment. It was often convenient for students craving fellowship and popularity to conform and adopt an English persona. Also manoeuvring from a position of outsider to insider was a useful means of learning about the inner workings of British society. But this was usually a temporary measure. As Gandhi and many others soon discovered to their cost, the expense of such a lifestyle (which was beyond the reach of most students) and the pitfalls of romantic entanglements presented difficulties. As a result it was impossible for most students to persist in this charade for a lengthy period. The superficiality of such imitation also soon dawned on students. Nehru described it as 'a soft and pointless existence' in his autobiography. The examples given here show that it was often a passing phase in student development. However, a key witness to the Lee Warner Committee did notice that a few students took their desire to assimilate 'to an absurd extent and refused to have anything to do with their countrymen, being anxious only to mix with the English'.[41]

Nevertheless, for the majority of Indians the process of assimilation was incomplete. Religion was an area where few inroads were made; even students who appeared to have wholeheartedly adopted English cultural norms, such as Aurobindo and Manmohan Ghose, showed partial or total resistance to attempts to convert them to Christianity. As already stated, they spent part of their childhood in England with a clergyman friend of their father, who also acted as their guardian. Dr Ghose wanted his sons to be fully immersed in English life, but was keen for them to choose their own religion. However when Mr Drewitt was in Australia, Mrs Drewitt, his mother, tried to convert the boys to Christianity. Aurobindo described his brother's reaction:

> One day at prayer time Manmohan was in an insolent mood and he said that old Moses was well served when the people disobeyed him. This enraged the old lady beyond measure and she said she would not live under the same roof with heretics. We felt relieved and I felt infinitely grateful to Dada.[42]

Even an Indian Christian such as Cornelia Sorabji expressed an aversion to evangelical missionaries, for whom she was a constant target during her years as a law student at Oxford:

> Dear old ladies were always trying to convert me – the heathen at their gates. And they would talk to me very loudly in Pidgin English. 'Calcutta come? Bombay come?' Only once did I try and undeceive a proselytising old lady. She regarded me reproachfully. 'But you look so very heathen!'[43]

Cornelia was anxious that the medical career of her sister Alice (later Mrs Theodore Pennel, the novelist) should not be financed by a missionary society. She wrote that they 'will bind Alice hand and foot and she will scarcely be allowed to breathe without their leave'.[44] The missionary society would agree to sponsor Alice only on condition that she became a medical missionary.

Although Pandita Ramabai became a Christian during her residence in England, her letters reveal that her conversion was fraught with difficulties and doubt. Much to the irritation of English missionaries, she continued to avoid animal products and stayed in communication with her Brahmo friends in India. Pandita's resistance to and questioning of the gospel also caused consternation to those around her. 'I believe Ramabai's questions and difficulties come from a native source', wrote Dorothea Beale, 'and in answering her questions we are answering those which come to her from Indian correspondence.'[45] According to Sister Geraldine, Pandita found the Anglican Church's conception of Christianity 'too narrow, tight and compact for her needs'.[46] Thus even in cases where acculturation appeared ingrained, Indians still clung to indigenous practices and rebelled against institutional constraints.

Missionary activities seem to have been more successful among ayahs and lascars than students, although organisations such as the London Missionary Society continued to show an interest in students. In 1895 the missionary Henry Morris wrote: 'Our hearts yearn over them, and we long that some systematic effort should be made to reach them and to win them for Christ. It is a scandal that they should ever leave this land without every nerve being exerted to bring them under genuine Christian influence.'[47] In the late nineteenth century pressure was brought to bear on the Indian Christian Union, a body established to bring Indian Christians residing in Britain in touch with each other, by the Church Missionary Society. The Reverend Fox strongly advised Christian Union members 'to exercise individual effort' in bringing their countrymen within the fold.[48] N. S. Subbarao described missionary activity among Indian students at Cambridge:

> [A]n individual fired with a fervid enthusiasm for the salvation of the heathen's soul, seeks him [the student] out in his obscure lodgings and reads the Bible with him, prays for him, takes him to the church on Sundays and to various meetings of a devotional character. He is a well-meaning and harmless sort of person, though at times he gets on one's nerves.[49]

The Indian student's indifference to religious questions perplexed missionaries. '[H]e will tell you that the spread and increase of religion is not his business', reported the *London Christian Mission Magazine* in 1922, 'that it would be impertinence on his part to concern himself with it. In such matters the mind of the educated Indian in London remains in the East, while too often he views with contempt that which floats in from the West.'[50]

STRENGTH OF INDIAN CULTURAL VALUES

The resilience of indigenous Indian social institutions, especially caste (*jati*) and kinship structures, was a major barrier to complete assimilation. Indian rejection of Christianity in Britain is further evidence of this.[51] No matter how westernised a student became, cultural attitudes based on original Indian habits of mind and upbringing did not dissolve away in England, as these cases demonstrate. At a fundamental level most Indians would have experienced some degree of cultural shock on their first exposure to Europe. Keshub Chunder Sen, the religious (*Brahmo Samaj*) and social reformer, for example, was struck by the sheer foreignness of the first European city he visited, Marseilles. He described it as 'so perfectly *bilati* [foreign]'. A period of adjustment was necessary to become accustomed to the new surroundings and objects. Sen was intrigued by spring mattresses: 'He felt he was going to sink through the floor and called his companion to see if he was still visible on the surface.'[52]

Patterns of everyday life – no longer governed by religious ritual – were disrupted. Even students who came from less orthodox families felt the contrast between the solitary existence associated with a London lodging house and the warmth and support of a large, joint family in India. Indian students used to the female company of unmarried sisters and sisters-in-law were plunged into an all-male environment. Not only did Indians in Britain have to adapt to a new environment, there were also the elaborate and unwritten rules surrounding codes of conduct. Confusion would sometimes arise when Indians tried to apply indigenous habits and customs to their relationships with British women. For example, when Rabindranath Tagore came to Britain as a young man he stayed with an English family. The daughter of the family was younger than Tagore and as a result he treated her as a sister, but he was disappointed when she did not reciprocate and treat him with the deference that Bengali older brothers expected of their younger sisters.[53] Clearly, while it is important to recognise the benefits of post-modernism in releasing Indians from the straitjacket of essentialism, cultural assumptions nevertheless did have some influence on the way Indians perceived Britain. Cultural attitudes and feelings of inadequacy also informed Indian criticism of British society.

BRITISH FAULTS

Although Indian students and visitors reacted positively to certain aspects of late nineteenth- and early twentieth-century British society, they were certainly not blind to what they saw were its numerous faults.

These were characterised as poverty, drunkenness, class inequality, materialism and individualism.

Rabindranath Tagore was shocked at the deprivation of the working classes: 'When you see them you do not feel that they are capable of human feelings, for they seem to be just a step higher than animals. I feel a shiver when I see the faces of some of them ... And I cannot tell you how dirty they are!'[54] T. N. Mukharji described poverty in Britain as 'a crime ... of the deepest dye'. He compared the position to India where, he argued, compassion was in greater abundance: 'In this country [India] you have only to look very pious and your poverty will be forgiven and society will worship you from the next day. The market for piety is extremely dull in England.'[55]

The nineteenth-century traveller Baijnath was struck by the vastness and insolubility of Britain's 'drink problem': 'about a quarter of a million of its people are yearly convicted for drunkenness ... drink mocks the legislator, the philanthropist and the patriot'.[56] Both Mukharji[57] and Nadkarni[58] noted that women were particularly vulnerable to alcohol addiction. The adverse consequences of drunkenness were dramatically underscored by R. C. Dutt's harrowing portrayal of a London labourer, who, unable to support his large family, resorts to one of London's many public houses, eventually resulting in violence, death and his children begging in the streets.[59]

Visitors who wrote about Britain blamed the glaring inequalities of English society, described by P. J. Ragaviah, as 'astonishing wealth and wretched poverty ... vast wisdom and sunken ignorance ... good and virtuous and ... the lowest depth of repulsive vice and sin',[60] on the class system. R. C. Dutt was pained to see that even in 'enlightened England' unreason and prejudice had survived.[61] On a lecture tour around Britain B. C. Pal was able to observe these distinctions in operation. At a Unitarian chapel meeting in Birmingham his host tried to console Pal by saying he 'had quality in the morning [a reference to the fact the chapel was located in an affluent area] and he assured me I would have quality in the evening'. Pal remarked:

> Their liberal religious creed notwithstanding, they had not been able to escape the general attitude of the wealthier classes of their society. These experiences brought home to me the very wide differences between India and England. The humanity of the British people is skin-deep, they have no castes, it is true, but the class feeling among them is really even worse, from the humanitarian point of view, than our caste feeling.[62]

Krishnabhabini Das was equally repelled by British class pride: 'In this country, [England] a dunce who happens to be rich thinks himself a very great man and hates a poor but learned man.' Like Pal, she also believed that class was more damaging than caste distinctions:

> It is because of this contempt of highly placed Englishmen that common people cannot, in spite of so many facilities, acquire knowledge and requirements ... In our country we only hear of rich men and poor men, but in England we often hear of gentlemen and vulgar men ... without money it is impossible to be recognised as a gentlemen.[63]

The implication here is that knowledge and learning were more valued in India than in Britain. Baijnath concluded that equality was a myth in England: 'English society, though it professes to be democratic, is really a very autocratic society.'[64] Like his contemporaries, Baijnath's admiration for Britain's democratic political system did not prevent him from delving beneath surface appearances to provide a critical analysis of his colonial masters.

All Indian observers agreed that materialism lay at the root of Britain's problems. Even the language used by writers to make this point is strikingly similar. Three of them likened the acquisition of money to a religion. Nadkarni wrote: 'Mammon is the god of the day.'[65] To Krishnabhabini money was 'the principal god worshipped by Englishmen'[66] and Baijnath was equally eloquent:

> The goddess of wealth has more votaries than the Church of England. To call a man a beggar is the greatest insult ... Nobody tolerates being under money obligations to another if he can help it. Your money is the test of your merit ... There it is the law of the survival of the fittest and the fittest is he who commands most money. There is feverish competition everywhere, and to earn money honestly if you can and to be a man of independent means is everybody's ambition ... it is not charity but money that covers a multitude of sins in England.[67]

These views were in line with P. J. Ragaviah's opinion that money was 'the key that opens all portals of pleasure and advancement, it is also the agent for the spread of wickedness'.[68] The financial hardship and poverty suffered by many Indian students made them particularly sensitive to the power of money in Britain.

Krishnabhabini was acutely aware of the foreign policy implications of such all-consuming greed:

> They have cast nets in all countries to gather money, and wherever they smell money they rush like the carrion-loving adjutant. In making money they care not for virtue or vice. Even if they make money by wrongful

means in a foreign country, they feel no compunction or self-reproach ...
How much money have they spent and how much blood have they shed
in order to force opium upon the unfortunate Chinese! ... Such is the
despotic hold of the demon of wealth upon the English people.[69]

Like Nadkarni, she believed that the advancement of material interests
inevitably sacrificed moral and spiritual requirements. In many respects
these writers were reiterating the arguments adopted by Vivekananda
and the Theosophists on the superiority of Indian spiritualism over
western materialism, a position later taken up by Gandhi in the
twentieth century.

R. C. Dutt praised the independent spirit and self-reliance of the
British, but these merits could have drawbacks when self-love became
too pronounced. He illustrated this point when he wrote: 'people ... do
not much trouble themselves with their neighbours' affairs. It would be
rude for one to show inquisitiveness about the private concerns of the
next-door neighbour.'[70] Krishnabhabini believed British individualism
had developed into something more sinister – an obsessional self-
interest: 'Englishmen do not put their hand into anything without a
desire to promote their own good, and there is nothing which they will
not venture to do in order to accomplish their own selfish ends.'[71] Several
commentators argued that the promotion of self-reliance was not
compatible with charity. They believed Indians had a greater charitable
sense than Europeans,[72] although Dutt argued that the dependence of
Indians on others and that the expectation of assistance conflicted with
the need to develop a national character.[73] Ironically, English independence had failed to counter a contradictory element of British life, noted
by Mukharji, namely, the tyranny of fashion.[74]

By residing in Britain students and non-students were able to observe
the British character. It was described variously as 'exclusive', 'cold',
'cynical' and 'reserved'.[75] Both Mukharji and Krishnabhabini viewed
Englishmen as hard-hearted because they exhibited so little family
affection. Mukharji wrote:

> The English people appeared to me to be wanting in family affection. As
> soon as a person attains majority, he or she leaves the paternal home to
> seek his or her fortune in the wide world ... On many occasions I saw
> Englishmen receive the news of the death of a very near relative with
> perfect indifference.[76]

Similar observations caused Krishnabhabini to note that Englishmen
were 'bereft of affection, kindness, humility, benevolence. They usually
oppress the weak and do not sympathise with those who are

unfortunate ... Thriftlessness and intemperance are two serious English faults.'[77]

In equally robust language Krishnabhabini condemned England as a nation of hypocrites: 'Very often they have one thing in their minds and another thing in their mouths. Their gentlemanly behaviour is often external and not sincere.' She felt that this failing was particularly prevalent among shopkeepers and traders:

> Many behave liberally towards foreigners, but that is mere show and ... commercial courtesy ... These Englishmen do everything, but feign not to know anything. As they think themselves purified after dinner by only rubbing with a piece of cloth the outer part of their mouths, so when they defile their hearts, they exhibit themselves as perfectly pure and sinless by assuming a grave and unconcerned appearance.[78]

R. C. Dutt also complained about the artificiality of British society. Sub Lal had noticed a similar quality to the importance attached to the 'ceremony of introduction in the social life of England' at Oxford, which he denounced as 'ludicrous and childish and worse than many of the old customs practised in India'.[79] But Dutt attributed such artificiality to the position of British women, a point I shall return to shortly.

Like her fellow male critics, Krishnabhabini accused the British of chauvinism, a superiority complex and xenophobia[80] combined with an ignorance of India:[81]

> They think the entire world lies low at their feet, and all other nations are inferior to them ... Towards foreigners in their own country they assume a very grave appearance and indulge in tall talk. To ordinary Englishmen, foreigners are simply an eyesore. It is their desire that they should go to all countries and bring home whatever they find there, but that no foreigners should come and settle in their country ... None need wonder that persons belonging to this nation should regard everything in our country as contemptible and treat us as beasts. It is the blood of India that enabled England to acquire such huge dimensions.

She warned the British against excessive national pride: 'It was pride of this kind that caused the decline and fall of the Roman Empire ... that humbled France ... at the feet of Germany.'[82]

POSITION OF WOMEN

Little more than 12 years separated the publication of R. C. Dutt's book and Krishnabhabini's work, yet their analysis of women's position in British society differed substantially. Although Krishnabhabini offered

the strongest and most emotive criticism of Britain and the British, citing
a catalogue of vices, she was also the most vocal in expressing her
admiration for British women, provoking one reviewer to praise her
contribution as the most balanced account of its kind.[83] According to her
there were three main areas that reflected the equal status enjoyed by
English women: marriage, domestic life and sibling relations. Krishnabhabini was impressed by the freedom of choice granted to children by
their parents on the subject of marriage. 'Neither Englishmen nor
Englishwomen marry except at their own free will', she wrote. 'Their
parents do not, as a rule, oppose their desire, they rather give them
consent.' She concluded that 'children are treated with greater care and
affection by English than by Indian parents'. She believed that while
the custom of separate accommodation for parents and adult children
reduced intimacy, it nevertheless increased 'mutual love' and lessened
domestic quarrels. Harmonious sibling relations were attributed to the
equal treatment given by parents to both boys and girls, smothering
any potential rivalry and disagreements, which she claimed were
common in India, where brothers from 'childhood learnt to hate their
sisters as their inferiors on account of their being women'.[84] Finally, she
advocated female emancipation in India on the lines of the policy of the
suffragette movement in England.

Dutt was also committed to female suffrage at a time when such views
had few male supporters in India or England; but he argued that, while
superficially British women had more freedom than Indian women, the
need to marry in British society diminished this freedom. As employment was closed to them, English women were obliged either to marry
or were 'shelved' and forced to depend on their parents. He wrote:

> To avoid this fate there is often a brisk competition among these fair
> commodities ... The education of a young lady is adapted ... to the
> formation of qualities which make her most pleasing to men ... in society
> the young lady must not be independent and dignified, but pleasing and
> amiable to affect a delicacy of feeling where perhaps none is felt, such are
> the arts and deceptions ... which civilisation and exigencies of society has
> [sic] taught the fair candidate for marriage in England.[85]

Dutt argued that the liberty to choose a partner in life did not guarantee
connubial happiness, as a young man in England knew as much about
the real character of his betrothed as his Indian equivalent.

Dutt blamed the false nature of English society on the fact that

> half the population have to act a part which they do not feel, and to assume
> a semblance of dignity with claims to special deference and privileges in

order to hide real and conscious disabilities, social as well as legal. Thus society is rendered artificial, promptings of nature are merged in the promptings of etiquette and social laws, and conduct and conversations are hampered and encrusted over with fixed forms and fashions.[86]

Dutt believed that the solution to this problem lay in the opening up of the professions to women: 'Create for her aims and aspirations of life higher and nobler than to court and feed upon the foolish admiration of men, and she will rise with the occasion and frivolities will give place to reflection and serious pursuits.'[87]

One Bengali student wrote to the *Journal of the National Indian Association* anonymously, describing the change he had undergone in England on the question of female emancipation. In India he had promised not to liberalise his views on the education and liberty of women and to steer clear of Manmohan Ghose's example. On his return from England Ghose had sought to promote his wife's education and remove restraints on her freedom. The student wrote:

> To say the truth, I myself was against him, and complained several times, in common with my countrymen, who tax him with adopting English habits to the sacrifice of native social bonds. But now I see that his example is noble ... Whence has my change come about? Simply from entering English society, from seeing it in the heart of the family. I now understand that women ought to be educated, not merely so far as bare utility dictates but for the very same reason for which men ought to be educated, for the development of a nobler being.

This fresh convert to the cause of female emancipation, no longer satisfied with the position of women in India, found reason to bemoan Britain's progress on the issue: 'The English themselves, so imperfectly carry out their principle, and in general by no means educate women so solidly as men.'[88]

Thirty years later the position of British women had improved relative to that of Indian women, but an Indian law student was surprised to find the professions still discriminating against women. When a young lady applied for admission as a pupil at his chambers in London, M. R. Jayakar was able to observe the reaction of his male colleagues: 'I voted in her favour with my Indian notions about women's rights, but curiously enough, my British colleagues unanimously voted against her, remarking that they did not want a "flapper" in the pupil room ... We developed a heated controversy in our room during the time Romer was considering the matter.'[89] Interpretation and expectation informed the differing perceptions of these commentators. Krishnabhabini was comparing her own poor quality of life as a woman in India with what she was able to observe of women's lives in England: 'I was locked up in the *zenana* just like you and I had no connection with anything of my country or the world.'[90] As a result anything which compared favourably with her own experience was applauded. She called on Bengali women to 'come out and see how happy the women of Germany, France and England are. There aren't any tears in her eyes! Look! Men here do not ignore women as good for nothing. Men do not treat them as pets and lock them up in the *zenana*.'[91] Despite its numerous faults, she viewed Britain as a place of freedom. This was partly influenced by the liberating effects of the travel process, which contrasted sharply with the seclusion and relative 'unfreedom' of her life in India. Dutt and later Jayakar came from different backgrounds (as male members of the colonial elite, their lives were not as circumscribed as women visitors') and had higher expectations of England; consequently when their experience failed to match their anticipations their disappointment was greater. Arguably Dutt's analysis was more profound as he attempted to pass beyond surface appearance, although Krishnabhabini's comments have a greater personal dimension. In much of the above discussion we have seen some agreement between Indian responses. By denigrating aspects of British life, Indians were able to defend their own culture from attack and occupy the moral high ground. But their criticism was also genuine, stemming from disappointment at what they encountered in Britain.

STUDENT SUSPICIONS AND COMPLAINTS

While the reactions of nineteenth-century visitors provide a general emotional response to encounters with British society, evidence is also available of a more immediate and reactive nature, involving specific complaints and responses to British criticisms of the Indian student population. Some of the grievances harboured by students over discrimination and financial problems have already been indicated, but this must be viewed as part of a broader climate of student suspicion and resentment. The English authorities' attempts to control and manipulate students provoked deep distrust, reflected in the London Indian Association's strong reaction to the Lytton Committee. It stated that all supervision was 'superfluous and offensive ... positively harmful to all parties' and 'the ultimate intention of the committee was to strengthen and perpetuate the humiliating machinery of special control'.[92]

The failure of the Indian Student Department was due to student animosity towards any type of officially-run institution. Surveillance operations carried out on students after the assassination of Curzon Wyllie and the cloak-and-dagger tactics employed to suppress the publication of the Lee Warner Report all militated against the success of the Department. Students failed 'to make any distinctions between one department of government and another' and declarations of interest in student welfare were regarded as a cover for intelligence-gathering operations.[93] Representatives of the Oxford Indian Majlis stated that 'Indian students are watched and their speeches in the Majlis and other sources reported. Naturally this engenders considerable bitterness and distrust and makes them suspicious of any interference from the authorities.'[94] Dr Bahl claimed that he had documentary evidence that speeches made at the university were reported and sent to the authorities. The speeches were often misreported and incorrectly attributed and could adversely affect students in their subsequent careers. K. R. Tampi of the Edinburgh Indian Association was able to give evidence of surveillance. Tampi's father was informed about his son's political activities by a British official, through information received from intelligence sources.[95] One man was caught stealing papers from the Edinburgh Indian Association. He claimed that he was obliged to spy because his remittance had not arrived.

Prakash Tandon was also surprised to find that when he went to seek advice on jobs in India, the official who interviewed him possessed a huge file of information on him. Tandon was mystified, as he had not visited the office in the eight years since his arrival in England. His first visit had given him the impression that British officials were not interested in student welfare. In his memoirs he reflected: 'We knew that Indian students in England were kept under careful watch, but I could not understand what valuable information could have made such a thick dossier on me. Apparently my every movement had been recorded.'[96]

Distrust of officialdom manifested itself in other ways. Indian history students refused to take special subjects relating to India because they were convinced that the India Office checked their papers.[97] Several students accused the local adviser at Edinburgh of being a government agent[98] and Miss Beck of the National Indian Association was aware that students she befriended were regarded as spies.[99] Two representatives at Cromwell Road believed it was the government connection which was at the root of the problem, creating a conflict of interests, as the warden of Cromwell Road was joint secretary to the Student Department as well as a student guardian.[100] Students expressed their anger at a meeting in Caxton Hall in 1914 when they called for the 'total and immediate abolition ... of the Department as injurious to their interests'.[101] Although the Lytton Committee denied any involvement in espionage, it was clear that political motivation underpinned the establishment of the department. The Lytton Report clearly stated the need for measures to 'counteract the harmful influences of the revolutionary movement'.[102]

It was not just the Indian Student Department which failed to secure the confidence of the bulk of the Indian student population; advisory committees in India were also of doubtful efficacy. Many students did not approach them, believing that they would not provide assistance. When Subhas Chandra Bose consulted a member of the advisory committee in Calcutta the adviser tried to dissuade him from travelling to England, claiming that it would be a waste of money and that he had little chance of acceptance. J. M. Sen, a postgraduate student at Leeds University, argued that the advisory committees not only provided little assistance for Indian students, 'but rather caused delay in forwarding of applications for admissions'. He also criticised the committees for failing to keep 'up to date regarding facilities and training in England', for giving 'wrong information and patronising advice' and for showing undue sensitivity to complaints of overcrowding from British universities rather than pressing the claims of Indian students.[103] Sen advocated the abolition of all advisory committees.

Numerous Indian students complained about the whole university admissions system. P. M. Chowdhury of Birmingham University was a typical example of a student who had been discouraged by the advisory committee but had managed to gain admittance when applying directly to an institution of higher education in Britain.[104] After the First World War R. N. Vaidya was told that there was strong competition for university places from demobilised soldiers. However, on the advice of a friend he decided to try his luck in England anyway. Dr Arnold, who had just returned from Scotland, told him that all the Scottish universities were full, but on personal enquiry both Edinburgh and Glasgow accepted him.[105] S. K. Rudra, writing in the student journal *Indus*, expressed the opinions of the majority when he said: 'Our numbers would go up still higher if most colleges did not adopt the practice of admitting only two Indian undergraduates per year ... We feel that these restrictions are working against us, not only at universities, but particularly in medical schools and institutions.'[106]

Engineering and industrial students felt a particularly strong sense of grievance. The case of N. B. Wagle, highlighted in Chapter 2, illustrates the enormous difficulties faced by Indian students seeking practical training. The Lytton Committee acknowledged there was some justification for the complaint. The Indian Student Department had relied on the work of a part-time individual who had no knowledge of industrial conditions in India. All his work was done through correspondence alone, using London as his base, consequently not enough had been done to search out opportunities for students.[107]

Indian students at British universities also objected strongly to their exclusion from the Officer Training Corps. As early as 1893 a Parsi student, J. P. Dastur, had complained to the India Office about his rejection from the Cambridge University Corps.[108] Indians were excluded on the grounds that they were not eligible for commissions in the British Army. But students from other parts of the empire were freely admitted, despite the fact that they were unlikely to seek commissions. The real reason the bar remained in place was fear that the admission of Indians would adversely affect recruitment of British students to the Corps, which was already suffering from a post-war decline, and might even result in the resignation of those who had already joined.[109] However, an Oxford ICS probationer believed that political rather than social imperatives were more significant. He had not detected any opposition among ex-service men towards Indians joining the Corps.[110] Feeble excuses were given for Indian exclusion: Indian riding skills were brought into question and at Scottish universities the wearing of kilts by Indians was regarded as problematic.[111] The idea of an exclusively Indian platoon attracted little support among students as it did not fulfil their main objective – equal treatment.

In addition, resentment also built up on the use of yet another mechanism designed to limit admissions; character certificates for the Inns of Courts. The regulations stipulated that Indian applicants not educated in the United Kingdom must produce a certificate from a high-ranking officer in the Government of India such as a collector, political officer or secretary to the High Commission. According to Dr Thomas Arnold, the rule was introduced by the Inns of Court because '90 per cent of the certificates of character bore the signature of one Indian barrister resident in London'.[112] Indian students complained that for other applicants not in permanent residence in the United Kingdom a certificate from a judge or magistrate was acceptable. Furthermore, Indian students also claimed that a collector or deputy commissioner was unlikely to have personal knowledge of an applicant. Consequently the certificates were based on police reports, which 'primarily related to political activities and opinions of the applicants and family'. Some students maintained that the advisory committees, on whose recommendation the certificates were granted, had demanded a guarantee of loyalty to the British government before awarding certificates. In this case the authorities appear to have responded to Indian concerns, since the unpopular regulation was rescinded in 1913.

Faced by mounting obstacles to admission to British universities, Indian students began to display an interest in America and Japan. By

1920 the Government of India had published a pamphlet written by R. K. Sorabji, Secretary of the United Provinces Advisory Committee, in order 'to meet the needs of students in the United Provinces, who constantly make requests for information about Education in the United States and Japan'.[113] Indian students were attracted to these countries by the prospect of low costs and the hope of earning money in the vacations. However, the author of the pamphlet was keen to stress that neither of these propositions was true. On the contrary, admission was difficult as Indian qualifications were not accepted in America. Indian students would have to enter as special cases. Also students wishing to follow technical courses in Japan were obliged to learn Japanese, pay fees of £100–150 per annum and compete with Japanese students for scarce places. Clearly this official publication was intended to limit the appeal of these countries for Indians.

REACTION TO BRITISH CRITICISM

Not only were Indian students suspicious of government agencies and critical about measures to exclude them from access to higher education, they also objected to British attacks on their personal conduct and lack of collegiate spirit. N. S. Subbarao responded to the three main criticisms levelled against the students by Cambridge authorities and students.[114] In reply to the criticism that Indians were aloof, he argued that such insularity was provoked by the Englishman's dislike of the Indian's presence. He claimed not to be exaggerating when he said that 'in Cambridge an Indian feels he is looked upon as an undesirable factor and an Englishmen is apologetic in claiming an Indian for an acquaintance of his'.[115] The root cause of this aversion was 'the honest British dislike for anything foreign'.[116] Subbarao also attributed Indian aloofness to the discriminatory college admissions policy at Cambridge. He concluded that Indo-British relations would be little improved by 'blunt declarations that at a particular college Indians are not taken as a rule, but a special favour will be shown to the individual concerned'.[117] As noted earlier, cost was also a major consideration. The expense of college life led many Indians to seek lodgings outside college, which often led to a solitary existence.

British complaints about Indians taking no part in sports were, he felt, largely justified. Subbarao could not envisage any remedy, as in his opinion the phenomenon was the result of an essential dichotomy 'between the "swot" who gets a first and a sporting man whose goal in life is a Blue'. He regarded Indians as fundamentally 'reading' men whose capacity for sports was, as a result, impaired. Indian success in examinations did not appear to improve their popularity. Such strengths, according to Subbarao, were more 'a matter for ridicule than otherwise'.[118] He also acknowledged that some students had been rather tardy in paying their bills. But he claimed that Indians were no worse in this respect than their English counterparts. It was their foreignness that was at issue, a point which he illustrated by the following comparison: 'Just as an Englishman in India is deceived by some coolie and writes furious letters to the papers about Indian dishonesty, so also the shopkeeper is wary of Indian customers.'[119]

British fears about Indian sexual immorality in Britain were partially reflected in Subbarao's concerns about students' involvement with prostitutes. Although he was vague about the number involved, he felt that it was greater than was tolerable. When citing the causes he was keen to stress the difference between India and England. First, in India strict restrictions were placed on any type of relations with women, apart from near relatives. Although Subbarao claimed to be an admirer of greater female emancipation, he felt such freedom could be open to abuse: 'In India a wayward man seeks the prostitute; in England she seeks him and solicits him.'[120] Secondly, Subbarao pointed to the fact that such behaviour was condoned. Indeed, he knew of three sportsmen at St John's College, Cambridge, who were arbiters of acceptable behaviour, but at the same time were 'notorious for their shameless disregard of the Eighth Commandment'. He continued: 'When dalliance with shop girls is a sure sign of manliness and men love to bask in the smiles of barmaids, it is but a step to sin.'[121] He believed the sanctioning of such vices and the bad example set by 'a large number of varsity men' in this sphere, acted as a further stimulus for Indians already beset by 'drawbacks and temptations'.

Two years later the President of the Cambridge Majlis was again obliged to defend the reputation of Indian students at the university, against the criticism of an anonymous writer in the university journal *Cambridge Review*. The article raised questions that had frequently been debated by British officials and the press – namely, the decline in the quality of Indian students studying in England and the political danger they represented. Subbarao used statistics to try to refute the view that Indians were intellectually unfit for a course at Cambridge. He compared the results of Indians who had matriculated between 1901 and 1905 and students in the university as a whole:

Indian students (%)[122]	*University students (%)*
honours 64.8	honours 46.3
pass degree 8.7	pass degree 32.9
wastage 23[123]	wastage 20.8

Indian students' results compared favourably with those of the majority of university students. Although the failure rate was approximately equal, Indian students distinguished themselves with a higher percentage of honours degrees compared with unclassified pass or 'poll degrees'. However, allegations of moral inferiority were harder to refute using quantifiable methods. Subbarao argued that it was unfair to indict a whole group on the basis of the behaviour of a few individuals.

Finally, criticism of the seditious nature of the Indian Majlis in campaigning for 'the dismemberment of the British Empire' was overstated. Subbarao claimed that recent unrest in India had led to discussions to which Indian visitors were invited but 'voting had not always gone the same way'. Lord Morley and other members of the Council of India had been invited to Majlis dinners, but declined. Subbarao felt that it was inevitable that Indians should discuss the future of their country: 'It is absurd to expect them to live in a sort of political vacuum in regards to Indian politics.'[124] Not only would political supervision be strongly deprecated, but it would also encourage the growing tendency among Indians to study in France, Germany or the United States, where contact with revolutionary thought could have serious consequences for India's relationship with England. Indian students responded vigorously to British complaints about their behaviour in England. Although it was acknowledged that there was a certain amount of truth in British allegations, nevertheless environmental factors were blamed and the British were often accused of either exaggerating or aggravating the situation.

STUDENT POLITICISATION

One of the main ways in which reaction to residence in England manifested itself among students was through the medium of politics. It is clear from the findings of the Lee Warner Report, discussed in Chapter 3, that many Indians did arrive in England hostile to the British government. This contention was supported by several Indian students. Deva Brata Muckerjea of Emmanuel College, Cambridge, claimed that Indian students had been inculcated with 'nationalist sympathies and yearnings before arriving in England'.[125] Pandit Bhagwadin Dube had observed 'a general awakening' in the sphere of politics in India, with students, in particular, exhibiting a marked interest: 'The idea of the distinction between what was one's own and what was foreign was taking deep root. The Gaekwar of Baroda could count on more personal loyalty than any provincial Governor.'[126]

Dube and Mian Sami Uddin, a Muslim law student, both attributed this growth in national consciousness to the dissatisfaction felt by educated Indians at their treatment by Europeans in India. This included restrictions on certain roads designated for white use only, exclusion from European clubs, and mistreatment by British civil servants. Dube felt that unless there was a change of attitude towards educated Indians, students in Britain would continue to march headlong to what he perceived to be the 'evil' philosophy of revolution.[127] J. C. Chatterjee, a postgraduate student at Trinity College, Cambridge, took a slightly different view. He blamed the anti-British views digested by Indian students before their arrival in England on the Anglo-Indian press in India, using offensive terms such as 'natives', 'ostyers' and 'babus' and the provision of 'Godless' education of a purely European type, which had led to a situation where Indians craved equality with the British. Chatterjee believed such 'false political hopes' of self-rule could never be realised and specific limits on political ambitions should be made known to Indians by the British.[128]

Even students uninfected by politics before reaching Britain experienced some degree of political awakening while residing there. For example, Fazl-i-Husain, who came to England in 1898 to study for the Indian Civil Service, revealed in his diary the enormous influence his studies had had on him. He wrote:

> I learnt something more ... I learnt what independent nations call 'Liberty' and understood ... the distinction between freedom and slavery. When attending lectures on History and Politics, I felt the perspiration of shame trickling down my forehead ... What did I want? Endowed with more than average intellectual capacities and ennobled with more than averagely noble blood and descent, not lacking moral weight or practice, not standing in want of tolerable symmetry or physique and yet I am inferior, simply because I am not English-born? Am I to be a slave because I am an Indian?[129]

Although Fazl-i-Husain was not completely ignorant of political philosophy before his contact with Britain (Islamic variations on similar themes of rights and liberties), clearly studying these concepts in England heightened his sense of injustice and provoked the question: Why were enlightenment theories not applied to non-Europeans?

Indian student associations, such as the Majlis and the revolutionary India House, provided students with political outlets. Rajani Palme Dutt remembered how the Majlis used to meet each week in a room in his father's house in Cambridge: 'As boys my brother and I used to listen to the fiery debates and impassioned controversies between moderates and extremists.'[130] M. C. Changla, in his Autobiography *Roses in December*, remarked that the Majlis was a revolutionary body, in line with the sympathies of most of the students at Oxford. He wrote: 'One heard the most bloodcurdling speeches at the meetings of the society. The speeches were anti-government, often highly seditious, calling always for the abdication of empire in India.'[131] Its reputation reached India; S. G. Velinker, the leading criminal lawyer of Bombay, requested Changla look after his son at Oxford. He added 'Please see that Vasant does not join that body, the Oxford Indian Majlis.'[132] K. P. S. Menon, who attended Oxford University at the same time as Changla, described the Majlis as 'a forum for letting off steam'.[133]

What proportion of Indian students became politicised in Britain? Did they merely harbour anti-British views or were they actively involved in revolutionary activities? One Indian student believed that 50 per cent of the whole body of Indian students in England were imbued with hostility. 'Of the remaining 50 per cent', he added, 'some were men of moderate and reasonable political views. Others were indifferent to politics and were interested mainly in social and religious matters. Thus the hostile section clearly predominated.'[134] Another Indian put the figure as high as 75 per cent. Nehru wrote in his autobiography: 'almost without exception' Indians in Britain were extremists.[135] Probably the most accurate indication was given by *The Times* on 1 September 1908. It calculated the student population to be approximately 800 (roughly in line with the Lee Warner Committee's estimates of 700). With this total in mind it reported: '[I]t still remains a conspicuous indication of the growth of a violent and unreasoning attitude, that so large a proportion of the total, as close upon 100, should gather in London on May 10th last to celebrate with joy the "Nationalist Rising" of the Indian Mutiny.' Even those who doubted the influence of India House, such as S. D. Bhabha, felt that the political aspirations of Indian students all ran in the same direction, namely, to acquire greater political rights. M. Z. Wicremsingh at Oxford argued that, although political beliefs differed on every question, in one matter, greater freedom of speech, they were unanimous. William Wedderburn also acknowledged that while Shyamji Krishnavarma may have had only a small following, nevertheless 'in a way he represented the general feeling of bitterness'.[136]

By the 1920s India House was no longer in existence. The search for world peace and the ideology of internationalism were gaining ground. The Indian student magazine *Indus* took up the theme of international brotherhood in a series of articles, urging students 'to forsake narrow nationalisms and instead show loyalty to mankind as a whole'. The Student Christian Movement House, founded in 1917 by the Student Christian Movement (SCM), was also guided by the spirit of internationalism.[137] Foreign students of all nationalities visited the house in Russell Square. But fewer Indians became involved with the SCM than Afro-Caribbean students.[138]

Although internationalism may appear to be a major departure from the parochial concerns of India House – which was limited to dismantling the colonial relationship between India and Britain – nevertheless, even during the first decade of the twentieth century when anarchist/ revolutionary ardour was at its peak in Britain, strains of internationalism were apparent. For example, in 1908 the Indo-Egyptian Association was founded in London to promote social intercourse between Indians and Egyptians.[139] Continuous attempts to establish an *entente* with other 'oppressed' nationalities, including the Turks and the Irish, were a notable feature of the Indian revolutionary movement in England. Events in Turkey and Ireland were important to the political development of Indians in Britain. The creation of the Irish Free State occurred while N. G. Ranga was a student at Oxford. He wrote: 'I saw, like all other Indian students at Oxford, how a revolutionary, armed revolt was proving successful against the armed might of England and her empire. Thus De Valera and Atatürk served as beacons of light to the Indian youths then in Europe.'[140]

Left-wing doctrines of socialism and communism also attracted Indian students in England during the 1920s.[141] Communist Party documents seized by Scotland Yard in 1925 reveal the inroads made by the Communist Party of Great Britain (CPGB). The Indian Communist MP for Battersea, Shapurji Saklatvala, was requested by the Colonial Department of the CPGB to meet selected Indian students in London before they completed their studies at Oxford. Saklatvala was provided with information regarding the political persuasion of the 66 members of the Oxford Majlis: 18 moderates (sought Dominion status),[142] 11 Swarajists, five socialists, 20 Indian Civil Service and Indian Forest Service, and 12 unclassified.

The Colonial Department had already distributed revolutionary literature to the Swarajists and the socialists, as success seemed most likely with these groups. But they still remained optimistic about the possibility of infiltrating the Civil and the Forest Service probationers[143] and those whose political opinions remained unknown to them.

The British Communist Party was not the only such organisation interested in Indian students. The Young Communist League had done a lot of work 'among Indian students in London and other university towns agitating against British imperialism'.[144] The Indian Bureau in London was formed for the closer study of communism and its propagation among students and seamen. But strained relations with the Communist Party and a membership of only about a dozen in 1925 hampered its progress. Lastly, the 'Indian group' also regularly circulated propaganda among students.[145] Lord Birkenhead, Secretary of State for India, was rebuffed by two college principals when he tried to crack down on communist activities. As a result, the Vice-Chancellor of Oxford issued an ultimatum to the students: requesting them to either renounce all contact with communism for the remainder of their college careers or face expulsion. The Vice-Chancellor's actions excited resentment from the undergraduate community. The Oxford Union voted against the decision on the grounds that it infringed freedom of expression, although the vote was reversed a week later.[146]

CASE STUDIES OF JAWAHARLAL NEHRU AND N. B. BONARJEE

Case studies show the process and impact of politicisation on individual students in England. An analysis of Nehru's political philosophy demonstrates the great importance of the ideas imbibed in England on his political career; while N. B. Bonarjee shows more clearly the development of an Indian student's political consciousness in Britain.

Jawaharlal Nehru entered Harrow in May 1905, aged 15. He left after two years to enter Trinity College, Cambridge. Having completed his science degree he went to London to study for the Bar and returned to India in 1912, a qualified barrister. Politics in India picked up momentum during these years and Nehru was kept up to date on any new developments by his father's first-hand accounts of Congress activities, as well as by regular consignments of Indian newspapers. His family's involvement in nationalist politics had attracted Nehru's interest from a young age and his residence in England enhanced this predisposition.

In his autobiography Nehru cites Meredith Townsend's book *Europe and Asia* as a particularly strong influence on the growth of his political consciousness. Its main premise is stated in the preface: 'inherent differences between Europe and Asia ... forbid one continent permanently conquering the other'.[147] Although Townsend was not completely free from many of the clichés which marred British writing on Asia, such as 'arrested progress', 'polygamy', 'enslavement of women' and 'cruelty', nevertheless he did attempt to provide a balanced account, highlighting weaknesses and strengths. According to him, Asians had achieved success in practically every field of human endeavour. He even suggested that the Asian excelled in certain areas: He 'is more quick-witted, especially in reading character; he anticipates his interlocutor's thought more rapidly; he invents with far more ingenuity and he is more capable of purely abstract reasoning'.[148] Although the book was positive about India's achievements and attempted to demystify some common falsehoods, it did not support the nationalist position nor was it overtly sympathetic to India's plight.

Presumably the book attracted the young Cambridge scholar's interest because of its proposition that British rule over India would soon end. Firstly, Townsend claimed that the Raj was 'built on nothing' except Indian opinion. 'Not only is there no white race in India, not only is there no white colony, but there is no white man who purposes to remain.'[149] He believed that the number of Englishmen there was smaller than London's black population and the loyalty of Indians could not be depended upon. Townsend wrote: 'There is no nation or tribe or caste in India which is certain in the hour of trial to stand by the white man's side.'[150] Without Indian support or at least apathy 'the "Empire" would collapse like a house of cards, and every ruling man would be starving prisoner in his own house'.[151] The self-sufficient Indians would be able to sustain themselves independently.

For Nehru, Townsend's hypothesis was given additional weight, since the book was published in the wake of Japan's victory over Russia. Townsend's remarks on the significance of the event echoed Nehru's opinion: 'An Asiatic power, not of the first-class either in area or population, has challenged and beaten by sea and land a first-class European state.'[152] Russia's defeat illustrated in graphic terms Townsend's assertions concerning European weakness. Nehru must have been immensely heartened to have come across a book in which a self-confessed supporter of the British Raj (he predicted anarchy would follow British withdrawal from India) openly admitted that the British people were suffering a crisis of confidence, with neither the will nor desire to put down an Indian revolt: 'They have become uncertain of themselves ... They doubt if they have any longer any moral right to rule anyone.'[153] By stressing the hollowness of British hegemony over India, Townsend had unintentionally given validity to the Indian nationalist cause. Although Nehru was already well acquainted with many of the contemporary ideas in Townsend's book, nevertheless he still found it inspiring.

Nehru exhibited a distinct preference for 'extremist' politics during his seven years in England. He came across two potential political role models for Congress while studying in Britain. He read about Garibaldi at Harrow, reflecting years later: 'Visions of similar deeds in India came before me, of a gallant fight for freedom and in my mind India and Italy got strangely mixed together.'[154] He was also impressed by Sinn Fein; quoting from the pamphlet *New Ireland*, he wrote to his father: 'Their policy is not to beg for favours but to wrest them. They do not want to fight England by arms, but to ignore her, boycott her, and quietly assume the administration of Irish affairs.'[155] He believed that if the Republicans continued to provoke consternation from the British government and receive mass support 'English rule would be a thing of the past before long.' All of these were arguments propounded by the 'extremist' wing of Congress. Indian leaders also influenced the young Nehru at this stage in his life. He later recalled the importance of Tilak: 'I remember that in my boyhood and youth, when I had not personally met him, how powerfully I was influenced by him.'[156] As a Congress moderate, Motilal Nehru disapproved of the way his son had 'changed' at Cambridge.[157] Nehru joined the Cambridge Majlis against his father's wishes,[158] reassuring him that the members 'were not as bad as they were painted'.[159] It was Nehru's shyness that prevented him from taking a more active part in its debates.

Most strands of Nehru's political philosophy can be traced back to his student days in England. In his *Discovery of India* he mentions three key elements: science, humanism and Marxism/socialism. Nehru believed that it was in the field of science that India had most to 'learn from the West'. Unlike other Indian visitors to England discussed here, Nehru failed to draw a distinction between the spiritualism of the East and the materialism of the West. In his *Glimpses of World History* he wrote that 'There is no question of a practical and materialist West and a spiritual and other-worldly East. The difference is between an industrial and highly mechanised West, with all its accompanying good and bad points, and an East which is still largely pre-industrial and agricultural.'[160] Nehru was following in the nineteenth-century European tradition of positivism, which gave primacy to empirically verifiable facts as the only form of valid knowledge. He admitted to being uneasy whenever he dabbled with metaphysical philosophy, from which he would happily escape 'with a feeling of ease'. His early confidence in the 'scientific method' can be seen when he wrote: 'My early approach to life's problems has been more or less scientific, with something of the easy optimism of the science of the nineteenth and early twentieth century.'[161]

Nehru also owed much of his humanism,[162] rationalism[163] and liberalism to the European enlightenment tradition. The British model of parliamentary government was adopted by Nehru after independence and the Indian Civil Service remained despite pledges to dismantle it. However, Nehru also used British concepts of constitutionalism and legality as tools against the British (as had earlier Congress leaders). He claimed that these notions had been subverted: in democratic countries a constitution 'controls the making of laws, it protects liberties, it checks the executive', but in colonial India 'laws can be promulgated by an irresponsible executive; at the shortest notice, the word "legal" simply means the will of the executive'.[164] Although Nehru's arguments were couched in terms of English political tradition, as one commentator has remarked: 'he did it in ways which accentuated the distinctively anti-colonial and pro-freedom aspects of the English'.[165]

Nehru acknowledged in an interview that his acquaintance with socialism began at Cambridge: 'I would say that it was really at Cambridge that, broadly speaking, certain socialist ideas developed.'[166] He attended a lecture at the university called 'Socialism and the University Man' given by George Bernard Shaw. Later he paid tribute to Shaw: 'like many of my generation, we have grown up in company with your writings and books. I suppose a part of myself such as I am today, has been moulded by that reading.'[167] Marx and Lenin had also 'produced a powerful effect', helping him 'to see history and current affairs in a new light'.[168] Nehru's commitment to internationalism, later reflected in his non-aligned foreign policy, can be seen by his unsuccessful attempts to apply these principles to his private life during his time as a student in England. When his father wrote to him on the subject of matrimony, Nehru favoured marrying outside the Kashmiri community: 'in my opinion, everyone in India should marry outside his or her community'.[169] But his father completely rejected the proposition. Similarly, early examples of his opposition to communalism are detectable in his letters from England. Relating Bipin Chandra Pal's speech at the Majlis to his father, he wrote: 'I objected strongly to his not taking the Mohammedans into consideration. Once or twice he did refer to them but then he was not very complimentary ... The Mohammedans here were, naturally not very pleased with him.'[170]

Several episodes in England involving racial discrimination caused Nehru to become more conscious of his nationality. Although it was not until he wrote *Discovery of India* that he focused closely on the foundation of his 'Indianness' – 'Blood', 'History' and 'Culture' – concepts usually associated with nationalists rather than internationalists. Firstly, there was the wrongful conviction of George Edalji.[171] Secondly, Nehru witnessed the imposition of quotas and attempts to reduce the number of Indians admitted to Cambridge.[172] Aware of the discrimination operated against Indians at Oxford, Nehru decided to post his application rather than visit in person in order to try and gain a place: 'If he [the college principal] once promised to take me', he wrote, 'it will be hard for him to get out of his promise when he finds out I am an Indian. If, however, I went to see him first he might refuse point blank to take me.'[173] Lastly, a similar incident took place when Nehru attempted to join the Officer Training Corps. Knowing that the Corps was barred to Indians, Nehru was convinced that the officer in charge was labouring under a misapprehension about his nationality when he was invited to a riding test: 'I do not suppose he knew I was an Indian when he wrote that, in spite of my un-English name ... I shall write to him and disillusion him about it and then ask him if I can join the M.I.'[174]

Although Nehru characterised his youth in England as a period of 'cyrenaicism',[175] when his political philosophy had only just started to emerge, nevertheless he subsequently conceded the enormous effect residence in England had on his outlook: 'Personally I owe too much to England to feel wholly alien to her. And do what I will, I cannot get rid of the habits of mind, and the standards and ways of judging other countries as well as life generally, which I acquired at school and college in England.'[176]

N. B. Bonarjee's experience of Britain was similar to that of Nehru. Both attended public school and university in England. However, Bonarjee underwent greater changes in his political outlook during his journey from schoolboy to young man than Nehru, who had come to Britain at an older age. By the time he left England, Bonarjee had moved from a position of complete acceptance of British rule to questioning Britain's imperial mission. Bonarjee had peculiarly strong British influences in his background. Both his grandparents had converted to Christianity; his maternal grandfather was half Scottish; and both parents had been educated in England. Bonarjee came to England with his family when his father entered Lincoln's Inn. The family settled in the south London suburb of Dulwich, where they were accepted by the middle-class community and invited to 'at homes', the ultimate test of approval.

His experience of preparatory school in Dulwich inculcated him with the British imperial ethos; as a result he was completely immersed in English values by his adolescence. Bonarjee was fascinated by G. A. Henty's rousing tales of empire building, as well as the classic works of Shakespeare, Scott and Stevenson. From history lessons he learnt that Britain was in India by 'divine ordinance' in order to benefit its inhabitants who, in Bonarjee's words, 'were on the whole not nice people at all, being addicted to burning widows, to incarcerating men and women in black holes or murdering them and throwing the bodies into wells, excessive stress being laid on such themes'.[177] These images were so powerful that he imbibed them subliminally with 'the air' he 'was breathing'. He even cheered and waved the Union Jack at King George and Queen Mary, 'with genuine feeling and enthusiasm', when they passed his school, along with all his other classmates. Bonarjee's only regret was his inability to share and become 'part owner of the Empire as the other boys appeared to be'.[178] Although he denied any resentment, he was clearly aware of the distinction between himself and his English companions: 'They had something which I had not, namely an Empire. They possessed, while I only belonged.'[179] The extent to which the educational system indoctrinated British schoolchildren with imperial propaganda is demonstrated by this account; it even captivated an Indian, destined to occupy a subordinate position within the imperial system. However, this 'early imperial period' of Bonarjee's life evaporated over the next ten years.

Several factors contributed to his politicisation in England; these included growing colour consciousness, radical influences, the First World War and the Amritsar massacre. The incident which first propelled colour into Bonarjee's notice as a child was the resounding victory of the black boxer Jack Johnson over the white Australian Tommy Burns, to become the heavy-weight champion of the world. The reverberations of the press outcry that followed reached Dulwich, 'even the placid "at home" day was not exempt'. The issue was debated: 'Was it right? Was it proper that such things should be?' Johnson's victory questioned white supremacy. It was even suggested boxing matches between an African and a European should be banned, 'for it was held that although the latter was culturally and mentally superior, he could not stand up to the former in the ring'.[180] This small incident had wider implications for Bonarjee: 'It was rubbed into my immature mind that human pigmentation was a most important factor in human relations.'[181] A few years later Bonarjee was again confronted by the race issue, this time in the guise of the 'Yellow Peril' as popularised by Sax Rohmer in the Dr Fu-Manchu stories: 'even at the age of fourteen of fifteen it struck me as odd that powerful, imperial Europe, which was ruling the world and looked like ruling it in perpetuity should have been so perturbed at the alleged "Yellow Peril"'.[182] These examples showed Bonarjee the depths of British insecurity. The publicity given to the 'Yellow Peril' and Jack Johnson were symbolic of a wider non-European menace, which frightened the British even during the heyday of empire. In the same way Townsend's book revealed to Nehru the weak foundations on which British rule was based.

Bonarjee was also exposed to radical influences outside his school environment. Like Jawaharlal Nehru's father Motilal Nehru, Bonarjee's father was a Congress moderate and his mother was involved with the Indian Women's Education Association.[183] It was through this connection that Bonarjee met S. K. L. Polak, a staunch supporter of the Indian National Congress and editor of *Free India*. Bonarjee's sister also supported the suffragettes and 'mixed in minor artistic and literary circles considered advanced for the period'.

Gradually Bonarjee began to question the allied war aims. This reached a peak when he gave vent to his views in a school essay, provoking uproar. He argued that successful governance of an empire was impossible without giving home rule to its component parts. Bonarjee's mother was informed that any repetition of such behaviour would adversely effect her son's entry into the Indian Civil Service. Bonarjee commented on the significance of the incident: 'even the mildest questioning of the alleged values of the Empire or a critical examination of its structure was thought to be in bad taste'.[184] Four years of wartime propaganda crystallised Bonarjee's distrust of British intentions, 'as one by one, much publicised war aims were thrown on the scrap heap'. However, it was the Amritsar massacre that most forcibly weakened the ideas he had been schooled in: 'I was no longer prepared to believe in the civilising mission of the Empire.'[185] He proceeded to Oxford in October 1919, with a great deal of political and religious scepticism. The following three years fed his numerous doubts and 'added a great many more to them'.

Bonarjee had come full circle in his political opinions, from waving the Union Jack in Dulwich to making seditious speeches at Oxford. He concluded that 'The happy memories of my boyhood were thus pushed into the background and the great mission of the Empire, which I had been taught to regard as a moral and civilising force, now appeared to me to be a complete myth.'[186]

This conversion, described long after the event, must be qualified, as Bonarjee's political scruples did not prevent him from joining the Indian Civil Service. Both case studies should be regarded with some degree of caution, as they are based either partly or wholly on autobiographies. In the case of Nehru, autobiographical material is supplemented by books he wrote in the 1930s and 1940s, in addition to contemporary letters to his father. Bonarjee, however, is more problematic, as his autobiography was written after independence. Consequently, Bonarjee may have wished to emphasise his nationalist credentials. He may, as a result, be vulnerable to charges of misrepresentation. Nevertheless, Bonarjee did spend 21 years in England, longer than most Indians, and his memories appear to be fresh and strong. If his motive was purely to bolster his reputation as a patriot, it is unlikely that he would have devoted so much space to his school days, when he was a loyal follower of the Raj. Instead he provides a relatively balanced, informative and extremely vivid account of his life in Britain. While it is important to be wary of possible distortions of the past, Bonarjee's autobiography is still an illuminating and comparatively rare study of the social and political development of an Indian in England from boy to man.

The examples of Nehru and Bonarjee show the way students' politicisation in Britain was closely tied to the development of national and racial consciousness. Radicalism was not just a product of negative forces. Discontent with British rule and government policy towards students in England also had a positive unifying effect which allowed students to strengthen their identity. In the conclusion I examine some aspects of the impact of residence in Britain on Indian students. This impact was affected by both British attitudes and the high hopes of fellowship with Englishmen many students brought with them. Feelings of disappointment and the experience of racism led students to become more consciously Indian and to rediscover indigenous traditions. In this way residence in England was a catalyst for change in the lives of Indians, producing varying degrees of radicalism, which had ramifications for Indian politics and identity.

To conclude: Indians in Britain simultaneously identified with aspects of metropolitan society, but they were also resistant to specific, racist, exclusionist policies they encountered. By examining Indian reactions to metropolitan society and British policy it is possible to investigate the way they negotiated identity. On the one hand, Indians flirted with European culture and fashion, internalising notions of freedom. But on the other, the strength of Indian cultural values, the failings of British society, the criticisms directed at students and the climate of political unrest in India all combined to highlight difference over similarity, exclusion over inclusion and nation over empire.

NOTES

1 See Chapter 1.

2 *The Times*, 15 January 1883, p. 5.

3 T. N. Mukharji, *A Visit to Europe* (Calcutta: W. Newman, 1889), p. 117.

4 Chowdhury, *British Experiences*, p. 7.

5 *Journal of the National Indian Association*, No. 5 (May 1871), pp. 94–5.

6 K. C. Mittra, *Memoirs of Dwarkanath Tagore* (Calcutta, 1870), pp. 88–9. Dwarkanath Tagore (1794–1846), grandfather of Rabindranath Tagore (see note 54), was a pioneer in the fields of commerce, social reform, philanthropy, education and publishing. Another visitor also believed that London had a magical quality, calling it 'Fairyland'. She praised the large variety of attractions: 'The condition of England, the beauty of the streets, the perfection of science, of music, the arsenals, female education, the unity of the people, the piety, the government, the respectability of the people, these and many other wonders have I seen.' Ragaviah, *Pictures of England*, p. 4.

7 R. C. Dutt, *Three Years in Europe: Extracts from Letters sent by a Hindu*, (Calcutta: S. K. Lahiri, 2nd edn, 1873), p. 59.

8 Gordon, *Brothers against the Raj*, p. 25.

9 See the following issues of the *Journal of the National Indian Association*, No. 40 (April 1874), p. 93; No. 172 (April 1885), p. 162; and (IOL) Annual Report (1906), p. 10.

10 Jayakar, *Story of My Life*, p. 64.
11 See Chapter 1 for additional examples.
12 L. Baijnath, *England and India* (Bombay: J. B. Karani, 1893), p. 117.
13 J. N. and H. M. Wadia, *Journal of a Residence of Two Years and a Half in Great Britain* (London: William. H. Allen, 1841).
14 Mukharji, *Visit to Europe*, p. 220.
15 Dutt, *Three Years in Europe*, p. 16.
16 Ibid., p. 55.
17 Ibid.
18 Ragaviah, *Pictures of England*, p. 52.
19 Jaini, *Fragments*, p. 121.
20 Ranga, *Fight for Freedom*, p. 80.
21 S. K Bose (ed.), *Netaji's Collected Works*, Vol. 1 (Calcutta: Netaji Research Bureau, 1980), p. 195.
22 Tandon, *Punjabi Century*, p. 207.
23 Das, *Life and Letters of Toru Dutt*, p. 63.
24 V. Chakrabarty, *Condition of Bengali Women around the Second Half of the Nineteenth Century* (Calcutta: Burdhan Press, 1963), p. 104.
25 G. Murshid, *Reluctant Debutante: Response of Bengali Women to Modernisation, 1849–1905* (Rajshashi: Rajshashi University, 1983), p. 86.
26 M. A. Bhore, 'Some Impressions of England', *Indian Magazine and Review*, 360 (1900), p. 309.
27 Pandita's father had left his family when they refused to accept his second wife.
28 N. Macnicol, *Pandita Ramabai* (Calcutta: Association Press, 1926). P. Ramabai, *A Testimony of Our Inexhaustible Treasure* (Kedgaon: Mukti Mission, 1917).
29 A. B. Shah (ed.), *Letters and Correspondence of Pandita Ramabai* (Bombay: Maharashtra State Board for Literature and Culture, 1977), p. 124.
30 Ibid., p. 60. There are parallels with Cornelia Sorabji. She had taught male students English literature at Gujerat College, Ahmedabad, before arriving in Britain and received a similar response: 'The society I think looks upon me rather as a moral leper … Mrs Gilmore … said they thought it not at all proper for me to teach in a men's college … Why are they so narrow and petty?' (IOL) MSS. Eur. F. 165/1, 3 October 1889.
31 Shah, *Letters*, p. 39.
32 Ibid., pp. 42–3. On her return to India, Pandita founded a school for widows. For additional information see K. Jayawardena, *The White Women's Other Burden: Western Women and South Asia during British Colonial Rule* (London: Routledge, 1995), Chapter 3.
33 Evans, *Thimmaya*, pp. 59–60.
34 Gandhi, *Autobiography*, p. 62.
35 Ibid., p. 75. She could have sued him for breach of promise.
36 Nehru, *Autobiography*, p. 25.
37 Baig, *Different Saddles*, p. 29.
38 Bonarjee, *Under Two Masters*, p. 33.
39 Menon, *Many Worlds*, p. 51.
40 (IOL) L/P&J/6/845, p. 90.
41 Ibid., p. 197.

42 Purani, *Sri Aurobindo*, p. 18.
43 C. Sorabji, *India Calling* (London: Nisbet, 1934), p. 52.
44 (IOL) MSS. Eur. F. 165/7, 29 September 1892.
45 Shah, *Letters*, p. 77.
46 Ibid., p. 400.
47 J. Salter, *The East and the West or Work among the Asiatics and Africans in London* (London: S. W. Partridge, 1896). Preface by Revd Henry Morris, 1895, p. viii.
48 *Indian Christian Guardian*, Vol. 2, No. 1 (January 1898), p. 10.
49 (IOL) L/P&J/6/845, p. 198.
50 *London Christian Mission Magazine*, Vol. 82 (1922), p. 123.
51 The durability of Indian social institutions is even more remarkable when compared with the disintegration of traditional cultural patterns in other parts of the British empire, namely Africa, where the length of contact was much shorter than in India. The tenacity of indigenous Indian practices may be attributed to the ability to adapt to new forces. See M. N. Srinivas, *Social Change in Modern India* (Berkeley: University of California Press, 1968).
52 M. Borthwick, *Keshub Chunder Sen: A Search for Cultural Synthesis* (Calcutta: Minerva, 1979), p. 105.
53 I am indebted to Professor Raychaudhuri for this information.
54 G. K. Mookerjee, *The Indian Image of Nineteenth Century Europe* (London: Asia Publishing House, 1967), p. 42. Rabindranath Tagore (1861–1914) was a Nobel-prize-winning Bengali poet, writer, artist, educationalist and humanitarian. See W. Radice, 'Letters from Europe', in K. Dutta and A. Robinson (eds), *Purabi: A Miscellany in the Memory of Rabindranath Tagore, 1941–1991* (London: Tagore Centre, 1991), pp. 39–53.
55 Mukharji, *Visit to Europe*, pp. 154–5.
56 Baijnath, *England and India*, p. 107.
57 Mukharji, *Visit to Europe*, p. 188.
58 Nadkarni, *Journal*, p. 384.
59 Dutt, *Three Years in Europe*, p. 56.
60 Ragaviah, *Pictures of England*, p. 112.
61 Dutt, *Three Years in Europe*, p. 53.
62 B. C. Pal, *Memories of My Life and Times*, Vol. 1, *1886–1900* (Calcutta: Yugayatri Prakashak, 1951), p. 237.
63 *Calcutta Review*, Vol. 32 (January 1888), p. xxiv.
64 Baijnath, *England and India*, p. 61.
65 Nadkarni, *Journal*, p. 384.
66 *Calcutta Review*, Vol. 32 (January 1888), pp. xxii–xxiii.
67 Baijnath, *England and India*, p. 44.
68 Ragaviah, *Pictures of England*, p. 112.
69 *Calcutta Review*, Vol. 32 (January 1888), pp. xxii–xxiii.
70 Dutt, *Three Years in Europe*, p. 175.
71 *Calcutta Review*, Vol. 32 (January 1888), p. xxii.
72 'We in this country know better how to treat our poor than the people of Europe.' Mukharji, *Visit to Europe*, p. 175.
73 Dutt, *Three Years in Europe*, p. 61.
74 Mukharji, *Visit to Europe*, pp. 159–65.
75 Baijnath, *England and India*, p. 45.

76 Mukharji, *Visit to Europe*, pp. 112–22.
77 *Calcutta Review*, Vol. 32 (January 1888), p. xxv.
78 Ibid., p. xxiv.
79 S. Lal, *How to Become a Barrister and Take a Degree at Oxford or Cambridge* (London: T. Whittingham, 1917), pp. 61–2.
80 H. S. S. Mahamed, *Journal of My Tours around the World, 1886–1887, 1893–1895* (Bombay: Duftur Ashkara Oil Engine Press, 1895), p. 280. 'John Bull is a sensible man … but he is reserved and repellent by nature. He does not mix soon with a stranger and is rather chary of making advances to him.' Nadkarni, *Journal*, pp. 380–410. 'Of recent years, under the garb of imperialism, a spirit of aggressiveness and arrogance, popularly termed Jingoism has unfortunately begun to manifest itself … dislike of the foreigner is an instinctive feeling with him [Englishman] and sometimes manifests itself in positive rudeness.'
81 Ibid., p. 380: 'It is astonishing how little knowledge the people, even leading statesmen, possess of our country.' Mukharji, *Visit to Europe*, p. 156: 'I came across many people in England who knew nothing else of India except the Mutiny.' Baijnath was also disappointed at the lack of interest shown in India. See Baijnath, *England and India*, p. 69.
82 *Calcutta Review*, Vol. 32 (January 1888), p. xxiii.
83 Ibid., p. xxv.
84 Ibid., pp. xx–xxi.
85 Dutt, *Three Years in Europe*, pp. 89–90.
86 Ibid., p. 91.
87 Ibid., p. 92.
88 *Indian Magazine*, No. 6 (June 1871), pp. 114–15.
89 Jayakar, *Story of My Life*, p. 41. Jayakar's progressive views on women show parallels with those of the members of the Edinburgh Indian Association. See Chapter 2.
90 Murshid, *Reluctant Debutante*, p. 85.
91 Ibid., p. 116.
92 (IOL) W1757, p. 151.
93 Ibid., p. 31.
94 Ibid.
95 Ibid., p. 120.
96 Tandon, *Punjabi Century*, p. 231.
97 (IOL) W1757, p. 35.
98 Ibid., p. 113.
99 Ibid., p. 225.
100 Ibid., p. 251, V. N. Sahai and P. V. Isaac.
101 *The Times*, 9 April 1914, p. 7.
102 (IOL) W1757.
103 Ibid., p. 103.
104 Ibid., p. 53.
105 Ibid., pp. 273–4.
106 *Indus*, Vol. 1, No. 2 (June 1921), p. 20.
107 (IOL) W1757, p. 33.
108 (IOL) L/P&J/6/360, No. 2181, 1893.
109 (IOL) L/P&J/6/360, 28 November 1895, E. S. Roberts, Commanding Officer of the Cambridge University Rifle Volunteers, to Adjutant of Rifle Volunteers, Captain Earle, 'It has been invariably our experience that the admission of these gentlemen

to our corps has *ipso facto* checked recruiting in the colleges to which they severally belong.'

110 (IOL) W1757, p. 37.

111 Ibid., p. 126.

112 Ibid., p. 210.

113 R. K. Sorabji, *Facilities for Indian Students in America and Japan* (Calcutta: Indian Bureau of Education, 1920). Richard Sorabji was the brother of Cornelia Sarabji.

114 See Chapter 3.

115 (IOL) L/P&J/6/845, p. 71.

116 Ibid., p. 197.

117 Ibid., p. 197.

118 Ibid., p. 198. It was not just the British who were guilty of essentialism.

119 Ibid., p. 199.

120 Ibid., p. 198.

121 Ibid., p. 199.

122 *Cambridge Review*, 20 May 1901, p. 404, Subbarao, 17 May 1909.

123 Two individuals from this group had technically not failed their examinations, since one still had Part 2 of a special paper to take and the other had returned to India at the end of his first year to take up a Government of India appointment. This reduced the total wastage or proportion who had failed to gain a qualification to 20.8 per cent, matching the university as a whole.

124 *Cambridge Review*, 20 May 1901, p. 404; Subbarao, 17 May 1909.

125 (IOL) Appendix 4, p. 207.

126 (IOL) Appendix 4, p. 95.

127 Ibid., p. 95.

128 Ibid., pp. 218–19.

129 (IOL) MSS. Eur. E. 352/2, 25 August 1900, p. 63.

130 British Communist Party Archives. R. P. Dutt Papers, File 3.

131 Changla, *Roses*, p. 34. For more information about the Oxford Majlis see Symonds, *Oxford and Empire*, p. 262.

132 Ibid., p. 35.

133 Menon, *Many Worlds*, p. 54.

134 (IOL) Appendix 4, p. 101.

135 Nehru, *An Autobiography* (London: Bodley Head, 1989), p. 21.

136 (IOL) L/P&J/6/845, p. 127.

137 *Student Movement*, Vol. 25, No. 4 (January 1923).

138 J. Green and R. Lotz, 'A Brown Alien in a White City', in R. Lotz and I. Pegg (eds), *Under the Imperial Carpet: Essays in Black History 1780–1950* (Crawley: Rabbit Press, 1986), pp. 208–17.

139 (IOL) POS 8960 Indian Home Dept. Pol, Part B, 30 January 1909.

140 Ranga, *Fight for Freedom*, p. 112.

141 Tandon, *Punjabi Century*, p. 216. 'It did not take a young Indian in England long to discover socialism as his political creed. We were vexed by the imperialist attitude of the conservatives, their easy assumptions that they were in India and elsewhere for the good of those countries.'

142 Communist Papers, Documents Selected from those Obtained on the Arrest of the Communist Leaders on 14 and 21 October 1925, Cd 2682. Letter to Saklatvala, 23 June 1925, p. 681.

143 These students had pledged allegiance to the government.

144 Communist Papers, p. 89.

145 Ibid., p. 96.

146 *Amrita Bazar Patrika*, 9 March 1926, p. 4.

147 M. Townsend, *Asia and Europe* (London: Constable, 1911), p. xxi.

148 Ibid., p. 387.

149 Ibid., pp. 85–6.

150 Ibid., p. 89.

151 Ibid., p. 87.

152 Ibid., p. ix.

153 Ibid., p. 115.

154 Nehru, *Autobiography*, p. 19.

155 Gopal, *Selected Works*, p. 38.

156 Ibid., p. 41, footnote 3.

157 Ibid., p. 49, Letter to mother, 5 April 1908, 'So father thinks I have changed in Cambridge.'

158 Kumar and Panigrahi, *Selected Works*, p. 129, 26 July 1907, 'Please do not go near the Majlis.'

159 Gopal, *Selected Works*, p. 36, 30 November 1907.

160 J. Nehru, *Glimpses of World History* (Allahabad: Kitabistan, 1935), p. 1000.

161 J. Nehru, *The Discovery of India* (Calcutta: Signet Press, 1946), pp. 10–11. Townsend also stressed the significance of science in Japan's victory over Russia, p. xiii, 'the Japanese have relied on what Europeans call science to a degree unprecedented in Asiatic warfare'.

162 Ibid., p. 11, 'Essentially I am interested in this world, in this life, not in some other or future life' and the indefatigable 'spirit of Man'.

163 Ibid., p. 15, 'we must hold to our anchor of precise objective knowledge tested by reason'.

164 Nehru, *Autobiography*, p. 423.

165 U. Baxi, 'The Recovery and Legitimation of Power in India', in V. T. Patil (ed.), *Explorations in Nehruvian Thought* (New Delhi: Inter-India Publications, 1992), p. 18.

166 R. C. Dutt, *Socialism of Jawaharlal Nehru* (New Delhi: Abhinav Publications, 1981), p. 15.

167 Gopal, *Selected Works*, p. 35.

168 Nehru, *Discovery*, p. 13.

169 Gopal, *Selected Works*, p. 67, 7 May 1909.

170 Ibid., Vol. 1, p. 62, 3 December 1908.

171 See Chapter 3.

172 Gopal, *Selected Works*, p. 65, 12 March 1909; p. 66, 18 March 1909.

173 Ibid., p. 55, 21 May 1908.

174 Ibid., p. 55.

175 Nehru, *Autobiography*, p. 21.

176 Ibid., p. 266.

177 Bonarjee, *Under Two Masters*, p. 40.

178 Ibid., p. 41.

179 Ibid., p. 41.

180 Ibid., p. 43.

181 Ibid., p. 43.

182 Ibid., p. 43.
183 See Introduction.
184 Bonarjee, *Under Two Masters*, pp. 60–1. Bonarjee's father (cousin of W. C. Bonarjee) returned to India after being called to the Bar in 1907, leaving his family in England. He had been offered the newly created post of Indian student adviser, but refused.
185 Ibid., p. 62.
186 Ibid., p. 78. K. P. S. Menon was one of Bonarjee's contemporaries at Oxford.

Conclusion

WE have seen that from the late nineteenth to the early twentieth century the number of Indians arriving in Britain to gain qualifications and learn about British society began to grow. The greater visibility of students at the Inns of Court and the universities fuelled British fears, arising out of popular culture and encounters with Indian princes, about the damaging effects of residence in Britain on students. 'The Indian student problem', as it became known in press and official circles, attracted most attention in the first decade of the twentieth century, with the establishment of a committee of inquiry, under the chairmanship of Sir William Lee Warner in 1907, and the assassination of the Political ADC, Sir William Curzon Wyllie, by an Indian student in 1909. The British authorities took measures to restrict the size of the Indian student population and control political activities, placing themselves in direct conflict with the students. Indians resented this encroachment into their lives, already beset by problems of racism, alienation and financial hardship. Many turned to politics. Indian experiences and reactions to British society highlight the issues of acculturation, discrimination, exclusion and politicisation. British attitudes and policy focus on paternalism, restriction and control.

The first generation of students and visitors excited interest from the host population rather than the hostility encountered by later arrivals, when the novelty had worn off.[1] For example, Keshub Chunder Sen and Rajah Rammohan Roy stayed with a variety of people in England and enjoyed their hospitality. Keshub Chunder Sen told the audience at his farewell soirée in England: 'Wherever I have been I have met with a cordial welcome from Her Majesty down to the poorest peasant in the Kingdom, I received sympathy and kindness … I came here almost penniless and you have fed me and clothed me during my residence in this country.'[2] Eyewitness accounts of individuals who had met Rajah Rammohan Roy eulogised the rajah's numerous qualities. One wrote that 'never was there a man of so much modesty and humility'.[3] The positive impression these men produced in Britain may have helped to create a more sympathetic environment for students arriving in the late nineteenth century. These visitors also had an ally in the orientalist Max Müller. He had established friendships with several Indian nationalists and intellectuals in England. As N. C. Chaudhuri has argued, the success of early Indo-British encounters was facilitated by the interest Müller drummed up in India.[4]

The editor of *The Times* also reported that Indian students had been warmly welcomed and aroused considerable interest in all groups of British society. He gave the example of Syed Mahmud, an undergraduate at Cambridge in 1869 and a great friend of Lord Tennyson, the Poet Laureate, who was entertained by aristocracy. G. Pillai reiterated this observation when he described how an Indian in England 'is admitted into the best English clubs, is seated under the gallery next door to a Bishop or a Judge, mixes freely with English ladies and realises he is a brother of man'.[5] N. L. Doss, who wore Indian costume while visiting Britain, claimed that the English exhibited definite signs of curiosity in him: 'They looked at me ... but none ever rudely stared.'[6]

Although animosity may have been less marked in this early period, particularly among the upper echelons of British society, Indians were not completely protected against incivility. In one of the earliest published Indian accounts of a first-hand encounter with British society, J. N. and H. M. Wadia wrote: 'The majority of the lower orders in England are very rude in their manners and behaviour towards strangers, whom they do not like to see in their own country.'[7]

The reception Indians received in Britain was closely tied to the political situation in India. Consequently, the different treatment Indian students received over the period reflected the changing political climate in India. Apprehension about the new radical direction of the nationalist movement in India led to a hardening of official attitudes towards Indian students in early twentieth-century Britain. This marked a move away from the comparatively liberal stance adopted by the British in the late nineteenth century, which was a period of relative tranquillity in India.

BRITISH ATTITUDES

Official concern about the undesirable consequences of a growing student population reached a peak in 1907, with the establishment of the Lee Warner Committee. The British realised that students were destined to play a key role in India's future and, as a result, their significance could not be ignored. Yet at the heart of the British stance on Indian students lay a contradiction. The implementation of English education in India, in order to create a 'class of persons Indian in blood and colour, but English in taste, in opinion and in intellect', had inadvertently sown the seeds of the Raj's downfall. Groomed as collaborators, Indians instead chose to challenge British hegemony.

The educated Indian occupied an ambiguous position within the imperial British psyche. The British were caught at a crossroads between a racially exclusive version of Englishness, to which Indians could never be admitted by virtue of their race (those who tried met tragic ends in plays and novels and were ridiculed), and an inclusive version of Englishness, in which Indians could be transformed, at least superficially, into Englishmen by adhering to gentlemanly norms, such as taking an active part in collegiate life and excelling on the sports field. The British were sending out conflicting messages. On the one hand, they claimed that English-educated Indians were not sufficiently westernised to wield power up to British standards; and on the other, they criticised the same men for not being Indian enough and for exhibiting hybrid tendencies. Excessive exposure to the West, they argued, had denationalised Indians and cut them off from the 'true India'. The inconsistency of British policy towards students is visible on another level. The desire to protect students from the temptations available in the West conflicted with the perception of students as the 'enemy within', representing a sexual and political threat which resulted in a 'moral panic'.[8]

British depiction of Indians in popular culture, shown in Chapter 3, created powerful myths which affected policy towards students, as well as the way Indians perceived Britain. To what extent did these myths correspond with reality? As with most myths, they contained a kernel of truth. A few Indian students, like the stereotypical 'Babu', took the desire to adopt English social habits to absurd lengths, by refusing to associate with fellow nationals in England and rejecting Indian culture in favour of English social mores on their return to India, especially during the 1860s and the 1870s, when such men were lampooned in the Indian press.[9] The student testimonies of Gandhi and Nehru, however, reveal that the assimilation of English customs was usually a temporary fad which lost its appeal after a few months. The 'discontented seditionist' fermenting revolution in London was another common character in Anglo-Indian literature, but this fostered misleading assumptions: many students entertained extremist views before their arrival. Ill-treatment in Britain, while significant, was not the only factor contributing to student discontent.

In some areas the British representation of Indians strayed even further from the truth and more into the realms of fantasy. One of the greatest fears surrounding Indians, both in popular culture and official circles, was miscegenation. While a few students married landladies' daughters and had relationships with English women (including prostitutes), the label of 'sexual predator' was inaccurate and exaggerated.[10] On the contrary, according to confidential official British opinion, it was often Indians who needed protection from certain European women. Attracted by their exotic appearance (presumably their skin colour, since most wore European clothes) and fairy-tale dreams of fabulous wealth and opulence, these women often mistook students for princes. Concerns about the behaviour of European women reflected British fears about female sexuality.

Another misleading stereotype attached to students was the complaint that they were reluctant to take part in collegiate life, specifically in sports. The British believed that nature had not equipped Indians (particularly Bengalis) as a race for athletic pursuits. Yet Indians such as Nehru, supported by his father, did take part in sporting activities. The myth of the 'bookish' Indian with no interest in sport was exploded in 1916 with the founding of the Gymkhana Club. Before then the success of Prince Ranjitsinhji (a Cambridge student) in cricket and the tour of a Parsi cricket team in 1886 should have refuted this prejudice. The Gymkhana Club rented sports grounds from Mill Hill Park Cricket Club in Acton. Only one year after the club was established for Indians its cricket team had played 22 matches, winning 13, losing six and drawing three. By 1920 the club had 270 members.[11]

The long-term impact of residence in England after a student returned to India is not something which can be examined fully here. The plight, however, of the England-returned was often featured in Anglo-Indian novels, as discussed in Chapter 3. Novelists such as F. E. F. Penny focused on problems of student denationalisation or hybridity and the difficulties of adjusting to Indian life. According to this fictional representation, the alienation of the England-returned was attributed to European action, as first-hand contact with Englishmen and women had challenged Indian values. In reality this depiction was an exaggeration. One England-returned Indian, Torrick Ameer Ali, argued that, although the restraints of life in India may have annoyed the England-returned temporarily, 'such feelings wore off when the young man discovered that there was no other society for him to enter and that his own offered compensation in the way of security and companionship'.[12]

The great difficulty which confronted students when they returned to India was not cultural readjustment but unemployment and low pay. This view is supported by the observations of Mrs Mary Trevelyan, warden of the Student Christian Movement House in Russell Square. After retiring from her post, Mrs Trevelyan decided to tour the world, visiting some of the foreign students she had met during the course of her working life and to publish her findings. In 1930 she visited India and reacquainted herself with 20 men from several regions. Of the 20 only five had 'fallen on their feet' economically. She wrote: 'Serious and widespread unemployment is the first fact which these men must grasp on their return home.'[13] Mrs Trevelyan also observed that of all the Indian students she saw in India, lawyers had fared the worse: 'Every young barrister I met was unhappy and all asked my advice as to the other possible professions.'[14] Although the men had been back in India for three to four years, 'few of them were earning anything like approaching a living wage'. In contrast, the ICS man was 'busy and well-contented'. The fact that an Indian who qualified in England for the Indian Civil Service received two-thirds of the salary of the average European was never referred to in English novels.[15] When students complained to Mrs Trevelyan about the lack of freedom available to them in India she assumed that this was due to cultural and emotional difficulties, rather than enforced economic dependence on parents.

Despite the negative stereotypes and assumptions fostered by some sections of British society there was also a strand of sympathetic opinion on questions relating to India. This may be seen not only in the hospitality offered to nineteenth-century visitors, but much later in individuals such as Harold Laski. Clearly British views were not monolithic. Just as Indian students incorporated a variety of attitudes towards the British, so British opinion also represented a wide spectrum.

FROM LIMITED IMPACT TO DISILLUSIONMENT

Some Indian students believed that the impact of studying in Britain was limited. According to Kamaladevi Chattopadhaya, a leading light in the Indian nationalist movement, who took a sociology course at Bedford College and attended some lectures at the London School of Economics, her residence in England contributed very little to her future career.[16] Similarly, an examination of Sukumar Ray's letters to his family from England between 1911 and 1913, when he was studying printing and photographic techniques at the London School of Photo Engraving and Lithography and the Manchester School of Technology, shows little evidence of any major changes in his general outlook. The calm passage of his stay in England, devoid of any major upheavals, enabled Ray to obtain the technical knowledge he had come to acquire. Ray encountered few of the difficulties which plagued many of his countrymen. He was sheltered from hardship by his association with a small but close-knit Bengali (Brahmo) community, centred around the homes of P. K. Ray and William Rothenstein, where Rabindranath Tagore stayed on a visit to England. Physically and mentally secure in this conducive atmosphere, he had little cause to criticise or question his surroundings, although Andrew Robinson has seen the roots of his future disenchantment with the Brahmo Samaj in an article he wrote for the journal *Quest* during his years in Britain.[17]

This view is partially supported by K. Vurgese Thomas, a Syrian Christian, who had lived in Britain for two years and was the first Indian member of Reuters. He cited three distinct kinds of Indian student in Britain. The third was profoundly affected and will be considered shortly. The first two groups appeared unchanged by their encounter, although the nationalists did become more radical and the Anglophiles became better acquainted with western mores. Thomas described them in the following manner:

> First there is the intensely nationalistic type, too critical, perhaps naturally, of the land of the Anglo-Indians. He comes full of prejudice and returns fuller of it, with possibly a feeling of hostility against his political adversaries. Next, there is the more frivolous type, who makes his acquaintance with dress suits and dances, visits theatres, and finally returns home a broken, a sadder but not a wiser man. If he can he would remain here a little longer and flutter a little more in the Butterfly Land he has discovered for himself; but finances are a consideration and he must return home.[18]

The unmoved, the nationalist and the socialite might all seem little changed by their stay in Britain. But most students were aware that residence had resulted in some degree of change in outlook, whether it was a complete transformation or a more subtle broadening of horizons. For example, on the eve of her departure, the poet Sarojini Naidu wrote to her friend Edmund Gosse: 'I cannot measure as yet my grief at leaving Europe, nor can I realise so soon the vast debt I owe these years of wandering among its people, its literatures, its arts … the ennobling and deepening and abiding influence of its culture, its ideas, its tradition on my whole nature.'[19] In addition, the effect of travelling to England may have been too profound to be consciously comprehended or rationalised. One Indian wrote: 'The whole environment exerts a tremendous influence on them, none the less potent because it is often unconscious.'[20]

Another Indian student, K. Zachariah, believed that any lasting beneficial effect of residence in Britain was undermined 'By a strange and disastrous irony, all that is worst is exposed to his eyes, and what is best is so effectively screened as to defy anything but a kindly chance or untiring persistence.'[21] Zachariah argued that the impact of the West on Indian students was limited, but that indifference was not the main obstacle; rather students were alienated and unimpressed by western pretensions to superiority. Ultimately the impression they took back to India was that 'there is nothing distinctive to learn from English society'. Instead, Indians were struck by the inferiority of British society in comparison with India: the Indian student, wrote Zachariah,

> sees politics controlled by the drink interest, reason overridden by partisanship, justice and mercy accounted vain names when opposed to state necessities. He sees an economic arena where labour is at war with capital, and the battle is too strong. Society, mindful of the threat to its self-interest, rather than of the problem of a just distribution, is alive to the economic peril; but it seems powerless to provide a solution that shall commend itself as fair and reasonable. He sees a state of morality, or rather immorality, which no casuistry can condone, but which flourishes unchecked in the midst of this professedly Christian society. In other words, the environment makes no constraining appeal to him at all – it is just silent or positively repellent.[22]

As a Christian, Zachariah was particularly concerned that there was little to challenge the faith of the non-Christian visitor.[23]

Evidence from student testimony suggests that most students did not remain indifferent to what they encountered in Britain. The impact ranged from a strengthening of opinions to more profound changes. This brings us to K. Vurgese Thomas's third group of Indian students. He wrote:

> Third, there is the type that takes work seriously, England and friendship seriously, who covets not only academic distinctions, but, as well, all mental and moral culture acquirable here. Perchance he is a little idealistic and, when he came, was looking forward to seeing a people who had as great a soul as their reputation had implied.[24]

Although all Indian students were disillusioned with their experiences of racial discrimination (both institutional and personal), surveillance and in some cases poverty, this last group of students, which formed the majority, were particularly disappointed. Thomas described the process of estrangement in detail:

> The Indian who at first imagines that the kindness and politeness he receives are marks of personal regard is soon disillusioned, and soon he finds out that these attentions are mere mechanical vibrations of society life, and that they are really the beginning as well as the end of the desire for human association. And so the Indian withdraws the feelers he threw out, after discovering in England nothing more than an expensive hotel,

the boarders of which are interested only in 'ballot boxes, cricket bats and joint-stock companies' and not a bit at all in humanity.[25]

These feelings of disenchantment were exacerbated by the extra-ordinarily high expectations of England harboured by many students, instilled in them by western education. One wrote of how 'he came willing and eager to fall in love with England ... At first sight everything is so easy and comfortable, that he [the student] imagines he has discovered an understanding people in a perfect land. Making friends should be as easy as railway travel.'[26] Vague hopes of an earthly paradise died early. Rabindranath Tagore felt deeply let down when the illusion of Britain he had fostered in India failed to materialise:

> I had thought that the Island of England was so small and the inhabitants so dedicated to learning that before I arrived here, I expected that the country from one end to the other would echo and re-echo with the lyrical songs of Tennyson; and I had also thought that wherever I might be in this narrow island, I would hear constantly Gladstone's oratory, the explanations of the Vedas by Max Müller, the scientific truth of Tyndall, the profound thoughts of Carlyle and the philosophy of Bain. I was under the impression that wherever I would go I would find the old and young drunk with the pleasure of 'intellectual' enjoyment. But I have been very disappointed in this.[27]

Britain's impact on Indian students was therefore affected by external factors such as discrimination and financial difficulties. British stereo-types of Indians had a detrimental effect on the way Indians perceived their stay in Britain, by contaminating the environment in which they lived. But internal factors were also important in creating expectations of an authentic England – in which Indians had the prospects of equal treatment, of cultural and intellectual discovery, and of fellowship with Englishmen. The real England inevitably disappointed these high hopes.

CULT OF FRIENDSHIP

As we have seen, some societies tried to put out the hand of friendship to Indian students in London. These included the National Indian Association, the Northbrook Society, the Society of Friends (Quakers), the Victoria League and the Student Christian Movement.[28] The Student Christian Movement (SCM) established a central home for foreign students, in Russell Square, in 1917 to try to alleviate the isolation endured by foreign students and to foster fraternity between students of the empire. In 1930 the following resolution was carried unanimously at the SCM Annual General Meeting:

> This conference of the officers of the Student Christian Movement recognises that there are numbers of overseas students in this country living in comparative isolation and suffering considerable disabilities on account of their colour. It also realises that the relationships of white and coloured peoples in the East and elsewhere are to a great extent determined by the quality of our thinking here in the West and by our treatment of students during their stay here ... This conference reminds itself of the clause in our Aim and Basis which says 'We seek the Kingdom of God, the recreation of all Mankind into one family without distinction of race or nation, class or capacity.' It therefore resolves to work with renewed earnestness for fellowship with these students and for the removal of their disabilities.[29]

The Student Christian Movement's desire to assist foreign students, of which Indian students were just one of numerous groups from many countries, did not stem purely from Christian obligation; other motives were at play. Friendship was seen as a safeguard against undesirable relationships between working-class English women and Indian students, which were believed to originate from loneliness. The SCM was also acutely aware of the potentially disastrous political repercussions of students from the empire leaving Britain embittered by the ill treatment they had received at the hands of English men, women and institutions. The foreign student secretary R. Brewster wrote: 'We have in London today the future leaders of the East, living lives of lonely study, longing to see what is best in England and unable to see it, trying to avoid what is worst and unable to escape.' But, as an Indian member of the SCM lamented: 'It is but rarely and by accident that he [an Indian student] can pass into the inspiring brotherhood of the Student Christian Movement, the camps or the Fellowships.'[30]

The editor of the *Spectator* also believed that Britain's position in India was undermined by Indian students' estrangement from British society. He wrote:

> In the course of our investigations one of the things which has consistently struck us is that much of the ill-feeling towards Great Britain in India today arises, not from a sense of political grievance, but some personal slight, imagined or real ... To our knowledge several of the most advanced leaders of Indian nationalism were formerly warm friends of Great Britain and it was owing to their treatment by white British subjects that their outlook changed ... Can we afford to send home [to India] every year hundreds of embittered and disillusioned students, with nothing but unhappy

memories of their stay? ... Those of us ... who are working for a peaceable solution of the Indian problem cannot afford to have work undone by the boarding houses of Bloomsbury.[31]

Clive Dewey has characterised the desire for fellowship, seen by the SCM in a more international perspective, as 'the Cult of Friendship' and applied it specifically to the ideology of one section of British civil servants in India.[32] This concept can be seen clearly in E. M. Forster's *A Passage to India*, in the characters and relationship between Dr Aziz and Fielding. The latter believes the world 'is a globe of men who are trying to reach one another and can best do so by the help of good will, plus culture and intelligence'. Fielding's outlook is similar to Dewey's Malcolm Darling, a high-ranking financial commissioner in the Punjab. It is significant that Forster was a friend of Darling. Like Darling, Forster's fictional creation, Fielding, placed great faith in the importance of good personal relations between Indians and Englishmen.

The novel starts by questioning whether it is possible for Indians and Englishmen to be friends. The character Hamidullah, who has as (Forster informs the reader) 'received a cordial welcome at Cambridge', believes friendship between Indians and Englishmen is only possible in England. This statement is based on the character's own experience in Britain:

> But take my case – the case of young Hugh Bannister. Here is the son of my dear, my dead friends, the Reverend and Mrs Bannister, whose goodness to me in England I shall never forget or describe. They were father and mother to me, I talked to them as I do now. In the vacations their rectory became my home. They entrusted all their children to me – I often carried little Hugh about – I took him up to the funeral of Queen Victoria, and held him in my arms above the crowd.[33]

Using this case to illustrate the difference between Indo-British relations in India and England, Hamidullah believes that the mind of Hugh Bannister, now grown up and working in India, has been poisoned against him by Anglo-Indians in Kanpur, something, by implication, that could not happen in Britain.

No doubt Forster provided a more accurate representation of India than populist English novelists, but Hamidullah's fictional experiences in the Bannisters' rectory did not correspond with the experiences of many Indian students in the real world. Close personal relations between Indian students and Englishmen and women were comparatively rare,[34] producing estrangement and personal alienation among students. As mentioned in Chapter 5, Vishnu Sahay and C. S. Venkatchar could not recall forming friendships with any Englishmen in the 1920s,[35] nor did Nehru mention any friends in his correspondence with his father.[36] Student remarks on this subject are often characterised by a sense of detachment. One wrote: 'In Cambridge I was more an observer than a participant in the university life ... I made no friendships with any Englishmen.'[37] J. N. Chaudhuri projected the same tone, although he was not referring directly to friendship: 'I was three years at Highgate School, a period I look back on without any particular pleasure or without any particular anguish. Parts of it were interesting, parts of it were dull, but it is three years I would not willingly repeat.'[38] However, he did not at any point view himself as an outsider during his time at Highgate; it was not until his reception at Sandhurst that he did so; he wrote: 'it was strange to find myself an alien at the RMC'.[39] M. R. A. Baig reacted in a much more emotive way to racial prejudice at Sandhurst; his disaffection is clear when he wrote:

> I entered Sandhurst in January 1923 and for the first time in my life encountered racial prejudice ... My reaction to all this was hurt more than outrage or indignation. My long and uninterrupted stay in England from 1910 to 1923, from 5 to 18 years old, had made me almost a young Englishman in everything except race, religion and colour. To be suddenly treated like this by those who up to now had treated me as one of themselves gave me a wound from which I never recovered.[40]

It is important to remember that Sandhurst was a special case. As may be seen from Chapter 5, suspicions about Indianisation along with other factors impeded good relations between English and Indian cadets. Nonetheless N. S. Subbarao, President of the Cambridge Majlis, reflected the views of many students when he claimed that, although he had not regretted his stay in Britain, he had not found it enjoyable as he had made no real friends. As a result, his 'expectations of free comradeship with Englishmen had been disappointed'.[41] Subbarao portrayed the impression of the English that Indians carried back as one of 'haughty repulse and petty slight, absolute want of consideration and entire lack of comradeship'.[42]

THE DEVELOPMENT OF NATIONAL CONSCIOUSNESS AND THE REDISCOVERY OF TRADITION

While most Indians returned to India with the qualifications they had originally come to obtain, emotionally they felt betrayed when they were not fully accepted into British society. The myth of British justice and fairness they had imbibed from law lectures and university textbooks was found to be untrue. Rejection by British society and the disappointment over lack of fellowship with Englishmen caused some students to become more conscious of their nationality. Student politicisation and the development of a national consciousness were two of the most abiding effects of first-hand contact with Britain for students. For many Indian students residence in England enhanced their sense of being Indian, as they were forced to justify themselves to a potentially hostile British society. This newly acquired racial consciousness was accompanied by a rejection of European notions of racial superiority, particularly when class relations became inverted in Britain.[43] Thus self-formation was effected by the reconfiguration of race and class.

Prakash Tandon and Subhas Chandra Bose were fascinated by the role reversals that took place in Britain. Indians were no longer in a permanently subservient position in relation to every class of European. Indian students in Britain were waited on by English servants, a situation unheard of in India, where so much depended on the outward preservation of white supremacy. An English servant was a contradiction in terms for Tandon and the strangeness of these new power relations was reflected in his remarks on the subject:

> We have heard that even the coolies of England were Englishmen dressed in coat, trousers and hat. Would I be able to ask one of them to carry my baggage? I had heard from one recently returned that in a public convenience you paid two annas to an English sweeper, dressed in a collar and tie, smoking a pipe and reading an English newspaper; what was more, he called you sir and thanked you if you gave him another two annas. There were girls who brought you food, and you did not call them Madam, they called you Sir instead. You lived in strangers' homes and paid them money and the lady cooked and washed for you and made your fire.[44]

The irony and the novelty of the situation was not lost on Subhas Chandra Bose when he was at Cambridge; he made no attempt to hide his pleasure, gleefully confiding that 'Nothing makes me happier than to be served by whites and to watch them clean my shoes.'[45] Nevertheless, he remained acutely aware of his subordinate position. Before leaving England, he wrote: 'Looking back upon my stay in England, I may say that I was never happy during my residence there. Our political relations with England are such that happiness is impossible. A sensitive Indian is reminded every moment of his stay in England about his position in the world. That reminder is of the most galling sort.'[46] This highlights Mary Louise Pratt's argument that contact zones (in this case metropolitan Britain) were sites of 'radical inequality' and 'asymmetrical relations of power'.[47]

Pride in race and nationality, accompanied by the military values of honour and allegiance to regiment, caused Indian cadets at Sandhurst to take practical measures to preserve Indian dignity and honour by developing an unwritten code of conduct over the years. When J. N. Chaudhuri arrived at Sandhurst in the 1920s, the rules were formally explained to him and that any deviation from them would result in ostracism by the Indian cadet community: 'The Indian Gentlemen Cadets were to use the most expensive balcony seats and not the cheaper stalls [at the cinema]. Visiting "Ma Hart" the military cadet's favourite pawnshop was taboo. Attendance at the end of term ball, a very colourful affair, was forbidden unless one could bring an Indian girl to it. Finally cutting in or filching another Indian GC's girlfriend was the greatest crime of all.' Chaudhuri speculated that the first three rules were designed to show that Indians were not 'a poor race'. 'Rule four made sense and rule five, looking at the shortage of girls who in those days would be seen out with Indians, was a safety device.'[48]

Estrangement from British society forced Indian students to fall back on Indian acquaintances, compounding allegations of aloofness. The annual Indian conference was one of the few venues Indians could come together as a group. According to the editor of the *Indus*, 1922 marked the fifth anniversary of the conference, which took place during one week in April and was attended by a broad cross-section of Indians resident in Britain, including students, businessmen and other professionals. The conference organisers hoped to establish an *esprit de corps* among the Indian community in Britain. In order to achieve this goal a deliberate decision was taken to limit discussion on controversial topics: 'politics was never in great favour.[49] Concerts, mushairas [meetings at which poets recited their writings], sports, excursions, mock parliaments, mock trials, mock elections, dramatic performances – these formed the greater part of the programme.'[50] Indian women played a prominent part; in 1922 Miss Bhagvat was elected honorary secretary. She was highly commended for her 'inborn executive capacity'. Women received a higher number of votes in the mock elections and their athletic prowess was also praised.

The conference helped to foster a group identity among Indians in Britain. One member wrote: 'The conference is becoming a centre of Indian social thought in England.'[51] Parochial differences were set aside and harmonious relations were established between Indians from different backgrounds and regions, prompting the assistant honorary secretary to remark: 'the whole atmosphere is so genuinely Indian'.[52] M. C. Changla made numerous contacts and enjoyed his year as conference secretary. The conference afforded N. G. Ranga his first opportunity of public speaking.[53] Many of those who attended the conference later became prominent politicians and administrators in India. The mock trials and parliaments gave them a unique chance to rehearse the roles they would eventually fill.

The Cambridge Majlis also contributed to the creation of a community spirit among Indian students. S. K. Rudra, a student at Pembroke College, proudly wrote:

> Almost all Indians, whatever their race or religion are members of the Majlis … It is a body where we feel our corporate and united existence. A living sense of oneness steals into our hearts as we meet Sunday after Sunday for debates or discussion or musical evenings … Religion and racial feelings are dissolved and forgotten for the common good.[54]

For Rudra the Majlis had gone beyond its original function as a debating society to become the students' guardian angel: 'It keeps a vigilant watch on the interests of Indian students as a whole.' However, relations between Indian students were not always harmonious. The student magazine *Indus* complained about the lack of camaraderie between Indian students and the need to dispense with unnecessary formality. Evidence suggests that some Indians remained stubbornly regional in their associations.[55] Another destructive Indian habit of mind, communalism, while dormant in England sometimes resurfaced when students returned to India.[56] Nevertheless, by the 1920s, most Indians believed that casteism and regionalism were on the decline in Britain.

This clearly represented an identification by these students with 'India'. Even students who appeared to be thoroughly anglicised asserted this allegiance. Both Kamaladevi Chattopadhaya and Cornelia Sorabji used clothing for this purpose. As we have seen, Kamaladevi came to Britain during the First World War to study sociology at Bedford College. The practical part of her course was in the East End of London. The Principal warned that she would be harassed if she wore a sari, but Kamaladevi adamantly refused to heed this advice and even had her nose pierced for the first time. The prediction did not come to fruition, although she did attract a great deal of attention.[57]

Cornelia Sorabji adopted Indian clothes, for the first time, when she came to England. The decision was made with the assistance of Miss Manning of the National Indian Association. She wrote to her family in India: 'the more I think of getting back to English garments the more I dislike the idea – so if no one at home objects, may I keep this attire, please?'[58] As both of Cornelia's parents were brought up by British Christians (her father was a minister) European clothes were the common mode of dress for her. She was concerned 'not to embarrass the family', by completely abandoning western attire. She intended to compromise by wearing dresses at home and saris to work, but she was unable to afford to buy any dresses in England. '[T]here is no help for it', she wrote; 'your friends will think me eccentric.'[59] Cornelia was puritanical about her appearance: 'The only laxity I indulge in is dropping my sari (sometimes) off my head in the sanctity of my room.'[60] Although a supporter of British rule in India, she felt strongly that all Indian students in Britain should take pride in wearing their national costume. But this stance had its drawbacks: her costume with its suggestions of foreignness was a magnet for unsolicited missionary interest.

Identification through clothing extended to identification with the achievements of fellow countrymen and women. Manorama Bose, who was studying teacher training and showed little interest in anything but Christianity during her time in England, wrote in her diary of her enormous satisfaction at the success of her compatriots in Britain:

> Yesterday I was very much interested in seeing the accounts of the Indian Breakfast in the 'Daily News' which took place at Westminster Palace ... I hope some good for India will come of it. I also read of a Mr Chuckerbutty who has taken the highest honour in the Indian Civil Service and has first passed the medical examination. I feel quite proud of my countrymen, specially of Bengalis.[61]

Toru Dutt expressed similar sentiments in England.[62] Living at a distance from their homeland often strengthened Indian patriotism, not least among women. Subhas Chandra Bose reflected: 'I believe a deep sense of patriotism develops in Indian women who come to this country.'[63] This statement was based on an Indian woman Bose knew, Mrs Mitra, who was an 'extremist' in politics; her husband Dr Mrigen Mitra, however, was a 'moderate'.

Exposure to the West sometimes allowed students to rediscover the value of Indian tradition, which had lost its prominence in the face of western education. The best example of this is Gandhi. Paradoxically, it was during his student days in London that Gandhi became truly acquainted with his Indian heritage by association with the vegetarian and theosophical societies. Both these movements valued eastern knowledge. As Stephen Hay has pointed out, it was only by imbibing the evangelical zeal of British vegetarians and theosophists that he was able to keep his promise to his mother and abstain from meat, alcohol and women in Britain.[64] Having stumbled across a vegetarian restaurant in London, Gandhi became more heavily involved with the movement during his last year there, when, apart from attending the obligatory dinners at the Inns of Court, he had more leisure time. He wrote for the Vegetarian Society's journal and attended meetings; at a practical level he regularly ate at vegetarian restaurants. His enthusiasm for the association led him to publish reasons why other Indian students should join the London Vegetarian Society. Not only did membership provide him with a supportive network of friends,[65] but also more importantly it enabled him to be a vegetarian out of conviction not merely out of duty. In Britain he became ideologically committed to a practice which had had little meaning for him in India, where he had secretly indulged in meat eating.

While vegetarianism satisfied his physical hunger, spiritual nourishment appeared in the guise of theosophy. Both organisations served similar functions of enlightenment for him and contributed to his growing knowledge of India. Gandhi was introduced to theosophy by two English friends. He had been greatly embarrassed when forced to admit his ignorance of the key Hindu scripture the *Bhagavad Gita*. They had approached him hoping for assistance in reading the original text. This admission caused Gandhi to write in his autobiography: 'I felt ashamed, as I had read the divine poem neither in Sanskrit nor in Gujarati.'[66] As a result he started to attend meetings and read the works of the theosophists' charismatic leader, Madame Blavatsky; but he was reluctant to take up membership of the society, excusing himself on the following grounds: 'with my meagre knowledge of my religion, I do not want to belong to any religious body'.[67] Clearly his ignorance of Hinduism was a sore point. However, Annie Besant's book *A Key to Theosophy* soon revived his interest: 'This book stimulated in me the desire to read books on Hinduism and disabused me of the notion fostered by the missionaries that Hinduism was rife with superstition.'[68] Gandhi left Britain able to justify and validate himself as a Hindu.

In the same way J. N. Chaudhuri had to leave his native Bengal and go to Britain in order to gain a true knowledge of India in its entirety. Chaudhuri met non-Bengalis for the first time on 'equal terms' in England. The arrogant insularity of Bengali society and the blinding parochialism of Chaudhuri's family – his father's interest in politics was limited to Bengal – had prevented him from perceiving Indians from other provinces as anything other than storybook caricatures, such as the 'lion-hearted Rajputs', or in a functional capacity: 'Rajputs for us were gatekeepers, Sikhs were taxi-drivers, Marwaris were father's litigious clients, Sindhis sold silk in the New Market, Coriyas were gardeners, Biharis were bearers, Pathans were usurious money lenders and Peshwaris, known as Kabuliwallas, came from time to time selling carpets.'[69] In the new contact zone of England, Chaudhuri, like many other Indians, experienced a major shift in identity; no longer just a Bengali he was an Indian as well. Arguably this was a false Indian identity, artificially created in an alien environment, but only to the extent that all nationalisms are 'imagined'.[70]

For Renuka Ray, who studied at the London School of Economics in the early 1920s, the expansion of her national consciousness went beyond an all-India perspective. Her mental horizons broadened substantially and incorporated an international dimension when she saw the affinity between India and other parts of the colonised world: 'I gained a wider perspective on human affairs and an insight into problems of other peoples, especially of those whose conditions were similar to our position. It facilitated free flow and interchange of ideas.'[71]

AMBIVALENCE

Indian reaction to residence in Britain was characterised by ambivalence: students responded positively to aspects of British life and even flirted with cultural assimilation; but this was continually offset by criticism and discontent, which produced radicalism. The hostility provoked by increased political consciousness could also serve more constructive ends, consolidating students into a community. Thus the response was twofold: on the one hand, many students admired British culture and thought; on the other, they remained estranged from British people and intellectually opposed to British rule. Aurobindo Ghose, who spent his childhood and adolescence in England, summed up this dichotomy: 'There was an attraction to English thought but not to England.'[72]

How were Indian students able to resolve this tension in their relationship with Britain? Most followed a model of selective adoption, viewing England as two nations, not north or south, rich or poor, but liberal and imperialist. 'The pull of England, the better and more idealistic side as opposed to the more raucous, imperialist attitudes of numerous Kiplings and Cecil Rhodes', attracted N. B. Bonarjee and his father before him.[73] As a child Bonarjee was convinced that Britain's 'inner voice, the so-called non-conformist conscience of Wales and the North, would make itself heard in the long run, however long that run might be', and triumph over 'full-throated imperialism'.[74] This aspect of England had appealed to Indian students since the nineteenth century, when a self-selected group of early Congress leaders became personally acquainted, through shared experiences as students in England.

The student journal *Indus* strongly advised students to be discriminating in what they chose to absorb from English society. *Indus* was balanced in its approach. It acknowledged the advantages of residence in Britain in broadening the students' outlook away from the narrow and provincial. One contributor was deeply impressed by the 'discipline, organisation and desire for progress, a higher standard of living and a uniformity in language, food and clothes'.[75] Another saw virtue in 'the queue system, natural desire for order and peace, respect for the rights of others'. He concluded that 'what England is able to accomplish by co-operation may serve as an incentive'.[76] Nevertheless, *Indus* was also keen that students should 'avoid the evils of western civilisation', as well as 'bitterness and disappointment as a result of unfortunate experiences at the hands of unworthy Englishmen'.[77] The journal was concerned that this underlying antagonism was preventing students from taking full advantage of their opportunities in Britain. It vainly exhorted its readers to exercise a 'sense of humour' and maintain 'a silence on many burning racial and political questions of the day, except when … views are sought',[78] in order to make the best of their stay in England. *Indus* summarised the dilemma that had faced Indian students since the nineteenth century:

> We do not wish to be transformed into indifferent Englishmen by our stay here, but we do desire to be better Indians by the wider outlook that we obtain in this country. We have to steer our course clear both of the Scylla of denationalisation and the Charybdis of obscurantist nationalism. The middle path is narrow and difficult to follow, especially for young men, but it is only if you succeed in taking it that you will justify your opportunities.[79]

Manmohan Ghose illustrates the way students managed to accommodate an aesthetic attachment to England with alienation from it and opposition to British rule in India. He came to Britain as a child and left as a young man, having completed his education. His chief interest was English poetry. By the end of his residence he was moving extensively in literary circles such as the Hobby Horse group and was being championed by Oscar Wilde. Yet he still felt a fundamental estrangement from British society; he revealed his innermost thoughts to his friend Lawrence Binyon in March 1899: 'I feel deeply that I must always seem a stranger to English people and only slight relations can ever grow out of this.'[80] He concluded: 'English in manner, culture and speech I have an Indian heart and nature and thus there is a perpetual division in me.'[81] This ambivalence is duplicated in one of Nehru's letters to his father:

> at times I am almost over-powered by a sense of my own solitary condition. When I arrived in England I had a feeling almost akin to that of a homecoming. The familiar sights and sounds had quite an exhilarating effect on me … It is strange but in spite of the homelike feelings I am constantly reminded of the fact that I am a foreigner, an intruder here.[82]

Ghose's English upbringing did not prevent him from despising British rule, to which he attributed India's poverty. In a letter to Binyon he described British rule as 'rotten to the core', citing the bribery of the law courts and police, the British salt monopoly, and incompetence in dealing with cholera epidemics:

> everything is in the favour of the rulers and to the destruction ... of the ruled ... India had a civilisation when the English were barbarians ... The people were much happier before the English came there ... [R]ather than have millions of people in the state they are now, I would rather the small minority of educated Indians were uneducated in the English sense of the term and Indian rule brought back.[83]

The Indian students' sophisticated and multi-dimensional response to Britain did not involve total rejection or assimilation. Like other South Asian visitors, they reacted both positively and negatively to different facets of British life; enviously admiring the freedom, democratic rights and liberties enjoyed by the British, while deploring what they perceived as British vices such as class distinctions, materialism and inequality. Perhaps because of their anomalous position, many students seem to have realised that absolute truths were a fiction, and that identity was something which had to be continuously renegotiated. Only by exploring their own tradition and western thought could a successful synthesis be constructed, by pragmatically accepting the benefits of residence in Britain and simultaneously rejecting the more unsavoury aspects of their English experience. This dualism was apparent to B. C. Pal, who wrote: 'There were both good and evil in English life and society as there was in our own. But while I was not blind to the dark side of English civilisation neither could I honestly ignore the bright side of it.'[84] While Indian students were able to adopt an eclectic approach rooted in experience and facts, the British, caught up in essentialist stereotypes based on theory and myth, were less able to resolve anomalies.

Evidently the impact of the colonial encounter was both uneven and multifaceted. British and Indian reactions resist monolithic interpretations. Consequently, the theoretical models, alluded to in the Preface, have been modified to reflect the complex, diverse and conflicting nature of colonial encounter and its historical specifics.

Another theme to emerge from this study is the gap between expectations and outcomes of encounter. The agency of encounter was fuelled by exaggerated expectations of England entertained by Indians and often contradictory British expectations of Indians. These unrealistic expectations were coloured by essentialism. Both British and Indian constructions of each other were heavily influenced by the notion of authenticity. Just as the British entertained a romanticised ideal of the 'real' India uncontaminated by the West, equally many Indian students came to Britain searching for the 'true' England – liberal, just and anti-imperialist. Both groups were searching for an idealised essence of the other and anything that did not fit this image was viewed as artificial. For the British, Indian students' cultural hybridity was unnatural. Similarly, for the Indian trained in the West, diehard imperialism was a subversion of western liberal values, working in opposition to the Englishman's 'real' nature. Gandhi later used this argument to claim that the Englishman was denying his 'better' (authentic) self by continuing to play the role of coloniser.

The discrepancy between expectation and outcome was also influenced by external factors. Official British policy was affected by negative imagery in British popular culture and the climate of opinion in India. Indian expectations clashed with the realities of racial discrimination, isolation and deprivation in England, all of which reinforced political and national affiliations.

Clearly, the colonial periphery was not the only terrain in which the coloniser and colonised encountered each other; imperial-metropolitan society also provided intriguing sites of exchange. By studying both terrains a fuller understanding of encounter may be achieved.

This study has also demonstrated the reciprocity between metropolitan British society and the periphery, as represented by India. The British became more anxious about Indian students as their numbers increased and as they seemed to represent more radical, nationalist responses in India. British anxiety about political developments in India provoked greater racial consciousness and resulted in increasingly repressive measures to control the Indian student population. Official intervention and the attitudes encountered by many Indian students in Britain led to a growth in political and national consciousness. Subsequently, they returned to India to swell the ranks of the nationalist movement, radicalised, at least in part, by British attitudes which had their origins in India, triggering the whole process again. Thus interaction between the periphery and the centre combined both centripetal and centrifugal forces, feeding off each other.

In this book I have examined how indigenous elites from dependent colonies, in this case India, were able to appropriate ideas and institutions to challenge, subvert and sometimes to prove their affinity with the metropolis. Issues of reciprocity and the contesting and evolution of identity through direct contact with metropolitan society need to be addressed further in relation to nationalists in other parts of the colonised world.

NOTES

1 There are exceptions to this, see U. K. Dutt in Chapter 5. Several suicides were
   reported among students in the late nineteenth century. See *Journal of the National
   Indian Association*, No. 78 (June 1877), pp. 165–6 (this also refers to students being
   robbed by women). P. C. Mozoomdar wrote in *Sketches of a Tour around the World*
   (Calcutta: S. K. Lahiri, 1884), p. 25, 'Another Parsee has blown his brains'.
2 Brahmo Tract Society, *Keshub Chunder Sen in England*, Vol. 2 (Calcutta: Writers
   Workshop, 1915), pp. 128–9.
3 M. Carpenter, *Last Days in England of Rajah Rammohan Roy* (Calcutta: Riddhi, 1915),
   p. 132.
4 N. C. Chaudhuri, *Scholar Extraordinary – Life of Professor, the Rt Hon Friedrich Max Müller*
   (London: Chatto & Windus, 1974), p. 294.
5 G. P. Pillai, *London and Paris through Indian Spectacles* (Madras: Vaijayanti, 1893), p. ii.
6 N. L. Doss, *Reminiscences: English and Australian* (Calcutta: M. C. Bhowmick, 1893),
   p. 37.
7 Wadia, *Journal*, p. 110.
8 This term is used in two sociological studies of the British media: Cohen, *Folk Devils*
   and S. Hall *et al.*, *Policing the Crisis: Mugging, the State and Law and Order* (London:
   Macmillan, 1978).
9 For an example see *Journal of the National Indian Association*, 63, 3 (March 1876) and
   Raychaudhuri, *Europe Reconsidered*.
10 MSS. Eur. C. 336/3. Torrick Ameer Ali's friend Sengupta had married his landlady's
   daughter.
11 *Indian Gymkhana Club* (London: Broad, 1928).
12 (IOL) MSS. Eur. C. 336/3, Chapter 16.
13 M. Trevelyan, *From the Ends of the Earth* (London: Faber & Faber, 1942), p. 172.
14 Ibid., p. 82.
15 N. C. Banerji, *At the Cross-Roads, 1885–1946* (Calcutta: Jijnasa, 1974), pp. 39, 82.
16 (IOL) MSS. Eur. T. 87/2. Kamaladevi Chattopadhaya (1903–) came from a wealthy
   family in south Karnataka. Widowed while still at school, Kamaladevi remarried
   Harin Chattopadhaya. She studied at Bedford College and the London School of
   Economics, and later toured Europe with her husband learning about theatre. On
   her return to India, she remained active in both the nationalist and the women's
   movements.
17 A. Robinson, 'Selected Letters of Sukumar Ray', *South Asia Research*, 7, 2 (1987),
   p. 176.
18 K. Vurgese Thomas, 'Indian Students in England', *Student Movement*, 25, 5 (1923),
   p. 104.
19 Cambridge University Library. Edmund Gosse Papers, Add 7023/80, Sarojini Naidu
   to Edmund Gosse, 13 August 1898. Sarojini Naidu went to England in 1895 with
   Annie Besant on a scholarship provided by the Nizam of Hydrabad. She studied at
   King's College, London and Girton College, Cambridge. She was a poet, speaker and
   a close associate of Indian politicians, particularly Gandhi.
20 K. Zachariah, 'An Indian in England – An Impression', *Student Movement*, 23 (1921),
   p. 6.
21 Ibid., p. 7.
22 Ibid.
23 Ibid., p. 8.

24 Ibid.

25 Ibid., p. 105.

26 Ibid., p. 6.

27 Mookerjee, *Indian Image*, p. 30.

28 The East and West Friendship Committee founded in 1921 described 'friendship as the vital element required to make non-European sojourn in England a success'. Its methods included private parties and sightseeing excursions. *Wayfarer*, Vol. 9, No. 2 (1930), p. 207.

29 *Student Movement*, 33, 1 (1930), p. 1.

30 Zachariah, 'An Indian in England', p. 7.

31 *Spectator*, 14 February 1931.

32 C. Dewey, *Anglo-Indian Attitudes: The Mind of the Indian Civil Service* (London: Hambledon Press, 1993).

33 E. M. Forster, *A Passage to India* (London: Marshall Cavendish, 1988), p. 7.

34 Exceptions include S. C. Bose's relationship with the Dharmavir family; Mrs Dharmavir was English. See Gordon, *Brothers against the Raj*, p. 34. Also Manmohan Ghose and Lawrence Binyon were close friends.

35 (IOL) MSS. Eur. T. 122.

36 Kumar and Panigrahi, *Selected Works*, p. 93, 23 November 1905, 'You do not also speak of any friendships you have formed at Harrow.'

37 (IOL) MSS. Eur. F. 180/85.

38 J. N. Chaudhuri, *An Autobiography* (New Delhi: Vikas, 1978), p. 17. 'The friendships I made at school were ephemeral to the point of being almost non-existent.' p. 20.

39 Ibid., p. 37.

40 Baig, *In Different Saddles*, p. 34.

41 (IOL) L/P&J/6/845, p. 197.

42 Ibid., p. 200.

43 This inversion is also prevalent in Anglo-Indian novels. See Chapter 3.

44 Tandon, *Punjabi Century*, p. 201.

45 Bose, *Netaji's Collected Works*, p. 195. Nehru was so struck by the curiosity of the situation that he felt obliged to mention it in a letter. During Christmas week in 1907 he attended a staff ball where guests waited on staff; when Nehru's cousin Birju asked a waitress to dance 'she answered "yes, sir". It was so funny her saying "sir".' Gopal, *Selected Works*, p. 41, 21 January 1908.

46 Gordon, *Brothers against the Raj*, pp. 65–6.

47 Pratt, *Imperial Eyes*, pp. 6–7.

48 Chaudhuri, *Autobiography*, p. 36.

49 In this respect it differed from earlier Indian organisations such as the London Indian Society, which also held an annual conference.

50 *Indus*, Vol. 1, No. 10 (February 1922), p. 109.

51 Ibid., Vol. 3, No. 9 (May 1924), p. 93.

52 Changla, *Roses in December*, p. 41.

53 Ranga, *Fight for Freedom*, p. 102.

54 *Indus*, Vol. 1, No. 2 (June 1921), p. 20.

55 Musharaful Huk, a student at Edinburgh University, accused Punjabis, Parsis and Eurasians of being particularly sectional in their associations. (IOL) L/P&J/6/845, pp. 300–1.

56 Zafar Ali Khan, 'The Basis of Common Indian Nationality', *African Times and Orient Review*, Vol. 1, No. 10 (1913), p. 295.

57 J. Brijbhushan, *Kamaladevi Chattopadhaya: Portrait of a Rebel* (New Delhi: Abhinav Publications, 1992), pp. 14–15.
58 (IOL) MSS. Eur. F. 165/8, 1 February 1893. Cornelia may have been influenced by the fact that a sari would have been more comfortable than the corset worn under a dress. She wore silk saris with velvet bodices, in different shades of the same colour.
59 (IOL) MSS. Eur. F. 165/7, 13 December 1892.
60 (IOL) MSS. Eur. F. 165/1, 2 November 1896.
61 (IOL) MSS. Eur. F. 178/69, 9 August 1884.
62 Das, *Life and Letters of Toru Dutt*, pp. 59, 90.
63 Bose, *Netaji's Collected Works*, p. 201, 2 March 1920.
64 S. Hay, 'The Making of a Late-Victorian Hindu: M. K. Gandhi in London, 1888–91', *Victorian Studies*, 33 (1989), p. 95.
65 At one time he shared lodgings with a vegetarian friend.
66 Gandhi, *Autobiography*, p. 76.
67 Ibid., p. 77.
68 Ibid.
69 Chaudhuri, *Autobiography*, p. 12.
70 Anderson, *Imagined Communities*.
71 R. Ray, *My Reminiscences –Social Development during the Gandhian Era and After* (New Delhi: Allied Publishers, 1982), p. 44.
72 Purani, *Sri Aurobindo*, pp. 82–3.
73 (IOL) MSS. Eur. F. 180/72. This illustrates the quest for authenticity.
74 Bonarjee, *Under Two Masters*, p. 30.
75 *Indus*, Vol. 6, No. 6 (March 1927), p. 184.
76 Ibid., Vol. 6, No. 3 (December 1926), p. 67.
77 Ibid., p. 68.
78 Ibid., p. 68.
79 Ibid., Vol. 7, No. 2 (November 1927), p. 38.
80 M. Ghose, *Collected Poems of Manmohan Ghose: Early Poems and Letters*, Vol. 1 (Calcutta: Calcutta University Press, 1970), pp. 195–6.
81 Ibid., Appendix 4, Musings, p. 286.
82 Gopal, *Selected Works*, p. 59, 29 October 1908.
83 Ghose, *Collected Poems*, pp. 141–2.
84 Pal, *Memoirs*, p. 228.

Postscript

CLEARLY, race relations have a much longer history in Britain than is commonly perceived. Although Commonwealth immigrants and their Indian predecessors differ in number and status, nevertheless parallels exist in the treatment they received. The main feature of British policy towards both groups was the desire to restrict numbers. The various devices used to contain the Indian student population have been discussed. However, as British subjects, Indian students had full rights of residence and, although it was possible to send destitute students back to India, a blanket ban on entry was not a practical option, not least because qualifications obtained in Britain were obligatory for some Indians and essential for the policy of indianisation. Restriction would also have provoked an outcry in Indian circles. The status of Indians was not enshrined in statute law until 1948, under the British Nationality Act. The 1948 Act reaffirmed the right to British citizenship of all Commonwealth citizens (including Indians) without restriction. But the division between citizenship and the status of subject was blurred, as no rights and privileges were attached to citizenship; they remained attached to the status of British subject. These included the entitlement to enter and leave Britain, service in the armed forces, work in the public services and voting rights.[1]

Why was it that by the 1960s the British government had moved away from an endorsement of the equal status of Commonwealth citizens to a policy of restriction? As with Indian students at the turn of the century, the authorities became alarmed at the number of South Asians and West Indians taking up their right of abode, a right that comparatively few had chosen to exercise during the colonial period. Although concern about the increased visibility of a black presence in a predominantly white society was instrumental in both cases, the decision to implement immigration controls in 1962, 1971 and 1981 was informed by additional considerations. In the early post-war period British policy-makers believed that Commonwealth co-operation and loyalty were vital for trade and foreign policy, and to help Britain to retain its position as a world power against the threat posed by the emerging superpowers.

In view of the importance assigned to the Commonwealth, any restrictive measures against Commonwealth citizens would have been highly controversial. But by the 1960s the Commonwealth no longer held out political and economic incentives; instead membership of the European Community reaffirmed British status as a European power. The category of British subject had become increasingly irrelevant. Restriction of citizenship to those with 'close ties to the UK' allowed Britain to fall into line with its Community partners. The 1962 Immigration Act signalled the end of Britain's open-door policy and a retreat from the Commonwealth. A series of extremely complicated immigration acts gradually reduced the rights of Commonwealth citizens to automatic British citizenship.

Apart from restriction, one of the areas of greatest continuity between post-war Commonwealth immigrants and their Indian predecessors was the concern over the size of the black presence. In both cases there was an invisible ceiling at which numbers became unacceptably high. In the early twentieth century educational institutions imposed limits on the number of Indian students. There was also an obsession with over-crowding and 'playing the numbers game' in the 1960s and the 1970s. The size of the black population in both these periods was important for two reasons. Firstly, Indian students and Commonwealth immigrants were identified as problems when their numbers increased. Secondly, British officials claimed that good race relations in Britain were dependent on keeping numbers down and maintaining the position of the established black community. While this was explicitly stated in the era of immigration legislation, Edwardian commentators were less specific, preferring to use concerns about the low quality of students, dragging down the reputation of Indian students as a whole, as an excuse to limit numbers. The lesson is that in both cases the ostensible reasons for restriction – whatever new situation had occurred, and the need to protect those on whom the restrictions were imposed – in fact concealed a continuity of attitude in Britain to non-British and especially non-white migrants.

On the other hand, another legacy of British attitudes towards students, paternalism (mentioned in Chapter 4), can be seen operating in the post-war period, namely, the persistence, particularly in the years immediately after the war, of the notion of Britain as the 'mother country'. The inhabitants of former colonies were still perceived as children even after independence. The 1948 Nationality Act was later criticised for pandering to sentimental paternalism, based on the view that, as a former colonial master, Britain was obliged to take some responsibility for her subjects. The Minister for Colonial Affairs remarked at the time : 'We still take pride in the fact that a man can say *civis Britannicus sum* whatever his colour may be and we take pride in the fact he wants and can come to the mother country.'[2] In this sense the continuation of more positive attitudes shown to Indian students helped to create the migration which the Immigration Acts sought to limit.

There are parallels to be drawn too in relation to the way British policy towards both students and Commonwealth immigrants was bedevilled by ambivalence and contradiction. British attitudes towards students exposed the ambiguity surrounding inclusive and exclusive notions of 'Englishness'. A clearer contradiction is evident in British policy in the later period. On the one hand, it restricted Commonwealth citizens' right to entry on racial grounds, through measures such as the so-called 'Grandfather Clause' in the 1971 Immigration Act, whereby a Commonwealth citizen who could show that one of his grandparents was born in the United Kingdom was entitled to entry clearance.[3] On the other, Britain had trumpeted the rhetoric of racial partnership and common identity within the multiracial Commonwealth throughout the 1950s and the 1960s. The case of Indian students in Britain had already exposed the limits of this ideal by the 1930s.

Finally, Indian students and Commonwealth immigrants are united by their experience of racial discrimination and exclusion. The reactions of modern black diaspora groups in Britain are similar to those of the earlier, transient, student population. Both groups experienced a situation in which formal institutions professed not to be racially biased, but in which discrimination and arrogance were often experienced at a personal level or as hidden in institutional practices. Denied full access to British identity by such practices, both groups sought to forge a new collective identity. In the case of Indian students this can be seen by the growth of a national consciousness. Modern ethnic minorities in Britain from different parts of the Caribbean, Africa and Asia have 'identified themselves politically as black'. But in the case of South Asian students the process was not complete: regional, linguistic and religious distinctions continued and could re-emerge into prominence. The same is true among ethnic minorities in Britain today. Nevertheless, within both groups a fluid and eclectic definition of self has managed to retain its attraction, either by the selective adoption model, or in Stuart Hall's analysis of modern black British experience, by 'diversity of identifications'.[4]

NOTES

1 See V. Bevan, *The Development of British Immigration Law* (London: Croom Helm, 1986) and Z. Layton-Henry, *The Politics of Immigration: Immigration, Race and Race Relations in Post-War Britain* (Oxford: Blackwell, 1992).
2 Bevan, *Development*, p. 76.
3 It was defended on the grounds of ancestry, but in reality it was a form of colour bar.
4 Hall, 'Old and New Identities', p. 57.

Biographies

THE following entries provide brief biographical summaries of some of the students discussed in this study. Although the list is not exhaustive, nevertheless it is hoped that these short sketches will enrich the text by giving additional information on the background and careers of selected individuals.

M. R. A. Baig (1905–   )

Baig's father was Oriental Translator to the Government of Bombay. In 1910 Baig and his family moved to England, when his father was appointed to the newly formed Secretary of State's Council of India in London. He lived in England for 14 years, attending Clifton College, and later passed out from Sandhurst as an officer in the Indian Army. Baig found army life in India intellectually barren and eventually left to pursue a career in commerce. He became more involved with Jinnah and the Muslim League, but resigned over the issue of Pakistan. He moved on to enter the diplomatic service, with posts in Goa, Pondicherry, Indonesia and the Philippines, rising to become Chief of Protocol. His final appointment was as Ambassador to Iran.

N. B. Bonarjee (1901–   )

Bonarjee was born into a highly westernised, middle-class family. Both of his grandparents were Christians and his father was a lawyer, journalist and landowner. He was educated in Britain, from Dulwich preparatory school through to Oxford University, where he qualified for the Indian Civil Service. On return to India he progressed from District Magistrate to Chief Secretary under the second Congress Ministry in Uttar Pradesh.

W. C. Bonnerjee (1844–1906)

Born into a middle-class Brahmin family in a village near Howrah, Calcutta, Bonnerjee started his career as a clerk to a Calcutta Supreme Court attorney in 1862. After four years studying for the Bar in England he was able to establish a reputation as a leading lawyer in India. Bonnerjee was the first president of the Indian National Congress. In 1902 he settled in England for health reasons and continued his political activities.

S. C. Bose (1897–1945)
Ninth child of a family of 14, Bose graduated from Calcutta University before proceeding to England for further studies. He returned to India in 1921, becoming the most prominent figure in Bengali nationalist politics by the 1930s, taking over the presidency of the Indian National Congress in 1938. During the Second World War, he established and directed the Indian National Army against British imperial rule.

M. C. Changla (1900–81)
Brought up in Bombay, Changla secured admission to Oxford and was subsequently called to the Bar. On his return to India he began practising in the Bombay High Court and rose to become a judge and eventually the first Indian Chief Justice. In the latter part of his career he occupied two key diplomatic posts, first as Ambassador to the United States and secondly as High Commissioner in England. Changla also entered Nehru's cabinet as Minister for Education, from which he later resigned; he also took over the external affairs portfolio.

General J. N. Chaudhuri (1905–83)
Although born in West Bengal, Chaudhuri spent the early part of his life in England, attending Highgate School and then as a 'gentlemen cadet' at Sandhurst. He joined the Indian Army during a turbulent period in Indian history. There was the problem of Kashmir, Goa and the Chinese invasion of 1962. Chaudhuri was promoted to Commander of the Indian Army, leading operations against Pakistan in 1965. After retirement he became High Commissioner in Canada.

R. P. Dutt (1896–1974)
Rajaini Palme Dutt was the son of a Bengali father and Swedish mother. A committed Stalinist, and influential Marxist theorist, he was a leading figure in the British Communist Party for over 40 years, becoming Vice-Chairman during 1950–65.

M. K. Gandhi (1869–1948)
Gandhi was born in Rajkot, western India, into the merchant caste. After studying law in England he practised in South Africa, leading Indian settlers in passive resistance campaigns. Later, on his return to India, he persuaded the Indian National Congress to adopt a policy of

non-violent, non-co-operation. Gandhi dominated Indian politics until his assassination by a Hindu extremist.

Faiz-i-Husain (1877–1936)
Hussain came from a Rajput Punjabi background. His father was a judge and commissioner. While studying at Cambridge he became a contributor to the *Observer* newspaper. He took up legal work and became a political worker and speaker in India. Hussain founded the Lahore branch of the Muslim League and in 1916 was elected to the Legislative Council espousing the Khilafat cause. In the 1920s he left Congress and League politics to establish and lead the Unionist Party and become a member of the Executive Council.

M. R. Jayakar (1873–1959)
Brought up in Bombay and educated at Elphinstone and St Xavier's College, Jayakar returned to India in 1905 after being called to the Bar. He became a judge in the Federal Court of India and a member of the Judicial Privy Council in London. Jayakar was also an educationalist and philanthropist.

K. P. S. Menon (1900–   )
Born into a Keralan Nair family, Menon attended Madras Christian College and spent over four years in Britain studying for the ICS examination. After a short time working in the divisions in India he joined the Foreign and Political Department. The remainder of his life was spent in high-profile appointments outside India. He was posted to Sri Lanka, Zanzibar, Africa and China. This experience enabled him to secure the then new post of Indian Ambassador to China. Menon also worked for the UN in Korea and his last position was as Ambassador to the Soviet Union.

J. P. Nehru (1889–1964)
The only son of an eminent lawyer, Nehru attended Harrow and Trinity College, Cambridge, before being called to the Bar. In India he joined the non-co-operation movement under Gandhi in 1920, was imprisoned several times and soon attained a leading position in the Indian National Congress. Nehru became the first Prime Minister of independent India, remaining in office until his death.

B. C. Pal (1858–1932)
Pal came from a traditional *Zamindari* (landowning) family. He started his career as a headmaster. It was his interest in theology and his close association with the *Brahmo Samaj* which enabled him to travel to

England on a scholarship, granted by the British and Foreign Unitarian Association. But he relinquished his scholarship and started lecturing on political and religious matters in Britain. Pal took up journalism in India, becoming proprietor of the nationalist publication *New India* and founder and editor of *Bande Mataram*.

G. P. Pillai (1864–1903)
Pillai was born into an affluent rural family. He had a varied working life as a journalist, author, social reformer, temperance worker, Congressman and constitutional agitator. He was also a devout Hindu and patriotic Trancorean.

N. G. Ranga (1900–)
Ranga came from a south Indian agricultural background. He studied at Oxford during the 1920s, where he came under socialist influences. He also became a member of the Colonial People's Freedom Congress. Ranga dedicated the rest of his life to championing the Indian peasantry and campaigning against untouchability.

C. Sorabji (1866–1954)
Cornelia Sorabji was born in Bombay presidency and obtained a first-class degree from Deccan College, Poona, before leaving to study law at Oxford. On her return to India, she was appointed adviser to the Court of Ward to deal with cases of *purdahnashin* (secluded women). In 1923 she was called to the Bar and practised as a barrister in India for five years, before settling in London in 1929.

P. Tandon (1911–)
Prakash Tandon was a West Punjabi Khatri by birth. His father was a sub-divisional officer. At 18 he left India to qualify as a chartered accountant in London. After eight years in Britain he took up employment with an Indian subsidiary of Unilever. Tandon worked his way up the company to become the first Indian vice-chairman.

General Thimayya (1906–)
Thimayya came from a prosperous family of coffee planters in Coorg near Mysore. He trained at the Military College near Dera Duhn and passed out from Sandhurst. He went on to pursue a successful career in the Indian Army.

Bibliography

PRIMARY SOURCES

1. Official Records

India Office Records and Library, London (IOL)

Public and Judicial Department Files, L/P&J/6
Political and Secret Department Miscellaneous Files, L/P&S/19
Indian Home Department (Political), Part A, POS 5943 and POS 5945 [microfilm]
Indian Home Department (Political), Part B, POS 8960–8962 [microfilm]
Crown Representative's Residency Records, R/2

Public Record Office, Kew

FO 371/4243

2. Official Publications

Calcutta University Commission Report, 1917–19 (Calcutta, 1919)
Communist Papers, Documents Selected from those Obtained on the Arrest of the Communist Leaders on 14 and 21 October 1925, Cd 2682
Indian Agitators Abroad, 1911, V/27/267/1
Indian Student Department Reports, (1912–13), Cd 7160, (1913–14), Cd 7719, Cd 8127, (1916) Cd 8418, (1916–30) V/24/832
Indian Technical Students Committee Report, 1912 (London, 1913) V/26/865
Quinquennial Review of Progress of Education in India, 1917–22
Report by the Commissioner for India on the British Empire Exhibition (Calcutta, 1925)
Report of Committee on Distressed Colonial and Indian Subjects (London, 1910), Cd 5133

Report of Indian Students Committee [Lytton Report], Part 1 (London, 1922) W1757, Appendix 4 contains the 1907 Lee Warner Report. Unpublished evidence volume, Lee Warner Report: L/P/&J/6/845, 1908

3. *Private Papers*

India Office Records and Library, London (IOL)

Ameer Ali Collection, MSS. Eur. C. 336
Curzon Collection, MSS. Eur. F. 111
Datta Collection, MSS. Eur. F. 178
Dunlop-Smith Collection, MSS. Eur. F. 166
Faiz-i-Hussain Collection, MSS. Eur. E. 352
Indian Civil Service Collection, S. H. Raza, MSS. Eur. F. 180
Lawrence Collection, MSS. Eur. F. 143
Lee Warner Collection, MSS. Eur. F. 92
Lytton Collection, MSS. Eur. F. 160
Morley Collection, MSS. Eur. D. 573
Royal Society for India, Pakistan and Ceylon Collection, MSS. Eur. F. 147
Sorabji Collection, MSS. Eur. F. 165

IOL Oral Archives

K. K. Banerjee, MSS. Eur. T. 79
N. B. Bonarjee, MSS. Eur. T. 81/2
K. Chattopadhaya, MSS. Eur. T. 87
B. K. Nehru, MSS. Eur. T. 113
M. S. Khan, MSS. Eur. T. 109
V. Sahay, MSS. Eur. T. 122
C. S. Venakchar, MSS. Eur. T. 112

British Communist Party Archives, London

Rajani Palme Dutt Papers

British Library, London

Lord Chamberlain's Plays
Ripon Papers, Add. MSS. 43, 580

Cambridge University Library

Edmund Gosse Papers

4. *Association Papers*

Edinburgh University Library

Edinburgh Indian Association Papers

Society of Friends, London
  Friends House Papers

University College, London
  College Minutes

Fawcett Library, London (FL)
  Indian Women's Education Association Report, 1932

Victoria League, London
  Minutes of the Executive Committee

Wellcome Institute, London
  Medical Women's Federation Papers

5. *Newspapers and Journals*

Advocate of India
African Times and Orient Review
Amrita Bazar Patrika
Bharat Bandhu
Bombay Gazette
Calcutta Review
Cambridge Review
Daily Mail
Daily News
Daily Sketch
Daily Telegraph
East and West
Edinburgh Review
Indian Christian Guardian
Indian Mirror
Indus
Journal of the National Indian Association [later entitled *Indian Magazine and Review* or *Indian Magazine*]
London Christian Mission Magazine
London City Mission Magazine
Nineteenth Century and After
Spectator
Student Movement
The Times
Times Literary Supplement
Times Educational Supplement

Umpire
Wayfarer
West Africa

6. Books, Pamphlets and Articles

Baig, M. R. A., *In Different Saddles* (Calcutta: Asia Publishing House, 1967)

Baijnath, Lala, *England and India* (Bombay: J. B. Karani, 1893)

Banerji, N. C., *At the Cross-Roads, 1885–1946* (Calcutta: Jijnasa, 1974)

Bhore, M. A., 'Some Impressions of England', *Indian Magazine and Review*, No. 360 (1900), pp. 286–313

Bhuyan, S. K., *London Memoirs from a Historian's Haversack* (Assam: Gauhati Publication Board, 1979)

Bonarjee, N. B., *Under Two Masters* (New Delhi: Oxford University Press, 1970)

Bose, S. C., *An Indian Pilgrim: An Unfinished Autobiography and Collected Letters 1897–1921* (Calcutta: Netaji Research Bureau, 1965)

Bose, S. K. (ed.), *Netaji's Collected Works*, Vol. 1 (Calcutta: Writers Workshop, 1915)

Brahmo Tract Society, *Keshub Chunder Sen in England*, Vol. 2 (Calcutta: Writers Workshop, 1980)

Brown, F. H., 'Indian Students in Britain', *Edinburgh Review*, Vol. 217, No. 443 (1913), pp. 136–56

Carpenter, M., *Last Days in England of Rajah Rammohan Roy* (Calcutta: Riddhi, 1915)

Changla, M. C., *Roses in December* (Bombay: Bharatiya Vidya Bhavan, 1978)

Chaudhuri, J. N., *An Autobiography* (New Delhi: Vikas, 1978)

Chettur, G. K., *The Last Enchantment: Recollections of Oxford* (Magalore, 1934)

Chowdhury, K., 'The Indian Student in England', *Student Movement*, Vol. 12 (1910), pp. 86–8

Chowdhury, P. M., *British Experiences* (Calcutta, 1889)

Das, H., *Life and Letters of Toru Dutt* (London: Oxford University Press, 1920)

Dicey, E., 'Hindu Students in England', *Nineteenth Century and After*, Vol. 66 (1909), pp. 349–60

Doss, N. L., *Reminiscences – English and Australian, Being an Account of a Visit to England, Australia, New Zealand, Tasmania, Ceylon, etc.* (Calcutta: M. C. Bhowmick, 1893)

Doyle, A. C., *Memoirs and Adventures* (London: John Murray, 1930)

Dutt, R. C., *Three Years in Europe: Extracts from Letters Sent by a Hindu* (Calcutta: S. K. Lahiri, 2nd edn, 1873)

Gandhi, M. K., *An Autobiography* (Harmondsworth: Penguin, 1982)

Gandhi, M. K., *The Collected Works of Mahatma Gandhi*, Vol. 1 (Delhi: Government of India, 1958)

Ghose, M., *Collected Poems of Manmohan Ghose: Early Poems and Letters*, Vol. 1 (Calcutta: Calcutta University Press, 1970)

Gopal, S., *Selected Works of Jawaharlal Nehru*, Vol. 1 (New Delhi: Jawaharlal Nehru Memorial Fund, 1984)

Gupta, J. N., *Life and Work of Romesh Chandra Dutt* (London: J. M. Dent, 1911)

Indian Gymkhana Club (London: Broad, 1928)

Jaini, J. (ed. M. Amy Thornett), *Fragments from an Indian Student's Notebook: A Study of an Indian Mind* (London: A. H. Stockwell, 1934)

Jayakar, M. R., *The Story of My Life*, Vol. 1, *1873–1922* (New Delhi: Asia Publishing House, 1958)

Kaul, B. M., *The Untold Story* (Bombay: Allied Publishers, 1967)

Kirk, K. E., 'Indian Students in England', *Nineteenth Century and After*, No. 66, (1909), pp. 598–606

Kumar, R. and Panigrahi, D. N. (eds), *Selected Works of Motilal Nehru*, Vol. 1, *1899–1918* (New Delhi: Vikas, 1982)

Lal, S., *How to Become a Barrister and Take a Degree at Oxford or Cambridge* (London: T. Whittingham, 1917)

Mahamed, H. S. S., *Journal of My Tours around the World, 1886–1887 and 1893–1895* (Bombay: Duftur Ashkara Oil Engine Press, 1895)

Menon, K. P. S., *Many Worlds: An Autobiography* (Delhi: Oxford University Press, 1965)

Mitra, K. C., *Memoirs of Dwarkanath Tagore* (Calcutta, 1870)

Mozoomdar, P. C., *Sketches of a Tour around the World* (Calcutta: S. K. Lahiri, 1884)

Muckerjee, M., *W. C. Bonnerjee – Snapshots from his Life and his London Letters* (Calcutta: Deshbandhu Book Depot, 1944)

Mukharji, T. N., *A Visit to Europe* (Calcutta: W. Newman, 1889)

Nadkarni, R. B., *Journal of a Visit to Europe in 1896* (Bombay: D. B. Taraporevala, 1903)

Nehru, J., *An Autobiography* (London: Bodley Head, 1989)

Nehru, J., *Glimpses of World History* (Allahabad: Kitabishen, 1935)

Nehru, J., *The Discovery of India* (Calcutta: Signet Press, 1946)

Pal, B. C., *Memories of My Life and Times*, Vol. 1, *1886–1900* (Calcutta: Yugayatri Prakashak, 1951)

Parekh, C. L. (ed.), *Essays, Speeches and Writings of Dadabhai Naoroji* (Bombay: Caxton Printing Works, 1887)

Pillai, G. P., *London and Paris through Indian Spectacles* (Madras: Vaijayanti Press, 1893)

Pinhey, M. A., 'England as a Training Ground for Young India', *Indian Magazine and Review*, No. 245 (1891), pp. 228–32

Ragaviah, P. J., *Pictures of England* (Madras: Ganz Brothers, 1876)

Ramabai, P., *A Testimony of Our Inexhaustible Treasure* (Kedgaon: Mukti Mission, 1917)

Ranga, N. G., *Fight for Freedom* (Delhi: S. Chand, 1968)

Ray, R., *My Reminiscences – Social Development during the Gandhian Era and After* (New Delhi: Allied Publishers, 1982)

Robinson, A., 'Selected Letters of Sukumar Ray', *South Asia Research*, Vol. 7, No. 2 (1897), pp. 169–236

Salter, J., *The Asiatic in England: Sketches of Sixteen Years Work among Orientals* (London: Seely, Jackson & Halliday, 1873)

Salter, J., *The East in the West or Work among the Asiatics and Africans in London* (London: S. W. Partridge, 1896)

Satthianadhan, S., *Four Years in an English University* (Madras: Varada-chari, 1893)

Shah, A. B. (ed.), *Letters and Correspondence of Pandita Ramabai* (Bombay: Maharashtra State Board for Literature and Culture, 1977)

Sorabji, C., *India Calling* (London: Nisbet, 1934)

Sorabji, R. K., *Facilities for Indian Students in America and Japan* (Calcutta Indian Bureau of Education, 1920)

Tandon, P., *Punjabi Century – 1857–1947* (London: Chatto & Windus, 1961)

Thacker's Indian Directory, 1896 and 1916

The Standing Committee on the Hindu Sea-Voyage Question, *The Hindu Sea-Voyage Movement in Bengal* (Calcutta: S. N. Banerjee, 1894)

Thomas, V. K., 'Indian Students in England', *Student Movement*, Vol. 25, No. 5 (1923), pp. 104–5

Underwood, T. R., 'Work among Lascars in London', *East and West*, Vol. 4 (1906), pp. 451–68

Wadia, J. N. and H. M., *Journal of a Residence of Two Years and a Half in Great Britain* (London: William H. Allen, 1841)

Wagle, N. B., 'An Indian Student's Experience of English Factory Life', *Indian Magazine and Review*, No. 361 (1901), pp.12–24

Wedderburn, W. and Gupta, K. G., *Female Education in India*, 10 February 1916

Zachariah, K., 'An Indian in England: An Impression', *Student Movement*, Vol. 23 (1920–21), pp. 6–8

7. Anglo-Indian Fiction

Anstey, F., *A Bayard from Bengal* (London: Methuen, 1902)

Anstey, F., *Baboo Bungsho Jabberjee, BA London* (London: J. M. Dent, 1897)

Campbell, H., *The Burqa – A Detective Story* (London: John Long, 1930)

Chandler, E., *Siri Ram Revolutionist: A Transcript from Life 1907–1910* (London: Constable, 1912)

Chandler, E., *The General Plan* (London: Blackwood, 1911)

David, W., *Monsoon – A Novel* (London: Hamish Hamilton, 1913)

Diver, M., *Far to Seek* (London: Blackwood, 1921)

Eyton, J., *Mr Ram – A Story of Oxford and India* (London: Arrowsmith, 1929)

Eyton, J., *The Dancing Fakir* (London: Longman, 1922)

Forster, E. M., *A Passage to India* (London: Marshall Cavendish, 1988)

Hukk, J., *Abdullah and his Two Strings* (London: Hurst & Blackett, 1927)

Kipling, R., 'The Bridge Builders' in *The Day's Work* (New York: Doubleday & McClure, 1898)

Mason, A. E. W., *The Broken Road* (London: Smith Elder, 1907)

Pennel, Mrs Theodore, *Doorways of the East: An Indian Novel* (London: John Murray, 1930)

Penny, F. E. F., *A Mixed Marriage* (London: Methuen, 1903)

Penny, F. E. F., *The Daughter of Brahma* (London, 1911)

Penny, F. E. F., *The Two Brides* (London: Hodder & Stoughton, 1929)

Penny, F. E. F., *The Unlucky Mark* (London: Chatto & Windus, 1908)

Savi, E. W., *The Daughter In Law* (London, Hurst & Blackett, 1913)

Thompson, E. J., *An Indian Day* (London: Knopf, 1927)

Wallis, A. F., *Slipped Moorings* (London: E. J. Larby, 1910)

SECONDARY SOURCES

8. Books and Articles

Abel, R. L., *The Legal Profession in England and Wales* (Oxford: Blackwell, 1988)

Abu-Lughod, I., *Arab Rediscovery of Europe: A Study in Cultural Encounter* (Princeton, NJ: Princeton University Press, 1963)

Adi, H., 'West African Students in Britain (1900–60): Politics of Exile', *Immigrants and Minorities*, Vol. 12, No. 3 (1993), pp. 107–25

Alatas, S. H., *The Myth of the Lazy Native: A Study of the Image of Malays, Filipinos and Javanese from the Sixteenth to the Twentieth Century and Its Function in the Ideology of Colonial Capitalism* (London: Frank Cass, 1977)

Anderson, B., *Imagined Communities: Reflections on the Origins of Spread of Nationalism* (London: Verso, 1983)

Aurora, K. C., *Indian Nationalist Movement in Britain 1930–1945* (Delhi: Inter-India Publications, 1991)

Ballhatchet, K., *Race, Sex and Class under the Raj: Imperial Attitudes and Policies and their Critics 1793–1905* (London: Weidenfeld & Nicholson, 1980)

Banton, M., *Race Relations* (London: Tavistock, 1967)

Barrot, R., *Bristol and the Indian Independence Movement* (Bristol: Bristol Historical Association, 1988)

Baxi, U., 'The Recovery and Legitimation of Power in India', in V. T. Patil (ed.), *Explorations in Nehruvian Thought* (New Delhi: Inter-India Publications, 1992)

Baxter, C., 'The Genesis of the Babu, Bhabanicharan Bannerji and Kalikata Kamalalam', in P. Robb and D. Taylor (eds), *Rule, Protest and Identity: Aspects of Modern South Asia* (London: Curzon Press, 1978), pp. 193–206

Bayly, C. A., *The Local Roots of Indian Politics: Allahabad 1880–1920* (Oxford: Clarendon Press, 1975)

Bhabha, H., 'Of Mimicry and Men – The Ambivalence of Colonial Discourse', in F. Cooper and A. L. Stoler (eds), *Tensions of Empire: Colonial Cultures in a Bourgeois World* (London: University of California Press, 1997), pp. 152–60

Bevan, V., *The Development of British Immigration Law* (London: Croom Helm, 1986)

Bolt, C., 'Race and the Victorians', in C. C. Eldridge (ed.), *British Imperialism in the Nineteenth Century* (London: Macmillan, 1984), pp.126–47

Borthwick, M., *Keshub Chunder Sen: A Search for Cultural Synthesis* (Calcutta: Minerva, 1979)

Brijbhusan, J., *Kamaladevi Chattopadhaya: Portrait of a Rebel* (New Delhi, Abhinav Publications, 1992)

Broomfield, J. H., *Elite Conflict in Plural Society: Twentieth Century Bengal* (Berkeley: University of California Press, 1968)

Carr, J. D., *Life of Sir Arthur Conan Doyle* (London: John Murray, 1959)

Carroll, L., 'The Sea Voyage Controversy and the Kayasthas of North India, 1901–1909' *Modern Asian Studies*, Vol. 13, No. 2 (1979), pp. 265–99

Chakrabarty, V., *Condition of Bengali Women around the Second Half of the Nineteenth Century* (Calcutta: Burdhan Press, 1963)

Chandler, E., *Youth and the East: An Unconventional Autobiography* (Edinburgh: Blackwood, 1924)

Chaudhuri, N. C., *Scholar Extraordinary – Life of Professor, the Rt Hon. Friedrich Max Müller* (London: Chatto & Windus, 1974)

Cohen, S., *Folk Devils and Moral Panics* (London: MacGibbon & Kee, 1972)

Curtin, P. D., *Image of Africa: British Ideas and Actions, 1780–1850*, 2 Vols (Madison: University of Wisconsin, 1964)

Dewey, C., *Anglo-Indian Attitudes – The Mind of the Indian Civil Service* (London: Hambledon Press, 1993)

Dewey, C., 'The Education of a Ruling Caste: The Indian Civil Service in the Era of Competitive Examinations', *English Historical Review*, (April 1973), pp. 262–85

Dutt, R. C., *Socialism of Jawaharlal Nehru* (New Delhi: Abhinav Publications, 1981)

Evans, H., *Thimayya of India* (Dehra Dun: Natraj, 1988)

Garnett, D., *The Golden Echo* (London: Chatto & Windus, 1953)

Ghose, L., *Manmohan Ghose: Makers of Indian Literature* (New Delhi: Sahitya Akademi, 1975)

Gopal, S., *British Policy in India, 1858–1905* (Cambridge: Cambridge University Press, 1984)

Gordon, L. A., *Brothers against the Raj – A Biography of Sarat and Subhas Chandra Bose* (New Delhi: Penguin, 1990)

Green, J. and Lotz, R., 'A Brown Alien in a White City', in Rainer Lotz and Ian Pegg (eds), *Under the Imperial Carpet: Essays in Black History* (Crawley: Rabbit Press, 1986), pp. 208–17

Green, J. P., 'West Indian Doctors in London: John Alcindor (1873–1924) and James Jackson Brown (1882–1953), *Journal of Caribbean History*, Vol. 20, No. 1 (1986), pp. 49–77

Greenberger, A. J., *The British Image of India: A Study of the Literature of Imperialism, 1880–1960* (London: Oxford University Press, 1969)

Guthrie, T. A., *A Long Retrospective* (London: Oxford University Press, 1936)

Hall, S., 'Old and New Identities, Old and New Ethnicities', in Anthony D. King (ed.), *Culture, Globalisation and World-System* (Basingstoke: Macmillan, 1991), pp. 45–68

Hall, S. *et al.*, *Policing the Crisis: Mugging, the State and Law and Order* (London: Macmillan, 1978)

Hardie, J. K., *India: Impressions and Suggestions* (London: Independent Labour Party, 1909)

Hay, S., 'Between Two Worlds: Gandhi's First Impression of British Culture', *Modern Asian Studies*, Vol. 3, No. 4 (1969), pp. 305–19

Hay, S., 'The Making of a Late Victorian Hindu: M. K. Gandhi in London (1888–1891), *Victorian Studies*, Vol. 33 (1989), pp. 76–98

Howe, S., *Novels of Empire* (New York: Columbia University Press, 1949)

Hunt, J. D., *Gandhi in London* (New Delhi: Promilla, 1993)

Hunter, W., *A Brief History of Indian Peoples* (Oxford: Clarendon Press, 1897)

Hyam, R., *Empire and Sexuality: The British Experience* (Manchester: Manchester University Press, 1990)

Inden, R., *Imagining India* (Oxford: Blackwell, 1990)

Jack, J. C., *The Economic Life of a Bengal District: A Study* (Oxford: Clarendon Press, 1916)

Jones, K. W., *The New Cambridge History of India: Socio-Religious Reform Movements in British India* (Cambridge: Cambridge University Press, 1989)

Kaushik, H. P., *Indian National Congress in England* (New Delhi: Friends Publication, 1991)

Kaviraj, S., 'The Imaginary Institution of India', in Partha Chatterjee and Gyandra Pandey (eds), *Subaltern Studies: Writings on South Asian History and Society*, Vol. 7 (New Delhi: Oxford University Press, 1992), pp. 1–39

Kopf, D., *The Brahmo Samaj and the Making of the Modern Indian Mind* (Princeton, NJ: Princeton University Press, 1970)

Lahiri, S., 'British Policy towards Indian Princes in Late Nineteenth and Early Twentieth-Century Britain', *Immigrants and Minorities*, Vol. 15, No. 3 (1996), pp. 214–32

Layton-Henry, Z., *The Politics of Immigration: Immigration, Race and Race Relations in Post-War Britain* (Oxford: Blackwell, 1992)

Lelyveld, D., *Aligarh's First Generation: Muslim Solidarity in British India* (Princeton, NJ: Princeton University Press, 1978)

Lorimer, D. A., *Colour, Class and the Victorians: English Attitudes to the Negro in the Mid-Nineteenth Century* (Leicester: Leicester University Press, 1978)

Low, R., *The History of the British Film, 1900–1914* (London: Allen & Unwin, 1949)

Low, S., *A Vision of India* (London: Smith Elder, 1906)

Maan, B., *The New Scots: The Story of Asians in Scotland* (Edinburgh: Donald, 1992)

MacKenzie, J. M., *Propaganda and Empire: The Manipulation of British Public Opinion 1880–1960* (Manchester: Manchester University Press, 1984)

Macnicol, Nicol, *Pandita Ramabai* (Calcutta: Association Press, 1926)

Majeed, J., 'Putting God in his Place: Bradley, McTaggart and Muhammad Iqbal', *Journal of Islamic Studies*, 4, 2 (1993), pp. 208–36

Mannsakar, F., 'The Dog that Didn't Bark: The Subject Races in Imperial Fiction at the Turn of the Century', in D. Dabydeen (ed.), *Black Presence in English Literature* (Manchester: Manchester University Press, 1985), pp. 112–34

Mcguire, J., *The Making of a Colonial Mind: A Quantitative Study of the Bhadralok in Calcutta, 1857–1885* (Canberra: Australian National University, 1983)

McLane, J. R., *Indian Nationalism and the Early National Congress* (Princeton, NJ: Princeton University Press, 1977)

Mehrotra, S. R., *The Emergence of the Indian National Congress* (New Delhi: York, Barnes & Noble, 1971)

Monier Williams, M., *Modern India and Indians* (London: Trubner, 1891)

Mookerjee, G. K., *The Indian Image of Nineteenth Century Europe* (London: Asia Publishing House, 1967)

Murshid, G., *Reluctant Debutante – Response of Bengali Women to Modernisation, 1849–1905* (Rajshasi: Rajshasi University, 1983)

Nandy, A., *The Intimate Enemy: Loss and Recovery of Self under Colonialism* (New Delhi: Oxford University Press, 1983)

Newcombe G. J., *White into Harvest* (London: Morgan & Scott, 1927)

Pandey, B. N., *Nehru* (London: Macmillan, 1976)

Parry, B., *Delusions and Discoveries: Studies on India in the British Imagination, 1880–1930* (London: Allen Lane, 1972)

Pinney, T. (ed.), *Kipling's India: Uncollected Sketches 1884–88* (London: Macmillan, 1988)

Prasad, B., *Indian Nationalism and Asia* (Delhi: B. R. Publishing, 1979)

Pratt, M. L., *Imperial Eyes: Travel Writing and Transculturation* (New York: Routledge, 1992)

Purani, A. B., *Sri Aurobindo in England* (Pondicherry: Sri Aurobindo Ashram, 1956)

Ray, R. K., 'Moderates, Extremists, Revolutionaries in Bengal, 1900–1908', in R. Sissons and S. Wolpert (eds), *Congress and Indian Nationalism* (Berkeley: University of California Press, 1988), pp. 62–89

Raychaudhuri, T., *Europe Reconsidered: Perceptions of the West in Nineteenth Century Bengal* (New Delhi: Oxford University Press, 1988)

Rees, J. D., *Real India* (London: Methuen, 1908)

Rich, P. B., *Race and Empire in British Politics* (Cambridge: Cambridge University Press, 1990)

Said, E. W., *Culture and Imperialism* (London: Vintage, 1994)

Schmitthener, S., 'A Sketch of the Development of the Legal Profession in India', *Law and Society Review*, Vol. 3, Nos 2 , 3 (1968–69), pp. 337–82

Seal, A., *The Emergence of Indian Nationalism: Competition and Collaboration in the Later Nineteenth Century* (Cambridge: Cambridge University Press, 1968)

Shephard, B., 'Showbiz Imperialism – The Case of Peter Logengula', in J. M. MacKenzie (ed.), *Imperialism and Popular Culture* (Manchester: Manchester University Press, 1986), pp. 94–112

Singh, B., *A Survey of Anglo-Indian Fiction* (London: Oxford University Press, 1934)

Singh, R. B., *The Imperishable Empire: A Study of British Fiction on India* (Washington, DC: Three Continents Press, 1986)

Sinha, M., *Colonial Masculinity: The 'Mainly Englishman' and the 'Effeminate Bengali' in the Late Nineteenth Century* (Manchester: Manchester University Press, 1995)

Strachey, J., *India – Its Administration and Progress* (London: Macmillan, 1911)

Street, B. V., *The Savage in Literature: Representations of Primitive Society in English Fiction, 1858–1920* (London: Routledge & Kegan Paul, 1975)

Sullivan, Z. T., *Narratives of Empire: The Fictions of Rudyard Kipling* (Cambridge: Cambridge University Press, 1993)

Symonds, R., *Oxford and Empire – The Last Lost Cause?* (London: Macmillan, 1986)

Townsend, M., *Asia and Europe* (London: Constable, 1911)

Trevelyan, M., *From the Ends of the Earth* (London: Faber & Faber, 1942)

Visram, R., *Ayahs, Lascars and Princes: The Story of Indians in Britain 1700–1947* (London: Pluto Press, 1986)

Voight, J. H., *Max Müller – The Man and His Ideas* (Calcutta: Mukhopadadhyay, 1981)

White, A., *Joseph Conrad and the Adventure Tradition: Constructing and Deconstructing the Imperial Subject* (Cambridge: Cambridge University Press, 1993)

Young, R. J. C., *Colonial Desire: Hybridity, Theory, Culture and Race* (London: Routledge, 1995)

9. Unpublished Material

Buckee, G. F. M., 'An Examination of the Development and Structure of the Legal Profession in Allahabad, 1866–1935' (PhD thesis, University of London, 1972)

Index